Madame Vestris and the London Stage

Madame Vestris

Madame Vestris and the London Stage

William W. Appleton

Columbia University Press

NEW YORK & LONDON   1974

Library of Congress Cataloging in Publication Data

Appleton, William Worthen.
  Madame Vestris and the London Stage.

  Bibliography: p. 217
  1. Vestris, Lucia Elizabeth (Bartolozzi) 1797–1856.
I. Title.
PN2598.V5A7   792'.092'4   [B]   73-10259
ISBN 0-231-03794-5

Contents

Illustrations

Preface

Madame Vestris was the subject of much catchpenny journalism during her lifetime. The garish accounts of her "public and private adventures" give one little sense, however, either of her importance in theatre history or of her complex personality. She was extravagant and self-indulgent, yet a disciplined and dedicated artist. She lived for many years in a blaze of notoriety, yet she was secretive and withdrawn. Her private letters are for the most part brief and impersonal, and though she was a pioneer in stage reform, she saw no need to commit her ideas to paper. Instead, she expressed them in the theatre. Her life was the life of the theatre.

In writing this book I have benefited from the help of many people, among them Shirley Allen, James Butler, Christopher Calthrop, Babette Craven, Denis Donoghue, Theodore Fenner, Malcolm Goldstein, Philip Highfill, Martin Meisel, Parmenia Migel, Evert Sprinchorn, the late Father Carl Stratman, and Hannah Winter. I am grateful to Christopher Murray for permitting me to make use of his unpublished study of Elliston, to Alfred Nelson for allowing me to quote from his transcript of the Winston diaries, and to Robert Eddison, Norman Philbrick, Burt Shevelove, and Mrs. John Wharton for generously giving me access to manuscript material in their private collections.

In addition, I am indebted to Helen Willard of the Harvard Theatre Collection, Paul Meyers of the Lincoln Center Theatre

Research Library, George Nash and Anthony Latham of the Enthoven Collection, Alexander Clark and Mary Ann Jensen of the Princeton Library, Louis Rachow of The Players' Club, and the staff of the British Theatre Museum. All of these have shown me every courtesy and made my work a pleasure.

Finally, I feel a special debt of gratitude to the late Alec Clunes, that charming and distinguished man of the theatre, who originally encouraged me to undertake this book.

New York City, 1972   *William W. Appleton*

Madame Vestris and the London Stage

chapter I

*P*rologue

During the autumn of 1882, in the course of clearing out the rubbish from the cellars of the Lyceum Theatre, a group of workmen came across a vast pile of decayed peacock feathers. It was all that remained from the spectacular production thirty-four years earlier of Planché's extravaganza, *The King of the Peacocks*, which had concluded with a dazzling vision of a peacock throne room. Madame Vestris, its producer, had been dead for a quarter of a century, but Londoners had not forgotten her. As a singer and actress she had delighted them for over thirty years, and as a manager she had set standards of production that had helped to alter the course of the English theatre. They remembered her also, however, as a personality. Her name still conjured up legends of scandals and indiscretions among the bucks and beaux of a gaudier era.

She had been born in London and had spent most of her life there, but, as one of her admirers put it, she belonged to all Europe.[1] Her father was Italian, her mother German, her first husband French, and her second husband English. Her paternal grandfather, Francesco Bartolozzi, had emigrated to England in 1764 and soon afterward the young artist was appointed engraver to George III. His success was immense and, as might be expected, his son Gaetano followed in his father's footsteps. The younger Bartolozzi was gifted enough, but he lacked his father's genius and found his greatest pleasure not in drawing but in music. His talents as a violinist made him welcome in London's artistic society, and in the course of a musical soiree he met Therese Jansen, the daughter of a dancing master originally from Aix-la-Chapelle. Like all of her family, Therese was musical. Her father played the violin. Her younger brother, Louis, showed promise as a composer, and her mother, Charlotte, was a gifted pianist. But Therese's talents were of a conspicuously higher order. Her piano teacher, Muzio Clementi, considered her one of his three best pupils, and Joseph Haydn also ranked her among the leading pianists in London.[2]

She was twenty-five when she met the thirty-seven-year-old Gaetano Bartolozzi. Their courtship was apparently a brief one, and on May 16, 1795, they were married in St. James's Church, Picadilly. Evidently the two families were pleased by the match for both Francesco Bartolozzi and Charlotte Jansen signed the register, and Joseph Haydn, also a witness, concurred with an approving flourish. The newly married couple moved into lodgings in 74 Dean Street, Soho, and there Gaetano established himself as a printseller, engraver, and drawing master. His young bride, it would seem, had no wish to pursue an independent career, and though Haydn subsequently dedicated to her no less than five major piano works, there is no evidence that she ever performed in public. Apparently she was happy in her role as wife to Gaetano Bartolozzi, and on March 2, 1797, their daughter Lucia Elizabeth was born.[3]

In all likelihood the child was named after her paternal grandmother, Lucia Feno. Francesco's wife was the owner of a small estate on the Venetian mainland which at the time of Lucia Elizabeth's birth was menaced by the armies of Napoleon. Alarmed by this threat, Francesco urged his son to go abroad as soon as possible and inspect his mother's property. Gaetano agreed. On June 23, 1797, he sold off his stock of prints, drawings, and copperplates, and shortly afterward he and his wife and child were on their way. Perhaps Gaetano was hoping to settle abroad permanently. Perhaps he merely found the change congenial. In any case, he was determined to extend their trip for as long as possible. They remained in Paris for a while, then moved on to Vienna and after a leisurely visit made their way down to the Adriatic. By the time they reached Venice two years had elapsed. There, as they had feared, they found the Feno property ravaged by the French army. Discouraged and no doubt short of money, they had no alternative but to return to England.

A melancholy notice in *The Times* on January 8, 1800, advised readers that Gaetano Bartolozzi was once again available to give instruction in drawing. One gathers that life at this period was not altogether easy for him. No doubt he found it difficult living in the shadow of his famous father—particularly since his father was growing increasingly irritable. Before long the two had quarreled, the older man accusing the younger of ingratitude and incompetence. Himself gregarious and extravagant to a degree, Francesco was more than usually hard up, and when the Prince Regent of Portugal offered him a pension he accepted it at once. In Portugal, he explained, he could stable his horse and drink French wines. In England he could barely afford a jackass and a pint of porter. His quarrel with his son perhaps confirmed him in his decision to leave England, but at any rate it did not impair his feelings for his lively young granddaughter, and in a letter written shortly before his departure he refers to her affectionately.[4]

After Francesco's departure Gaetano's fortunes declined still further. He contrived to eke out a living by adding fencing and music to the subjects in which he gave instruction, and though his relationship with his wife was becoming increasingly cool, in 1807 their second child, Josephine, was born. Like her older sister she had pale skin, dark hair, and dark, flashing eyes, but there the resemblance ended. Young Josephine was passive and withdrawn, her older sister quite the opposite. Even in infancy Lucia Elizabeth's spirit had begun to assert itself. Rather than study piano, she had insisted on studying voice and at a very early age received instruction, often gratuitously, from a number of teachers, among them Domenico Corri. As one of her early biographers put it: "She was indefatigable in her studies, and never lost an hour which she could appropriate to the purpose of improvement; and some months before she had completed her thirteenth year, she had sung at several concerts of the nobility, where her powers were greeted with the most enthusiastic shouts of admiration and applause." [5]

At the age of fifteen she met Armand Vestris, *premier danseur* at the King's Theatre. He was ten years her senior, of medium height, with the compact build of a dancer. "His face was chubby and inexpressive, and his eye had an expression of dissipation that was unpleasing—the gloating of passion without fire," [6] according to one account, but he had the allure of a great name. His grandfather, Gaetano Vestris, had emigrated from Italy to Paris where he was acclaimed as "Le Dieu de la Danse." His father, Auguste, was no less famous. For over thirty years he had been *premier danseur* at the Paris Opera, and his elevation and *batterie* were still legendary. As performers and teachers Gaetano and Auguste had made the Opera ballet the most celebrated in Europe. Young Armand, born in 1787, was carrying on the great tradition, and when he made his debut, at the age of twelve, three generations of the Vestris family had danced together. London had first applauded him in 1809 in James D'Egville's ballet *Les Amours de Glauque*, and subsequent appearances in Portugal and Italy had established him as a dancer of international reputation.

He had also acquired some notoriety as a ladies' man. Rumor had it that during his stay in Lisbon he and Junot, chief of Napoleon's forces, had feuded over the dancer Julie Petit.[7] It was also rumored that he enjoyed the favors of Fortunata Angiolini, his partner at the King's Theatre since 1809. In any event, Vestris was strongly attracted to Lucia Elizabeth Bartolozzi, with her perfect figure and vivacious manner. He proposed to her and she accepted. Her parents saw no reason to oppose the match, and on January 28, 1813, they were married at St. Martin's-in-the-Fields.

No doubt the Bartolozzis considered him a catch, and no doubt their daughter had reasons of her own for marrying him. Perhaps she was genuinely in love with him. Perhaps she saw in him primarily an opportunity to advance her own career. The prospect of appearing at the King's Theatre would have dazzled any young singer. Twice a week, on Tuesdays and Saturdays, all of London society gathered there to applaud the opera and the ballet. It was no longer fashionable to patronize the two

Armand Vestris in the ballet of *Macbeth*. (*Princeton Theatre Collection*)

great patent houses, Drury Lane and Covent Garden, except on those rare occasions when Mrs. Siddons emerged from retirement to stalk the boards as Lady Macbeth or Queen Katharine.

The evening's entertainment was as ritualistically prescribed as the dress of the gentlemen. Performances began at eight o'clock, a concession to the increasingly late dinner hour, and concluded, nominally, by midnight. (The Bishop of London had sternly prohibited any performance after that hour.) In the course of that time it was customary to present not only a full-length Italian opera, with a divertissement between the acts, but a full-length ballet as well. In addition, the audience insisted upon an interval of at least a half or three-quarters of an hour. As a result, despite the Bishop's prohibition, performances often went on until one o'clock.

If the singers were not as good as those at La Scala, nor the dancers as brilliant as those at the Paris Opera, the audience was probably the most dazzling anywhere. The theatre was a large one. The pit and gallery each held about a thousand spectators, but it was the boxes, upholstered in rose-colored silk, that drew all eyes. There sat the ladies, a glittering constellation of fashion. Hardly less resplendent were their escorts, each in his frock coat, knee breeches, and ruffled shirt, a *chapeau à bras* tucked under one arm and a dress sword at the side. Other fashionable bucks adorned the two omnibus boxes on each side of the stage. There and in Fop's Alley, a section of the pit, they gathered to applaud their favorites before sauntering backstage to flirt and gossip in the Green Room.

Madame Vestris had good reason to hope that she might eventually appear before this audience. The Napoleonic wars had sharply curtailed travel and the roster of singers was sadly depleted. The company was fortunate, however, in having a number of good dancers and a notable *maître de ballet*—Charles Didelot. He had studied under Noverre and Armand's father, Auguste Vestris. His best work, *Flore et Zéphire*, first produced in London in 1796, had led to his engagement in St. Petersburg, but during the Napoleonic Wars he had returned to the King's Theatre. Madame Vestris was perhaps too young to appreciate his gifts, but he was a man after her own heart, a perfectionist who drilled his dancers mercilessly and exercised a nearly total control over his ballets. He devised the choreography, wrote the libretto, selected the music, and approved the costume and scenic designs. He also collaborated with the engineers on machinery for spectacular effects—a soaring flight by Zéphire or the apparition of a forest from the bowels of the stage.

From 1812–14 Didelot presided over the ballet with Armand Vestris as his *premier danseur*. It was during the last of these seasons that England and her allies achieved a series of victories over Napoleon. Audiences at the King's Theatre marked these occasions by patriotic outbursts, and the dandies testified to their undying hatred of Bonaparte by refusing to adopt the latest French fashion—the opera hat.

As a result of these victories Didelot decided to leave the King's Theatre. He had been in disfavor in France and had many enemies there, but the altered political climate led him to hope that a production of his spectacular ballet, *Flore et Zéphire*, might at last be feasible at the Paris Opera. Appointed in his place was Armand Vestris.

The new ballet master and his wife probably made a trip to Paris during the autumn of 1814, for when the 1815 season began, a number of French dancers joined the company at the King's Theatre. Also on hand were various members of the Vestris family, notably Armand's father, Auguste, still active as a dancer at fifty-five. Carlo Vestris, a cousin, who had appeared with the company during the previous season, was reengaged, as was his father, Stephano, who was appointed official librettist. If it was not quite clear to anyone just what function Stephano performed, there was no doubt that Armand, at least, was more than earning his salary. He was acting in a triple capacity as ballet master, dancer, and choreographer, and within three months he had produced three new ballets.[8] In *Mars et l'Amour* he appeared as the God of Love while his father took the role of Mars. (It would probably not have amused Auguste to know that balletomanes jovially referred to him as "Le Père d'Amour.") Of more consequence, however, were Armand's two ballets *Les Petits Braconniers* and *Le Prince Troubadour*. Like Noverre and Didelot he relied extensively on pantomime and spectacle, but in his emphasis on setting and in his evocation of local color he was breaking new ground. The vision of Scotland in *Les Petits Braconniers* and the medieval splendors of *Le Prince Troubadour* anticipated the world of the Romantic ballet.

Toward the end of each season the principal artists in the company were each permitted a benefit night—usually on a Thursday. On these occasions they were allowed to make up their own bill. They sold the tickets as advantageously as they could, and, after paying the house charges, pocketed the difference. Armand's benefit fell on July 20, 1815. As the main attraction he proposed to appear in his own ballet, *Le Prince Troubadour*. To fill out the bill he suggested a revival of Peter von Winter's two-act opera, *Il Ratto di Proserpina*, with his wife in the title role.

It was daring, no doubt, for Madame Vestris, at the age of eighteen, to make her debut in a leading role, but the choice had much to recommend it. The limpid, neo-Mozartian melodies of Winter suited her voice, and the part was dramatically not a demanding one. Furthermore, although the opera was a popular one, it had not been performed for some years. Nonetheless, the prospect must have filled her with dread. The role of Proserpina had been created by Signora Josephine Grassini, a gifted soprano, whom many music-lovers remembered. (In 1815 she was living in Paris where rumor had it that she was the mistress of the Duke of Wellington.) Equally dispiriting was the thought that at least four members of the Vestris family would be watching her from the wings. Between the acts of Winter's opera Armand was to dance a bolero and Auguste a *minuet de cour*. Carlo Vestris was also billed to appear and Stephano would doubtless be lurking somewhere backstage.

However nervous she may have been at eight o'clock on the evening of July 20, her initial stage fright soon passed. Accompanied by Madame Fodor as Ceres, she rode on stage in a chariot drawn by dragons. At the conclusion of her first aria the audience warmly applauded. Princess Charlotte, the popular daughter of the unpopular Prince Regent, was observed tapping her fan in approbation and even opera-goers who remembered Grassini joined in the applause. It was true that her acting was rudimentary. She confined herself to the simplest of gestures, crossing her arms or waving her right hand gently, but the richness and purity of her voice, her "perfect symmetry" and "beautiful countenance" [9] more than compensated for these deficiencies, and such was her success in Winter's opera that it was repeatedly performed during the remainder of the season.

With the closing of the King's Theatre in August, Armand and his wife departed for Paris. The triumphant forces of the Allies, fresh from their victory at Waterloo, had swept into the French capital two months earlier, and in their wake came streams of visitors. Presumably Armand and his wife returned there to visit his family and to recruit dancers for the following season. In any event, by December they had returned to London and Madame was busily studying new roles in Winter's *Zaïre* and Martin y Soler's *La Cosa Rara*. She also added to her repertory Dorabella in *Cosi Fan Tutte* and Susanna in *The Marriage of Figaro*. Her earlier success had perhaps made her a trifle overconfident, for her appearances during the 1816 season disappointed expectations. Not without reason was the King's Theatre known as the tomb of singers. There was no disguising the fact that her voice was still undeveloped and that she was forcing it in her new roles. Even though Susanna's music was transposed for her to a lower key, she achieved only a modest success in the part. As the critic of *The Times* somewhat equivocally put it: "She sang delightfully some very trying passages." [10]

In the course of the same season Armand produced his best-known work, *Gonzalve de Cordoue*. Set in Granada during the Moorish dominion, the ballet was acclaimed by the public. Of the choreography little is known, but the libretto, reminiscent of Dryden's *Conquest of Granada*, gave him an opportunity to interpolate the regional dances he had studied during his stay in Portugal and Spain. As usual, the production was an elaborate one. Bands of peasants and troubadours swarmed across the stage, and so splendid were the scenes in the Alhambra and the surrounding countryside that the spectacle threatened to overwhelm the dancing.

Cast as the leader of a Moorish tribe was Oscar Byrne, an English dancer, who in later years became Madame's chief choreographer. Also in the cast was Julia Mori, dancing the role of a rival chieftain. Since the departure of Fortunata Angiolini from the company in 1814, gossip had linked the names of Armand Vestris and the young *figurante*. In all likelihood the rumors were true. The vain ballet master had a penchant for his young pupils, and quite prob.bly he had already begun to tire of his wife. She was spirited ar;d independent, and like him ambitious, self-centered, and extravagant.

By 1816 the Vestrises had run up substantial debts and at the conclusion of the opera season, so one of Madame Vestris's biographers informs us, "[Armand] was arrested for debt, cleared himself by bankruptcy, and went to Paris with his wife." [11] The statement is open to question, however. Contemporary newspapers make no allusion to his arrest. His name does not appear on the lists of bankrupts, and his wife seems to have remained in England until late autumn. On November 14, 1816, Stephano Vestris, in a chatty letter from London, refers to "Madame Armand's" impatience to see Giovanni Benelli, the regisseur of the Théâtre des Italiens in Paris.[12] Evidently she was in communication with him soon afterward, and Benelli arranged for her to make her Paris debut on December 7 as Proserpina.

Some time shortly before that date she arrived in Paris. Whether she was with Armand or not is uncertain. Her use of the name Bartolozzi-Vestris upon her arrival suggests that she and Armand may already have parted company. Perhaps she used her maiden name to avoid confusion with Carlo Vestris's wife. Perhaps she felt that the name Bartolozzi would be to her advantage at the Théâtre des Italiens. Certainly she stood in need of every such advantage. The Théâtre des Italiens no longer offered any real competition to the Paris Opera. Its patentees were the flamboyant soprano, Madame Catalani, and her disagreeable husband, Paul Valabrèque. They took a contemptuous view of the musical public in Paris and Valabrèque's managerial policy was a simple one: "My wife and four or five puppets are all we need." [13] Productions were makeshift, and the orchestra and chorus minimal.

Madame Catalani was to be on tour until August and Benelli was anxious to present a short operatic season as inexpensively as possible. Experience had taught him that English singers were far less demanding than those from other countries. He had already engaged Mrs. Dickons, an English soprano somewhat past her prime. He also had under contract an Italian basso. With these two as Ceres and Pluto, Madame Vestris in the lead, and a modest chorus of nymphs and demons, he could produce *Il Ratto di Proserpina* at minimal expense.

The announcement that Madame Bartolozzi-Vestris would shortly appear in Winter's opera did not cause much stir nor, for that matter, did her debut. Opera-lovers found the work cold and monotonous and Madame a poor substitute for Grassini. Describing her performance, one critic observed: "Cette cantatrice, dont la taille et la figure semblent plutôt convenir à l'opéra-comique qu'à l'opéra-seria, a une voix de contralto resserrée. . . . Sa voix manque de timbre et trahit toujours l'expression qu'elle tâche de donner à son chant." [14] Others were more generous, but a British correspondent waspishly hinted that even these were perhaps more swayed by her personal attractions than by her musical attainments.[15]

She appeared in Winter's opera six times, and on March 27, 1817, participated in a benefit concert. Both *Cosi Fan Tutte* and *Zaïre* were in the company's repertory, but Benelli did not cast her in either production nor did she appear at the Italiens after Catalani's return in August. Tradition has it that she subsequently performed at the Théâtre Français as Camille in Corneille's *Horace*, with Talma in the lead, but the story is probably apocryphal. During the years 1817–18 Talma was in England for some weeks and on tour for part of the time. On those occasions when he appeared in *Horace*, debuts by other members of the cast were carefully noted. Madame Vestris's name is not cited in this connection. She had no talent for tragedy and in all likelihood the story had its origin in the fact that Rose Gourgaud

Vestris, a tragedienne, had been a member of Talma's troupe some years earlier. Eliza Bartolozzi-Vestris is also said to have appeared at the Odéon, but this too is suspect, particularly since the theatre was burned to the ground in 1818. If indeed she did make any professional appearances in Paris after March 1817, they made singularly little impression. One can only conclude that after her disappointing reception at the Italiens she realized that she needed further preparation and decided, for the time being, to leave the stage.

Little as we know about her professional career during this period, we know still less about her private life. Her husband, she tells us, "left her at Paris, under the care of her father." [16] Armand had accepted an engagement at the Teatro San Carlo in Naples and departed for Italy accompanied by Mlle. Mori. He and his wife never saw each other again. Doubtless they were happier apart, and no doubt Madame Vestris found consolation soon enough. Her early biographers assert that she promptly plunged "into the dissipation of the French metropolis." [17] Perhaps she was indeed swept into the circle of fashionable English visitors who flocked to Paris to enjoy the cuisine at the Rocher de Cancale and to gamble the night away at the Salon des Etrangers, but neither Lady Morgan nor Captain Gronow in their gossipy accounts of the English in Paris makes any allusion to her. A fragmentary letter addressed to the Marquis de Marigny and attributed to Madame Vestris probably dates from this period but in no way does it suggest that she was a hardened demimondaine. Written in a childlike mixture of French and Italian, designed to baffle prying eyes, the letter is touchingly genuine and direct. "Je te prie en grâce," she writes, "de me donner une heure ou le matin ou le soir ou l'après-midi que je t'embrasse mille fois." [18]

She remained in Paris from 1816 to 1819, but we know virtually nothing about her during those years. Perhaps her father was teaching there and after Armand deserted her she remained with him. Perhaps she was supported by admirers. Presumably she continued to study singing and often attended the opera and the theatre. One imagines that she did not much care for the melodramas of beggar-maids and brigands at the Porte-Saint Martin or the frigid rhetorical tragedies at the Comédie Française. Far more attractive were the spectacular *féeries* at the Gaité and the comedies at the Vaudeville, as light and insubstantial as a soufflé. But it was evidently Paris itself that most strongly affected her and most deeply influenced her taste. She had not forgotten England, however, nor had she abandoned her hopes for a career, and by September 1819 she was back in London.[19]

chapter 2

$\mathcal{A}$donis in $\mathcal{B}$reeches

She returned at an auspicious time. After an eventful career at the Surrey, the Olympic, and various provincial theatres, Robert William Elliston was about to launch his first season at Drury Lane. He was a versatile and experienced actor, outstanding in genteel comedy, but he was at his best as Robert William Elliston, the great lessee. Quick-witted and persuasive, he knew how to cajole an irate audience into a good humor and how to cope with almost any backstage calamity. Nonetheless, he faced a formidable challenge. Since the turn of the century the prosperity of Drury Lane and Covent Garden had been increasingly threatened by a growing number of minor theatres. The situation was paradoxical. The two patent theatres, each of which accommodated about three thousand spectators, were ill-suited to the legitimate drama but were licensed to present it. The minor theatres, on the other hand, were admirably suited to the legitimate drama but were forbidden to produce it. Instead, they had turned to melodrama, burletta, and spectacle. In theory they were not permitted to compete with the patent theatres, but in practice the patent theatres had been compelled to compete with them. The results had been murderous. The lower scale of admissions at the minor theatres had lured away so substantial a portion of the audience that Covent Garden had not had a profitable year since 1809, and the receipts at Drury Lane had steadily declined since 1812.

The quality of the company had also declined. With the exception of Edmund Kean and a few of the comedians, the troupe was lackluster. But Elliston was an optimist, and with the aid of his acting stage manager, James Winston, he began a purge of the incompetents. Some he replaced by actors who had been under contract to him at the Olympic and the Theatre Royal in Birmingham. Others he sought out in the provinces. In comedy he had little to fear, but in tragedy Drury Lane was woefully inferior to Covent Garden. Determined to bolster his strength in this line, Elliston attempted to raid the theatres of Bath and Liverpool. His efforts were unavailing. He failed equally in trying to lure Mrs. Siddons from retirement. Still worse, he almost lost the one actor who was essential to his plans. Edmund Kean, who had himself hoped to become the lessee of Drury Lane, threatened to defect, and only by consummate maneuvering did Elliston persuade him to stay on. Covent Garden had no performer of comparable stature, but its two leading tragedians, the aging Charles Mayne Young and the youthful William Charles Macready, had at least one advantage—they were competently supported.

These disappointments made Elliston anxious to build up his company in other ways. Both patent houses had a number of singers under contract. Ordinarily they confined themselves to light opera, but occasionally they also undertook more ambitious works. The success of an opera in Italian at the King's Theatre not infrequently led to a rival version in English at Drury Lane or Covent Garden, but in such instances the level of performance was generally depressingly low. Typical was the production of *The Marriage of Figaro* offered at Covent Garden in March 1819. Only Mrs. Dickons, as the Countess, and Miss Stephens, as Susanna, were in any way competent to cope with the music. Others in the cast, principally recruited from the comic wing of the company, were left to struggle with Mozart's score as best they could.

It was Elliston's hope that in opera, at least, he could surpass

Covent Garden. He made a good beginning by engaging John Braham, the great tenor. Braham was short and unprepossessing but he was the master of a showy bravura style that had made him an enormous favorite. In Madame Vestris, Elliston saw a further opportunity to strengthen his company. Her career to date had not been a particularly distinguished one, but she was still young, attractive in appearance and manner, and might well prove an effective rival to Kitty Stephens, the leading soprano at Covent Garden. For some weeks he and Madame argued over terms, but finally they reached an agreement. She was to receive £200 for thirty performances. Elliston also agreed to allow her a benefit, subject to the usual charges.[1]

The death of George III in January brought about a temporary closing of the theatres, but on February 19, 1820, Madame Vestris made her delayed Drury Lane debut as Lilla in Cobb's comic opera, *The Siege of Belgrade*. Grafted onto Cobb's absurd libretto of love among the Balkans, with songs by Stephen Storace, was a subplot with music from Martin y Soler's *La Cosa Rara*. The opera had been popular for nearly thirty years and consequently the familiarity of the songs gave critics the opportunity to concentrate upon her performance. Leigh Hunt, for one, was enthusiastic: "This theatre is justly said to have had a great acquisition in Madame Vestris, who sang at the opera some time ago. Why she has not performed there again is to us incomprehensible, for she is a true singer, a pleasing actress, and a handsome woman; three graces not very frequently united in the same woman."[2] His admiration was seconded by Henry Crabb Robinson who noted in his diary: "[She] will become, I have no doubt, the darling of the public . . . she is by birth English and her articulation is not that of a foreigner, but she looks and walks and gesticulates so very French that I almost thought myself in the Theatre Feydeau."[3] Robinson's impression is substantiated in Hunt's account of her acting in the scene of a lovers' quarrel.

> We [liked] . . . that appearance of involuntary tenderness which she throws into the question, "No more?" when she and Leopold have been agreeing never to see each other again, and they stand nearly back to back, he pretending to huff, and she

making little elbow approaches to him, throwing down her eyes the while and looking at her lifted fingers. The transport with which he turns around and dances headlong with her into a merry chorus was never more warranted.[4]

While there was general agreement that she was an effective actress, opinion was divided as to her vocal talents. The role of Lilla in *The Siege of Belgrade* and also that of Adela in *The Haunted Tower*, in which Madame Vestris next appeared, had both been created by the composer's sister, Ann Storace, who had a voice of considerable range and power and tended to embellish her songs with florid ornamentation. Many at Drury Lane were disappointed by Madame's unadorned vocal style and found fault also with her subsequent performance in the title role of Arne's opera, *Artaxerxes*. Her singing of the famous aria "In Infancy" was condemned as trite and her vocal inadequacies sharply criticized: "Her singing is simplicity itself, for she cannot manage the most transient shake or the slightest cadenza, as there is a rawness in her high notes which the greatest dexterity is wanted to conceal." [5] No doubt the higher notes did, indeed, give her trouble. A true mezzo-soprano, she was often tempted to go outside her vocal range. Even her most ardent admirers admitted to this, but her "simplicity," while it dismayed some, captivated others. The critic of *The Morning Post* commended her rendition of a fresh and unassuming song, with words by John Clare, which she interpolated into the score of *The Siege of Belgrade*, and Leigh Hunt, far from condemning her interpretation of "In infancy," praised her for its exquisite simplicity.

Her notices were on the whole satisfactory, but she had not made the impact upon the public which Elliston had hoped for. In April 1820 he produced *Shakespeare versus Harlequin*, an adaptation of Garrick's *Harlequin's Invasion*. Undertaking the role of Dolly Snip, Madame sang a number of songs agreeably enough, but the modest success of the production could be attributed almost entirely to the pantomime device that permitted "Joey Snip, the tailor, [to] have his head cut off and walk with it about the stage." [6] The adaptation, like Garrick's original, celebrated the triumph of Shakespeare and the downfall of Harlequin, but Elliston had reason to doubt the conclusion. He had launched the 1819–20 season hoping that Shakespeare and Kean would restore the fortunes of Drury Lane. His hopes had not been realized, however. An elaborately costumed production of *Richard III* failed to draw. *Coriolanus*, with the original text restored, expired after four performances. Only *King Lear* had proved a success, and though Covent Garden had rushed into production a rival version of Shakespeare's tragedy, Booth's feeble interpretation could not match the fire and intensity of Kean's performance.

Elliston had clearly scored a victory, but early in May he suffered a defeat. For some months James Sheridan Knowles had been laboring to complete his tragedy of *Virginius*, assuming that Kean would play the title role. Upon completing it he discovered to his surprise that Elliston had already accepted a tragedy on the same theme, but he soon found another outlet for his product. Covent Garden at once put it into rehearsal with Macready in the lead. The role of the heroic Roman centurion admirably suited Macready's abrasive personality, and the success of the play was instantaneous. In the meantime Kean was rehearsing the same role at Drury Lane, but not even he could breathe life into the marmoreal Drury Lane version. To counterbalance its certain failure, Elliston hit upon the notion of reviving *Giovanni in London*, an afterpiece which had proved highly successful at the Olympic three years earlier.

The work had been suggested by Mozart's *Don Giovanni*, performed for the first time in England in April 1817 at the King's Theatre. Within a month Covent Garden had produced its own version, *The Libertine*, adapted by Henry Bishop. Despite the fact that Charles Kemble, as the Don, could not sing a note and made no attempt to do so, the production had proved a success. W. T. Moncrieff's burlesque version *Giovanni in London*, had followed in December. Resuming the story at the approximate point at which Da Ponte's libretto concluded, Moncrieff began his two-act burlesque with Giovanni's attempt to seduce the Furies and his subsequent ejection from Hell. Having ferried the Styx, he makes his way to London accom-

panied by three females, and after a reunion with his valet Leporello, he embarks on a series of adventures. A seduction and a
duel lead to his confinement in the King's Bench, and the piece
concludes with his release and his marriage to a young lady of
fortune.

The burlesque's topicality, its breezy dialogue and slangy lyrics, set to well-known airs, amused playgoers. They were
equally diverted by Moncrieff's impudent hero. The part had
originally been played by a man, but subsequently it had been
performed with even greater success by a hawk-nosed, raw-
boned actress, Mrs. "Jo" Gould. It occurred to Elliston that the
role might well be suitable to Madame Vestris—or Madame,
as her contemporaries called her. After all, she had already appeared *en travestie* as the young Persian prince, Artaxerxes.

Madame at first hesitated. No doubt she was deterred by the
thought that in assuming the role she might impair her operatic
career. Finally she reluctantly agreed, and the piece had its
Drury Lane premiere on May 30, 1820. Its success was
even greater than Elliston had hoped for, and overnight it made
Madame famous.

Actresses *en travestie* were hardly a novelty in the English
theatre. Charles II and his courtiers had ogled Nell Gwyn as a
young gallant in Dryden's *Secret Love*. Mid-eighteenth-century
playgoers had flocked to see Peg Woffington as Sir Harry Wil-
dair, and their grandchildren had applauded Dorothy Jordan in
the same role. All were conspicuously feminine, and all known
for their amorous proclivities. Their swaggering appearance in
male dress heightened their allure and added a new dimension to
their appeal. As one versifier put it in his tribute to Madame
Vestris:

> In breeches then, so well she played the cheat,
> The pretty fellow, and the rake complete;
> Each sex was then with different passions moved,
> The men grew envious and the women loved.[7]

For the first time in her career she had found a role that really
suited her. Attired in doublet and hose, sporting a plumed hat

and brandishing a riding crop, she strode through her role with an air of high good humor and well-bred nonchalance. There was little intrinsic merit to Moncrieff's afterpiece, but Madame lifted it conspicuously above the usual level of operatic travesty. In contrast to the usual coarse and exaggerated style of burlesque,

Madame Vestris in *Giovanni in London*.

her performance had elegance, charm, and restraint. For twenty years she continued to appear in entertainments of this type, and through them she was to exercise an extraordinary influence on both production and acting styles.

Until the close of the season, on July 8, *Giovanni in London* packed Drury Lane nightly, and such was the popularity of the Don that he was resuscitated at various other theatres in various other guises. At the Adelphi, home of melodrama, audiences applauded *Giovanni Vampire*, and at Astley's Circus spectators thrilled to *Giovanni on Horseback*.[8] Madame had perhaps already begun to tire of the role, but it had brought her a gratifying number of offers, among them one from David Morris, lessee of the Haymarket. The prospect of an engagement at that theatre appealed to her. Only the Haymarket was licensed to present legitimate drama during the summer months. The sociable little playhouse held only about sixteen hundred persons, approximately half the number that could be accommodated at Drury Lane or at Covent Garden.

But if Madame had any idea that her talents were to be used in legitimate drama, she was quickly disabused. Within a fortnight she was appearing at the Haymarket as Macheath in *The Beggar's Opera*. Gay's Newgate pastoral was a stock repertory piece which managers often attempted to freshen up by unusual casting. (On one occasion it had been performed "with all the characters metamorphosed, men being substituted for women, and women for men.")[9] Nonetheless, critics were not altogether reconciled to such novelties. While they agreed that Madame's voice was well suited to the traditional ballads, one complained that she was no more like a highwayman than "a duck-legged drummer to General Washington,"[10] and even her admirer Leigh Hunt gently took her to task.

> If Madame Vestris goes on in this manner we must really insist, with whatever violence to ourselves, upon her putting on her petticoats. The more we are pleased with her in trousers and boots, the more we long to see her out of them. She so divests Macheath of his blackguardism—renders him so unlike himself and his sex, converts him really into something so taking and so genteel, so un-Giovannis him as she does the Spaniard —in short, makes him such a very gentlemanly sort of man, that he and his wives seem like three females playing a frolic in masquerade. Her red frock-coat and white trousers become her by the feminine mode of wearing them, and the elegance of her figure, a sort of compromise between the dress of an English

buck and that of a Turkish lady. They are masculine enough as a dress, and yet feminine enough for her to wear them with ease. The only thing at which she seems awkward is her hat: and as we like her ease in the rest, so we like her awkwardness in this. . . . In a word, we never remember an instance of an actress who contrived to be at once so very much of a gentleman and yet so entire and unaltered a woman.[11]

Most theatregoers, however, did not share his reservations. Leering through their quizzing glasses, they pronounced her an Adonis and applauded her to the echo. Her popularity made her sought after by many managers, but Elliston's offer to increase her salary persuaded her to return to Drury Lane in the autumn.[12] He was particularly eager for her services since John Braham had deserted him and Edmund Kean had left for America. Although he had engaged no less than three tragedians— Junius Brutus Booth, James Wallack, and John Cooper—to replace his star actor, Elliston, with reason, was doubtful that they could do so. His season began, somewhat ominously, with *The Road to Ruin* and *Giovanni in London*. He was pinning his hopes, however, on his own production of *The Beggar's Opera* which had its first performance one week later. It had been strongly cast, with Joseph Munden, the great low comedian, in the role of Peachum, and to give it the fillip of novelty Elliston had added an extra scene to the original—Macheath's betrayal at Marylebone Gardens "as they appeared in the time of Gay." Madame insisted on receiving an extra £10 a night to repeat her performance as Macheath,[13] but the extra expense proved more than justified. So warmly was the production received that receipts skyrocketed to over £300 a night. Audiences, it seemed, could not have enough of Madame in breeches, and in short order Elliston was presenting her as Apollo in *Midas* and as Little Pickle, the Blackwall tar, in *The Spoiled Child*. As one critic put it: "The town ran in crowds to see Madame Vestris's legs, though they had been somewhat lukewarm about her singing, and hundreds who 'made mouths at her' while attired in the becoming dress of her own sex, discovered that her proportions were most captivating when set off to advantage by a tight pair of elastic pantaloons." [14]

But if Madame was doomed to appear for the time being in transvestite roles, she saw no reason for confining herself to one theatre. When Elliston refused to allow her to appear at the Opera House, she countered by refusing to perform any male characters at Drury Lane. Grudgingly, he gave her permission to appear at the rival theatre once a week at £25 a night. John Ebers, the new lessee, had engaged as his leading singers Madame Camporese and Ronzi de Begnis. Madame Vestris was hardly in their class, but her popularity was immense and her voice had taken on a new richness and assurance. Like Elliston, Ebers was eager to make use of her in breeches parts, and consequently she returned to the King's Theatre, after an absence of nearly five years, as Pippo, a village youth, in Rossini's *La Gazza Ladra*. Her performance, however, disappointed some critics who doubted that she belonged on the operatic stage. "To us she appears completely cast into obscurity by the simple brown doublet and subdued style of acting which she is there compelled to assume. The effrontery, slang, feathers, and switch of Don Giovanni suit her far better." [15] Others, such as Leigh Hunt, found her completely in her element. Describing her performance as Pippo, he wrote: "She suits it as a rose does her native tree, or a bird the company of birds." [16]

For the remainder of the season she shuttled between the Haymarket and Drury Lane. Rossini's opera had caught the public's fancy and it was repeatedly performed, but Elliston was also clamoring for Madame's services. He had been offering theatregoers a succession of standard plays, strongly cast, but the response had been languid. As a result, he was turning increasingly to opera and spectacle. John Braham had returned, and the operatic wing of the company had been strengthened by the engagement of a new soprano, Mary Ann Wilson. She was unprepossessing in appearance, even by operatic standards, but her voice was much admired and the king himself attended her debut, on which occasion she appeared as Mandane in

Arne's *Artaxerxes*, with Madame Vestris in the title role. Comparisons were inevitable, and Elliston did all that he could to encourage them. Arne's work was subsequently much performed, and in *Dirce*, the most ambitious production of the season, Elliston again paired the two sopranos. The opera was a dull affair, with music by Braham, Charles Horn, and an assortment of Italian composers, but it gave audiences the opportunity to assess the two rivals. They agreed that as a singer Miss Wilson perhaps had a slight edge. They also agreed that as an actress she was woefully inferior to Madame. (Some spectators were evidently disappointed that Miss Wilson, in the title role, was not dragged across the stage at the tail of a wild bull, as the legend required.)

As a further stimulant to the box office, Elliston also devised a number of spectacular entertainments. On June 18 he commemorated the anniversary of the Battle of Waterloo with a program of plays, a masquerade ball, and a supper.

> In order to accommodate the dancing, Elliston boarded over the pit, thus making an enormous stage, decorated in suitably patriotic style. Following two farces, and a concert in which the favourites Miss Wilson and Eliza Vestris were featured, the masquers descended from the boxes and flooded the huge stage with their fancy dress forms. Five bands struck up varied kinds of music, and strongmen, tumblers, slack-rope vaulters and the like went through their acts. . . . Supper was announced at 1 A.M.; the revelry did not finish until seven.[17]

The Coronation of George IV on July 19, 1821, gave Elliston the opportunity to cap even this entertainment. Within a fortnight he had produced his own version of the ceremony, duplicating the ritual at Westminster as lavishly as possible and playing the monarch's role himself. So exactly did he reproduce George's dress that at his entrance the audience rose spontaneously, and so carried away was Elliston by his own grandeur that in subsequent performances he bestowed his blessing upon the spectators.[18]

The spectacle kept Drury Lane open throughout the summer. Miss Wilson, who had proved a short-lived attraction, defected from the company. Wallack and Booth also left Elliston. Madame, while she had no part in the Coronation pageant, occasionally performed as Giovanni, but she was compelled to remain in London for another reason. Her father and mother had had a serious disagreement. He was hard up, in poor health, and had retired to a country retreat. In a letter to her dated March 4, 1821, he complains grumpily of the inadequacies of the local apothecaries, of the stifling religiosity of the place, and in a despondent postscript he adds: *"Everything goes against my will."* [19]

On August 18 he died. Madame Bartolozzi had evidently neglected him, but Madame, according to one of her early biographers, did all that she could to ease his last days.

> He had been so reduced by his thoughtless extravagance as to be unable to procure the attendance of a surgeon; on being informed of which, Madame Vestris immediately ordered that he should have the best medical advice money could procure; and when he shortly after died, under an operation for the stone, he was buried in a very respectable, perhaps we might say, magnificent manner, the expenses being entirely defrayed by Madame Vestris.[20]

Following his death, she paid a brief visit to the Continent, but by November she had rejoined Elliston at Drury Lane. Kean had returned from America, and although Elliston was as determined as ever to encourage legitimate drama, audiences were equally stubborn in clamoring for spectacle. The Coronation pageant had worn thin, but in December Elliston conceived an idea for a new spectacle. The new monarch was to visit Ireland to preside an the installation of the Knights of St. Patrick. Audiences had begun to tire of *Giovanni in London*. Why not send Giovanni to Ireland to witness the ceremony? In short order a sequel had been concocted with music set to Irish airs, and late in December 1821 it had its premiere. As before, Madame Vestris played the Don and Harley Leporello. On this occasion, however, audiences were not amused. Giovanni's escapades— his advances to the ladies, his firing of a convent, and his subsequent trial—were too reminiscent of his earlier adventures.

Elliston was once again playing George IV, but he too failed to win over the spectators. They took exception to the shabby scenery, they found the heraldry indecipherable, and within a week the piece was withdrawn.

The new year began equally dismally. Madame was not offered an engagement at the King's Theatre.[21] Kean found that he could no longer bring audiences to their feet, and Elliston discovered that only by featuring his two star performers on the same bill could he hope to fill the house. As a result, he called upon them to perform almost nightly. While Kean was on stage hoarsely whispering the dying words of Hamlet or Lear, Madame Vestris was in her dressing room donning her breeches for the afterpiece.

Toward the end of the season playgoers observed that she appeared fatigued. It was hardly surprising. Not only was she performing continuously, but she was also troubled by family problems. She felt a real sense of responsibility toward her mother and sister, but the two of them obviously taxed her patience. Josephine was in her early teens and already attracting admirers. Captain Best, a middle-aged man-about-town, felt an urge to protect her, but her mother favored Lord Petersham, a rich young peer. Alarmed by his persistent attentions, the young girl fled from her mother's household. But Madame Bartolozzi was not easily deterred. On the pretext that Josephine had stolen several china cups and saucers and also various chimney ornaments, she applied to the Bow Street police station for a warrant to apprehend her. The young girl was found without difficulty and appeared in court on the arm of Captain Best. Under examination by a magistrate, she timidly asserted that the articles belonged to her. A servant corroborated her evidence. Suddenly, to the astonishment of the court, she blurted out, "The reason which forced me from my mother's house was the continued persecutions I received from Lord P[etersham]." [22] She further revealed that her mother had urged her to become Lord Petersham's mistress in exchange for a settlement of £500 a year. Mrs. Bartolozzi indignantly denied the charge, but a shocked magistrate, after determining that Josephine was only fifteen years old, ordered her placed under the care of a female friend. The notoriety of Lord Petersham (the future husband of Maria Foote) and of Madame Vestris inevitably drew attention to the episode, and despite Madame's later deposition categorically stating "that her said mother never bartered with Lord Petersham, or with any person whatsoever to dispose of her child Josephine," [23] the scandal lived on.

A short summer engagement at the Haymarket left Madame still more exhausted, but at its conclusion she escaped to Brighton for two months. Parading on the Steine and admiring the newly completed Pavilion, she enjoyed the sea breezes while Elliston and Samuel Beazley, the leading theatre architect, were busily renovating Drury Lane. They gutted the stage area to allow for more space behind the scenes, transformed the auditorium from a three-quarter circle to a horseshoe shape, and added private boxes.

By the time the theatre was ready to open Elliston had also vastly improved his company. Through lavish salary offers he had lured away from Covent Garden John Liston, Charles Mayne Young, and Kitty Stephens. He was hoping not only to weaken the other theatre but to stimulate the public's curiosity by encouraging rivalries within his own company. Liston and Munden, the two great low comedians, were to be paired off against each other. Charles Mayne Young, the stately tragedian, was to be pitted against Kean, and Miss Stephens was to provide competition for Madame Vestris. In theory, at least, the plan was a politic one.

On October 16, 1822, the theatre had its official opening. After a round of applause for the renovations and a dutiful rendition of the national anthem, Elliston led the company through *The School for Scandal.* Another old favorite, O'Keefe's comic opera, *The Poor Soldier,* with Madame as Patrick, brought the evening to a close. But it was on the second night that he provided a real surprise for her admirers. On that evening Young performed *Hamlet.* Playing opposite him was Madame Vestris as Ophelia. The tragedian had often played the role at Covent Garden and perhaps for that reason the performance attracted little critical attention. One critic tantalizingly observed that he found Madame "most interesting in look, demeanor, and voice." [24] Another noted that she sang prettily and acted with pathos and simplicity.[25] Other scattered observations are equally laconic. Presumably she was drawn to the part by the musical opportunities in the mad scene and by the entree it might give her into the world of Shakespeare, but evidently she was disappointed by her reception for she played Ophelia only on four more occasions [26] and not until years later did she again undertake a serious role.

chapter 3

The Siren of Mayfair

Giovanni in London made Madame Vestris famous on stage. In private life she was almost equally celebrated. Until her father's death and her mother's quarrel with Josephine, she had been living with her family, but by November 1822 she had taken up independent residence at Number One Curzon Street. Before long the scandalous journal, *The Age*, was referring to her as "The Siren of Mayfair," and she had become the subject of widespread gossip. No doubt she was often slandered by fashionable bucks, eager to boast of their imaginary conquests. Equally certainly, some of the scandals were true. She enjoyed the company of men and she enjoyed intrigue. The society in which she moved was tightly knit. Its members lived on a plane of easy intimacy, and by the time the fourth bottle of port had circulated around the dinner table they had few secrets from one another. But even the most insolently libertine among them found that a pretense to discretion and morality lent an agreeable zest to their adventures. Adept as they were in amorous maneuvres, they met their match in Madame Vestris. She played the game with cool detachment, as acutely aware of her "honor" and at the same time as active in her intriguing as any heroine of Wycherley or Congreve.

Abetting her in these intrigues was Charles Harris, a mysterious figure who for some years played an important role in her life. He had a small house in Half Moon Street, a modest place in the country, and a taste for hunting and the theatre. He lived on the perimeter of society, but a number of men of fashion enjoyed his company and found him useful as an agent in financial matters.

Some cryptic letters, watermarked 1816 and shuffled in among his papers, suggest that he and Madame may first have become acquainted while she was still living with Armand Vestris. The letters indicate that Harris was acting as an intermediary in some clandestine affair, though on whose behalf cannot be established.[1] In any case, by 1822 Madame was on intimate terms with him and showered him with notes asking for advice. The easy intimacy of these messages implies that he made no demands on her and that their relationship was probably an asexual one.

Many others, however, were anxious to make a conquest of Madame. In November 1822 she received a number of ardent letters from Montague Gore. The young man was unknown to her. Madame was curious, but she was not eager to antagonize her other admirers by openly encouraging a new one. She had accepted an annuity of £500 a year, probably from Horatio Clagett, a rakish young ne'er-do-well, but she was finding the arrangement distasteful. Hearing that her unknown admirer was a man of means, she professed herself willing "to listen to the offer of another." [2] She did not propose to jeopardize her current annuity, however, and consequently any meeting with Gore would have to be arranged with the utmost discretion.

Since Harris's house was only around the corner from Curzon Street, Gore was directed to send all his letters under cover to that address. Madame had a passion for secrecy. Her private letters are almost all unsigned and undated. Often no addressee is indicated. When necessary she made use of initials or nicknames, but whenever possible she preferred anonymity. Together she and Harris drafted her letters and dispatched them to her admirers who were instructed to return them with the answer. However suspicious she may have been of her correspondents, she at least trusted Harris, and as a result a fair number of her letters have survived.

Since Harris's papers were disposed of at auction shortly after his death, the letters are now widely scattered, but some notion of Madame's private life may be gathered from her correspondence with Gore, much of which remains intact.[3] Before a meeting between the two took place, Madame and Harris put their heads together and devised a scenario which would permit such a meeting with a minimum risk of scandal. The plan they outlined is an extraordinary one—a preliminary sketch for a scene from Feydeau:

I [Harris] shall call on Monday being sent for by her and that she shall walk with me into Half Moon Street that M[ontague] G[ore] shall meet us there that she shall come up that she shall appear to know him well shall introduce him immediately to me—We shall walk towards my house—I shall ask her in of course—and I shall ask him out of politeness but as though I did not expect he should accept the offer—but he does assisted by her—that after a few minutes have elapsed she will ask me for a little scent bottle which I shall decline getting saying I cannot find it she appearing disappointed not being able to send me out of the room when Frederick [the valet?] comes in with a letter I apologize and go out to write an immediate answer. When she commences—you will think it very strange our meeting thus but the fact is I am watched every place I go to—but coming here never excites the slightest suspicion C[lagett] and him are very great friends and H[arris] keeping a Lady of his own C[lagett] never thinks anything of it and indeed he has no reason although I believe he is more my friend than C[lagett]'s at least I am certain that he would not for the world do me the slightest injury and not being very bright there isn't much difficulty in deceiving him [Clagett] although I never risked it until today.[4]

Gore at first balked at the arrangements, but he reconsidered, and after their initial meeting he gave Madame Vestris a pledge guaranteeing her "the sum of £300 per annum for her life."[5] It initiated a torrent of letters whose sequence is impossible to establish. Madame's letters, drafted with Harris's help, are unsigned and undated. Even her stationery—usually without a watermark—seems to have been selected with a view to secrecy. Gore also avoided dates, salutations, and signatures, punctiliously returning all their correspondence to Harris as she had requested.

The letters make somewhat chilling reading and do little honor to Madame. Gore aroused in her only feelings of cupidity and boredom. To judge from the following sample of his correspondence, her boredom, at least, was justifiable.

> Tribute of respect to Madame Vestris. In the person of Madame Vestris are united all those attractions which have often flitted as phantoms in the brains of poets and artists, but were never before embodied in the full reality of Nature. Lives there the man with breast so cold as to view unmoved her countenance which is tinged with fairest and most delicate hues of Beauty's pencil, her glossy locks parted in graceful ringlets over her unruffled forehead, her ebon eyes that shed around the loveliness of their brilliancy, or the pure marble of her breast? Breathes there the wretch of so degraded a taste as not to gaze with respectful rapture on the symmetry of her person and the graces of her mien? [6]

The gift of a diamond necklace somewhat softened the heart within that marble breast and the subsequent gift of a diamond comb and a pair of diamond earrings further quickened her interest, but their relationship remained a business one. Madame was not impressed by the settlement he initially proposed. Acting as love's deputies, her solicitors persuaded him to raise his offer to £700 a year. Even then, however, they were unable to arrive at any mutually satisfactory arrangement, for Gore insisted upon inserting a clause into their agreement—"as long as she is faithful." Madame as vigorously opposed it and returned to him both his settlement and his check for £700.

Despite the precautions they had taken, rumors of Madame's latest conquest were soon in circulation. Gore was convinced that one of his servants was spying upon them, and before long his offer of a settlement was common gossip. Commenting on this development, a frustrated admirer suggested to Harris that more properly Madame should have settled £700 a year on

Gore. "At first it may seem a little hard that she should give so much money to him for lying with her, but on reflection he is to lie with her tomorrow night and the next night after, and every night, and perhaps not once embowell her." [7]

Apparently she was not an easy conquest, although in another letter the same correspondent reports to Harris his strong suspicion that Thomas Duncombe, a rich and fashionable young Yorkshireman, had had his way with her. It was hardly a matter of consequence, except perhaps to Montague Gore. By February 1823 he had had enough. In the chilliest of terms he informed her that he considered "the connection as finally and irrevocably broken off." [8] No less politely she replied:

> This I consider to be my last letter. It is finished. I thank you for giving me the opportunity of serving and beg of you to believe me
>
> Ever yours,
> Sunday Feb 15th 1823   E. Vestris [9]

To try and unravel the tangled skein of her amours during this period, or to list the "Vestry-men," as they were called, would be an exercise in futility. Without a doubt she was involved with a number of men. Her tastes were extravagant. She entertained to perfection and had a passion for clothes and jewelry. She had a mother and sister to support, and she was generous to a fault. She could hardly be expected to meet all these expenses out of her theatrical salary. Like Lady Teazle she had convinced herself that she was no more extravagant than a woman of quality ought to be. There was little in the Regency ethos to contradict such a line of argument, and for a decade she was pampered and protected by her rich admirers.

One suspects that she felt a secret contempt for many of them. The society in which she moved was for the most part self-centered, spoiled, and dull to an astonishing degree. Anatomizing the English dandies, Prince Pückler-Muskau observed that they could talk only of sports and gambling and were deplorably ignorant.[10] James Grant in his dissection of pre-Victorian society echoes these sentiments.[11] Happily Madame could name a few exceptions among her friends. Lord Alvanley was famous as a host—on one occasion he had organized a water fête for five hundred guests—but he was also a man of intelligence and wit. Above all there was Thomas Duncombe—politician, playgoer, and music-lover.

After Gore's withdrawal, Madame seems to have abandoned Clagett for Duncombe, and for the time being the gossip about her subsided. She had arrived at a critical stage in her career.

The Select Vestry-Men.

She had tired of the Don and longed to play light comedy, but managers seemed reluctant to indulge her. As a singer she was also in a difficult position. Though she could take some satisfaction in the fact that Ebers reengaged her for the King's Theatre, it was becoming increasingly apparent that she could never attain the status of a prima donna.

The Opera reopened in January 1823. Soon after, Ebers revived *La Gazza Ladra* with Madame in her original role. The following month he produced Rossini's *La Donna del Lago*, inspired by Scott's poem, with Ronzi de Begnis as Ellen and Madame Vestris as Malcolm. Subsequently she also appeared as Zamira in Rossini's *Ricciardo e Zoraide* and as Edoardo in the same composer's *Matilde di Shabran*. Her roles were admittedly subsidiary to those of Camporese and de Begnis, but Ebers found her a useful member of his company and a "universal favorite."

The "universal favorite" enjoyed playing to the glittering assembly at the King's Theatre and she exercised her prerogatives to the full. Describing the performers' privileges, Ebers writes:

> A prima donna is entitled to a separate dressing-room, with a sofa and six wax candles; a second donna, a dressing-room, without a sofa, and two wax candles. The same principle obtains with the chief male performers, and with the first and second dancers of both sexes. Ludicrous as it may seem, these marks of precedency are insisted upon with the greatest exactness. Madame Vestris went beyond all others and furnished herself with two additional candles; and one night, there not being, by some inadvertency, candles enough in the house, she stood on the stage behind the curtain and refused to dress for her part until the required number of lights was obtained.[12]

Throughout much of the summer she remained in London, performing at the King's Theatre until the close of the season and occasionally appearing at the Haymarket. In August, accompanied by her mother, she set out for Edinburgh. The wide, clean avenues and bracing air of that city delighted her,[13] and after completing an engagement at the Theatre Royal she returned to the Haymarket. David Morris, the lessee, had offered her a chance to put on petticoats for a change. Madame was increasingly anxious to establish herself as a comedienne and welcomed the opportunity to undertake such roles as Letitia Hardy, the resourceful heroine of Mrs. Cowley's *The Belle's Stratagem*.

Both Elliston at Drury Lane and Charles Kemble at Covent Garden were eager to engage her, and during the summer she artfully played one against the other. By September, Elliston had capitulated to her terms and grudgingly agreed to allow her to appear at the King's Theatre provided that she also appeared three times a week at Drury Lane.[14] As usual, he was hoping to restore the legitimate drama to its former eminence, and, as usual, his expectations were disappointed. Charles Mayne Young had returned to Covent Garden. In his place Elliston had engaged William Charles Macready, but Kean refused to appear with the rival actor and as a result attendance fell off sharply. As he had before, Elliston fell back on opera and spectacle. The sensation of the season was indubitably Moncrieff's melodrama, *The Cataract of the Ganges*, featuring a waterfall, a forest fire, and a stud of horses. Hardly less popular was a series of Shakespearian comedies, "operatized" by Frederick Reynolds and Henry Bishop. It was a measure of the taste of the times that while Macready in *Measure for Measure* and *The Winter's Tale* played to empty benches, Shakespeare "operatized" drew crowded houses. Even the sour prophets who predicted future musical versions of *Macbeth* and *Romeo and Juliet* confessed to their enjoyment of the Reynolds-Bishop *Merry Wives of Windsor*. With Dowton as Falstaff, Braham as Fenton, and Miss Stephens and Madame Vestris as Mrs. Ford and Mrs. Page, it could hardly fail. Encouraged by its reception, Elliston next produced a musical version of *The Comedy of Errors* with Liston as Dromio, Miss Stephens as Adriana, and Madame as Luciana. He followed this with a revivial of *The Tempest*, featuring Madame as Ariel and Macready as Prospero. No doubt Macready regarded this as the ultimate indignity. Only a few patches of Shakespeare's text had survived, and even these were trimmed to make room for musical interpolations by Purcell, Haydn, Mozart, and Rossini.

The rage for Shakespearian opera coincided with the excitement occasioned by Rossini's visit to London during the early months of 1824. Accompanied by his wife, Isabella Colbran, he arrived in January to supervise a season of his own operas to be presented at the King's Theatre by Giovanni Benelli. From a balcony on Regent Street, with a brilliantly colored macaw perched on his shoulder, the great composer delightedly watched the crowds and the traffic below. The fascination was mutual. Hostesses lionized him, George IV royally welcomed him at the Brighton Pavilion, and Rossini, though he knew no

English, tactfully responded by humming a few bars of *God Save the King*.

The season had been designed to capitalize on the vogue for Rossini and to show off the talents of Isabella Colbran. The company which Benelli had engaged was almost exclusively Italian, but he had also reached an agreement with Madame Vestris. Although he had made only minimal use of her talents at the Théâtre des Italiens, she had since become a London celebrity. As a result, he engaged her to appear in the first opera to be performed—Rossini's now-forgotten *Zelmira*. Cast in the leading role, of course, was Madame Colbran. The audience at the King's Theatre on the evening of January 24, 1824, was an expectant one, and when the composer seated himself at the pianoforte and gave the signal to begin, excitement ran high, but by the end of the evening disappointment was widespread. Madame Colbran could no longer produce the glittering cascades of sound which had so delighted Italian audiences, and the role of Emma proved too taxing for Madame. The season had started badly and it continued so. The indisposition of Ronzi de Begnis caused Madame at short notice to undertake the role of Rosina in *The Barber of Seville*, and though Ebers tells us that she enjoyed "a happy success in the histrionic part," [15] the music was clearly too much for her. So were many other roles in the repertory, and consequently she appeared only occasionally during the latter part of the season. It concluded dismally. Pasta and Catalani, at ruinous expense, were called in to bolster attendance. Rossini failed to complete the new opera which had been commissioned for a London premiere, and Benelli fled the country leaving behind him a trail of bad debts.

But if Madame was distressed by the failure of the season, her admirers were not. Like Byron they had had enough of "lasciamis and quavering addios." [16] They preferred her in entertainments of another sort. As one of her admirers put it: "Only think of her leg, sir—there's shape!—there's symmetry!— Bravo! Encore!" [17]

Audiences in Dublin apparently shared these sentiments. Madame Vestris first appeared there on October 25, 1824, in a breeches role.[18] She had wearied of such parts but agreed to play Macheath provided that the scene with his doxies was omitted. The engagement was a successful one, but she was happy to return to London in the latter part of the autumn.

Ebers had reengaged her for the 1825 season, but pending the reopening of the Opera House she accepted an interim engagement at the Haymarket. (Her prospects at Drury Lane seemed increasingly bleak, and consequently she had made no effort to reach an agreement with Elliston.) While Ebers effected some necessary alterations in the opera house, he arranged for his company to appear twice a week at the Haymarket, and as a result Madame Vestris for a brief time appeared there under two managements. On Tuesdays and Saturdays she performed in Italian, on the other evenings in English.

The arrangement was convenient, but when Ebers moved his company back to the King's Theatre she ran into a series of difficulties. She refused to appear in Rossini's *Semiramide* on the grounds that it had been insufficiently rehearsed. She also refused to appear in Meyerbeer's *Crociato in Egitto*. Signor Velluti, a *castrato*, had been engaged for the leading role. It had been nearly thirty years since a *castrato* had performed in England and the excitement occasioned by his forthcoming appearance recalled the days of Farinelli. Nevertheless, Madame was so opposed to appearing with the tall, spectral soprano that she begged Ebers to find a replacement for her. A replacement was found. Perhaps Ebers had had enough of Madame, or perhaps the episode convinced him that she was not indispensable. In any case, it was the last year during which she regularly performed at the King's Theatre.[19]

Shortly afterward another link with the past was broken. For almost ten years she had been separated from her husband Armand. From the Teatro San Carlo in Naples he had moved on to Vienna where he was active as a choreographer at the Hofoper. His pupil Amalia Brugnoli had caused something of a sensation by her novel manner of dancing *sur pointes*, and most recently he had created a number of roles for the young Fanny Elssler.[20] On May 17, 1825, at the age of thirty-seven, he died.

There is no reason to believe that Madame was much affected by his death. She had long since ceased to think of him. She had other reasons to feel depressed. Neither Elliston nor Ebers seemed likely to reengage her, and her career seemed at a standstill. Then, suddenly, she had the satisfaction of participating in an enormous success. On September 13, 1825, John Poole's three-act comedy *Paul Pry* had its premiere at the Haymarket. Not since *Giovanni in London* had an entertainment so captivated the public. The hero of the occasion was indisputably John Liston. For years he had delighted London, mugging his way through a succession of burlettas and farces. In Poole's comedy, which recalls Dryden's *Sir Martin Mar-all* and Mrs. Centlivre's *The Busybody*, he found the ideal vehicle. As Paul Pry, the irrepressible meddler, with his button eyes and flat nose, baggy trousers and umbrella, he achieved national status, and his recurrent apology, "I hope I don't intrude!" became a byword. But Madame Vestris also contributed to the comedy's success. In her subsidiary role as Phoebe she introduced the fresh and appealing song of "Cherry Ripe" to such effect that from then on it was inevitably associated with her. Such was the play's popularity that before long Liston's porcine features stared out of every printshop window and ceramic Paul Prys adorned innumerable mantelpieces. Performed one hundred and fourteen times during the season, it enjoyed perhaps the longest initial run since the original production of *The Beggar's Opera*.

Madame remained at the Haymarket until November 1825. Since March she and Charles Kemble had been dickering and finally she agreed to appear at Covent Garden for sixty performances at £10 a night.[21] She had altogether given up the notion of returning to Drury Lane. For some time Elliston had been drinking heavily and his behavior had become increasingly irrational. He had developed an obsessive habit of kicking those with whom he disagreed. In addition, he had suffered a crippling stroke, and though he retained the direction of the theatre, the burden of management had fallen on the shoulders of his unpopular deputy, James Winston. Kean had returned to America, Munden had retired, and Miss Stephens' and Macready's status was in doubt. Understandably, the remaining members of the company were thoroughly demoralized.

At Covent Garden, on the other hand, an air of optimism prevailed. Kemble had commissioned a new opera, *Oberon*, from Carl Maria von Weber, and it was to have its world premiere in the spring. For months he had been corresponding with the composer in Dresden, urging him to visit London and supervise the rehearsals. The opera, a singspiel with a libretto by J. R. Planché, contained considerable stretches of dialogue and required singers who could act and actors who could sing. Madame had been engaged primarily to fill the important role of Fatima. Needless to say, she was delighted. During the autumn she resigned herself to performing in breeches, though Kemble indulged her by occasionally allowing her to play Letitia Hardy or Lydia Languish. She had a number of secondary obligations to fulfill—a series of concerts at Vauxhall and a brief engagement in Dublin during the latter part of January—but by February she had returned to London and was ready for rehearsals.

The excitement caused by Weber's arrival revived memories of Rossini's visit, though the emaciated, ailing German bore little resemblance to the robust, jovial Italian. Weber had taken to heart Planché's warning that only set pieces such as duets, ballads, and choruses could hold the attention of a London audience, but nonetheless he faced many problems. Drury Lane had rushed into production a rival *Oberon*, "a new grand romantic fairy tale." Braham and Miss Paton, the leading singers, persisted in improving his music with embellishments of their own. With the exception of Madame Vestris, none of the singers could act and none of the actors could sing. In addition, the libretto called for a series of unusually complicated scenic effects.

By the time the premiere took place, on April 12, 1826, the difficulties had miraculously evaporated. Dazzled by the singing and the music, audiences overlooked the fact that Braham looked like a dumpling and Miss Paton acted like one. Storms and shipwrecks took place on cue and in the conjuration scene rocks changed into faces "gleaming with many-coloured flames and lurid light." [22] Within a few days the ailing composer was dead, but he had at least lived long enough to witness *Oberon's* triumph.

Until the end of the Covent Garden season Madame continued to appear as Fatima. Subsequently she returned to Ireland for an engagement in Dublin, followed by concerts in Cork and Waterford. The unpretentious provincial theatres were not to her taste, however. She preferred boxes to benches and wax tapers to tallow candles, and she was happy to return to the Haymarket for another short season. Her repertory there was a familiar one, but she appeared as well in a number of novelties, among them an absurd bit of chinoiserie entitled *Pong Wong*. Written by Charles James Mathews, the son of the great comedian, it was designed to show off the comic talents of John Liston, but it expired after one performance.

Madame could tolerate professional disappointments with equanimity. She was far less tolerant, however, in personal matters. Shortly afterward some jaunty verses entitled *Madame Vestris's Catalogue* appeared in a new periodical appropriately entitled *The Wasp*.[23] The poem begins thus:

> Come tell me, said Duncombe, as kissing and kissed,
> Fair Vestris reclined on his breast,
> Come tell me the number, repeat me the list,
> Of the youths whom your favours have blest.

The boudoir *Iliad* continues with an account of her marriage to Vestris, her subsequent adventures in Paris, and her decision to return to London.

> I roved unrestrained, tasting each tempting flower,
> And revelled in passion's delight,
> Nor paused in my course till a favouring hour
> Brought dear England again to my sight.

> Ah Tommy! though pleasures in Paris abound,
> In England more profit I see,
> For here lovers are wealthy and fools too are found
> To shower much of that wealth upon me.

The poem concludes with a catalogue of her lovers' names and Madame's vow to prove faithful—until Duncombe is out of her sight.

Madame had good reason to feel annoyed—on professional grounds, at any rate. Her reputed stable of lovers would have taxed the energies of a full-time courtesan, let alone those of an extraordinarily busy actress. During her recent engagement at Covent Garden she had appeared no less than seventy-six times, in eighteen different roles, in five of them for the first time. On fourteen occasions she had performed both in the main entertainment and in the afterpiece as well, in one instance playing both Lydia Languish in *The Rivals* and Susanna in *The Marriage of Figaro* in the course of the same evening.[24]

She was even more angered by the subsequent publication of a pseudonymous volume entitled *Memoirs of the Life, Public and Private Adventures of Madame Vestris*.[25] John Duncombe, the publisher, was one of the pack of literary scavengers who fed on scandal and libel. Two years earlier he had regaled readers with a gloating account of Maria Foote's breach-of-promise suit, and in 1825 he had treated them to an even nastier account of Edmund Kean's affair with Mrs. Cox.

It was not in Madame's nature to let such an attack go unanswered. The scandalous *Memoirs* were initially scheduled to appear serially. After the appearance of the first number, Madame warned Duncombe to suspend publication. When he failed to do so, she took legal action. On November 25, 1826, she was granted a hearing before the Court of the King's Bench.[26] In a detailed affidavit, also signed by her mother, she categorically denied almost everything in the *Memoirs*. Point by point she challenged the account of her early days, reputedly passed in Italy, Spain, and Portugal. She rejected as well the stories of her amorous escapades in Paris and London, denying even an acquaintance with most of her reputed lovers. Occasionally her denials have comic overtones. Her solemn assertion that "she never had thoughts of taking the veil and becoming a nun at Minorca or any other place," no doubt brought a smile to the Bench. Probably the court was also amused by her indignant rejection of the rumor that she had played "hunt the barber" on shipboard with a crew of naked sailors.

Though Madame perhaps protested just a shade too much, the court found in her favor and she was awarded £100 in damages. Unfortunately, however, she did not succeed in suppressing publication, and the legends and scandals were incorporated into subsequent slapdash collections such as Oxberry's *Dramatic Biography*.

Madame soon resigned herself to this. She recognized the value of publicity in any form—but she was upset by any reflections on her as a performer. Many accused her of greed. It was true that her demands were high—she insisted on at least £40 a week—but managers could be assured that she would earn her salary, for she frequently appeared in two or three entertainments in the course of an evening. It was also true that she exacted fees from songwriters for promoting their songs. By 1826 she was probably the most popular of the ballad-singers. Since then she had introduced a number of songs which had enjoyed great popularity—"The Banners of Blue" by her uncle, Louis Jansen, "I've Been Roaming," and, most notably, Alexander Lee's "Broom Song," first performed during Liston's Haymarket benefit on September 18, 1826. Understandably, Madame felt that she was entitled to some part of their profits. Equally understandably, songwriters resented the assumption.

Some also took offense at her high-handed manner in musical matters, but it was a failing she shared with many of her contemporaries. Like Miss Stephens and Miss Paton she altered scores at will, omitting some songs and adding others, regardless of their musical or dramatic propriety. As Susanna in *The Marriage of Figaro* she interpolated into the score the popular ballad of "I've Been Roaming." The addition was not to everyone's taste, but Mozart's score was in no sense sacrosanct. It was usually a guess as to who would sing "Voi Che Sapete"—the Countess, Susanna, or Cherubino. Singers in general had a cavalier attitude toward composers, and some months later Madame repeated the offense. If she was unembarrassed by Mozart's prestige, she was not likely to be intimidated by contemporary composers. She bullied Alexander Lee into altering his music until it suited her. In like manner she insisted upon the prima donna's prerogative of dressing a role as she saw fit. Ordinarily her choice of costume was discriminating, but in some instances her vanity overcame her sense of propriety. Cast as a country girl in Henry Bishop's *Clari; or, the Maid of Milan,* she wore a silk skirt and lace-edged petticoat that were far more suited to a worldly Parisienne.

Although she was still a favorite with playgoers, she was well aware that time was not on her side. As an opera singer her career was coming to an end. She was engaged at the King's Theatre during the winter of 1827 but performed only as Pippo in *La Gazza Ladra.* In Covent Garden she played almost entirely in afterpieces, though on occasion, particularly during the benefit weeks in May and June, she had the opportunity to perform in legitimate comedy. At her own benefit, on May 24, 1827, she elected to play Lady Teazle in *The School for Scandal,* "being her first and only appearance in that character." But the choice was a questionable one. Neither then nor later did she ever really succeed in conveying the impression of a girl "bred wholly in the country." She was shrewd enough, however, to surround herself with an admirable cast—William Farren as Sir Peter, Charles Kemble as Charles Surface, and Charles Mayne Young as Joseph Surface.

Between engagements at Covent Garden and the Haymarket she traveled widely, offering provincial managers a choice of some fifteen roles, most of them musical, but, as always, she jumped at the chance to play legitimate comedy. Although she was anxious to advance herself, she was also concerned about Josephine. Her younger sister had reached the age of twenty-one and she too wanted a career on the stage. She was taller than Madame and very like her in appearance, but curiously languid and remote in manner. She was also a mezzo-soprano, but so modest were her talents that a debut at the King's Theatre was out of the question. Instead, she made her first appearance at the more intimate Haymarket, on June 17, 1828, as Rosina in *The Barber of Seville.* Though critics were kind to the trembling young soprano, they expressed little enthusiasm and suggested that the music lay too high for her. Her subsequent performances in roles in which Madame had also appeared—Apollo and Susanna—provoked even cooler comments: "We do not think it quite prudent in Miss Bartolozzi or her advisers to force

Josephine Bartolozzi as Susanna in *The Marriage of Figaro*.

comparisons upon the public betwixt that lady and her more talented sister; Miss Bartolozzi is exceedingly deficient in spirit and is completely devoid of the dash and ease Madame Vestris throws into characters." [27] Madame was also anxious to avoid such comparisons. She was ready to encourage Josephine in every way, and applauded conspicuously from a stage box at her debut, but she tactfully refrained from performing in London during her sister's engagement.

After a provincial tour Madame returned to take part in Josephine's benefit in early October, and on the twenty-first of that month she rejoined her colleagues at Covent Garden. In the course of some necessary alterations to the theatre, Kemble briefly transferred the company to the English Opera House, better known as the Lyceum. The temporary move gave playgoers the opportunity to test a question which had often been asked: could the legitimate drama be seen to better advantage in a smaller house? There, for once, they could see every flicker of expression on Kean's face and catch every inflection in his voice as he blazed his way through Richard III and Shylock. But so accustomed were they to the vast reaches of the patent theatres that the performances made no lasting impression, and when Kemble returned to Covent Garden, the season went on as before. For Madame it was an undistinguished one, her performances being confined almost entirely to trivial operettas by Henry Bishop and Alexander Lee.

At the season's close she embarked on her most ambitious tour to date. With her was Josephine, and together they made the circuit of Worcester, Warwick, Leamington, and Manchester. Their reception was a mixed one. Although they drew good houses and although Madame had evidently coached Josephine to good effect, the latter was hardly a favorite. As the Countess in *The Marriage of Figaro* "her singing [of] 'Tyrant, soon I'll burst thy chains,' would have been hissed at any minor theatre in London," complained one reporter.[28] Nor was Madame exempt from criticism. Describing their performance in *Charles the Second* the same critic observed: "Madame Vestris's personation of Mary was by no means correct. Mary is a simple unsophisticated girl; she gave her all the meretricious airs of a modern barmaid. Miss Bartolozzi's page was as cold and inanimate as usual. This lady seems more engaged with admiring herself than with her part." [29]

They prolonged their tour through the autumn of 1829,

appearing in October in Edinburgh and Newcastle. They had little incentive to return to London. Elliston had finally gone bankrupt and Drury Lane had fallen into the hands of Stephen Price, an American entrepreneur who was already regretting his speculation. Charles Kemble's situation at Covent Garden was not much healthier. His taxes were in arrears and the Duke of Bedford's ground rent was unpaid. But in October a theatrical miracle occurred. The youngest member of the Kemble family, Fanny, made a sensational debut as Juliet, supported by her father, Charles, in his famous interpretation of Mercutio. At Drury Lane, the following month, James Wallack scored an almost equal triumph in Planché's sensational melodrama, *The Brigand*. For the moment, at least, the lessees had been reprieved.

On returning to London Madame at once began negotiating for an engagement. Neither Kemble nor Price was clamoring for the services of Josephine, but before long Madame had coaxed Price into an agreement. She was to perform at Drury Lane for £25 a night while Josephine was to be placed on the payroll at £20 a week.[30] They had struck a fair bargain. Madame by then had a sizable repertory and she had no aversion to undertaking new roles. Her appearance with Josephine in a new comic opera, *The National Guard*, did not cause much of a stir, but she enjoyed a real success in *Hofer, or Tell of the Tyrol*, a production which featured music from Rossini's *William Tell* and spectacular Alpine settings by Clarkson Stanfield.

The number of Madame's admirers had not perceptibly diminished. Some, like the elderly Beau Page, contented themselves by expressing their feelings in verse. Recovering a glove which she had mislaid, he returned it to her, enclosing with it the following couplet:

> If from that glove you take the letter G,
> Then glove is love—and that I send to thee.

Madame's reply was brief and to the point:

> If from that Page you take the letter P,
> Then page is age—and that won't do for me.[31]

Among her more serious admirers was "Handsome Jack" Phillipson, the heir to a substantial estate in Wales, with whom Madame had a short-lived affair.[32] But Josephine also had her admirers, in particular a young tenor at Drury Lane. His name was Joshua Anderson, and though Madame was hardly in a position to find fault, she expressed her vigorous disapproval. According to the backstage gossip, she curtly informed the young man that

> some person had offered Miss Bartolozzi 300 a year & 1000 down and [she] wished to know if he [Anderson] could do so or give her up—his reply was as long as she would stay with him no one would take her from him after which Vestris said Phil[l]ipson should see him. He said he had better not for he should certainly kick his arse. This produced the coolness between them.[33]

Anderson was also angry for another reason. For years Madame had been reluctantly performing Macheath in *The Beggar's Opera*. On April 13, 1830, she did so again, though Anderson had been led to believe that he was to play the role on that evening. In the course of the performance she was hissed. Convinced that Anderson was responsible, two friends of Madame lodged a complaint in Bow Street charging that he had conspired to prevent her from performing. In a contemporary ballad by a twopenny poetaster Madame Vestris states her complaint thus:

> Signor Anderson, you have behaved like a scamp
> And I'll tell you as much to your teeth;
> Neither you nor your creatures my courage shall damp,
> Nor prevent me from playing Macheath.
>
> Recollect, my bold fellow, you're young on the stage,
> And had best mind your P's and your Q's;
> For, whether you like it or not, I'll engage
> The breeches to wear when I chuse.[34]

For some time the backstage tension ran high. Madame and her sister were not on speaking terms, and Josephine was observed glaring at her from a stage box. Chance casting threw Madame and Anderson together in *Guy Mannering* and during a love scene they made a ludicrous attempt to remain in character in spite of outbursts of hissing and applause from rival factions in the audience. The matter was finally settled only when the court found for Madame, but she wisely did not choose to be vindictive. She patched up her difference with Anderson by agreeing to play Lucy to his Macheath. She also made her peace with Josephine, and, perhaps hoping to set her a good example, shortly afterward parted from "Handsome Jack."

If Josephine's future seemed bleak, Madame's was also clouded. Early in July, Stephen Price, the lessee of Drury Lane, declared himself bankrupt. Charles Kemble seemed likely to follow suit. Although Madame had agreed to appear in Dublin, she changed her plans in order to remain closer to London, and during the summer of 1830 she toured the Midlands, competing with such attractions as Hector, the canine star, and Mlle. D'Jeck, the Elephant of Siam, who had created a sensation in a melodrama of that name. The two great patent houses were apparently floundering, and Madame was aware that she would have to adapt herself to the changing times. Accordingly, she began a correspondence with Frederick Yates, the Adelphi lessee. It was under his auspices that Mlle. D'Jeck had made her debut. Though Madame perhaps felt some distaste at the notion of appearing in such company, she was a professional who recognized the increasing importance of the minor theatres. Evidently she and Yates could not come to terms, but her subsequent negotiations with John Chapman, of the Tottenham Street Theatre, proved more satisfactory and she agreed to appear there. The theatre was an inconsequential one, pitifully small and dingy, and remote from the theatrical center, but the lessees of the patent houses had twice brought legal action against it for presenting legitimate drama.[35] In both instances the charges, for technical reasons, had been dismissed.

During the course of Madame's engagement, which began on November 15, Charles Kemble took action against Chapman for the third time. Public sympathy ran high in the defendant's favor, but it was clear that he had infringed on the rights of the patent theatres and in consequence the judge found for the plaintiff and the season came to an abrupt end. The little theatre hardly posed a threat to Covent Garden, but to Kemble the victory had a symbolic importance. Within a month he discovered that while he had temporarily silenced Chapman, he was facing far more serious opposition from a new and unexpected competitor.

chapter 4

The Olympic Muse

On December 6, 1830, John Chapman announced that the Tottenham Street Theatre would close at the end of the week. On the same day Madame Vestris leased the Olympic Theatre from John Scott at an annual rental of £1,000.[1] Her move was a bold one, particularly for a woman, but for ten years she had been active in the theatre, nor was it unprecedented for a woman to take such a step. Mrs. Henry Siddons, after the death of her husband, had for a time directed the Theatre Royal in Edinburgh, and Harriet Waylett, the popular singer, had recently had a brief fling at management.

The Olympic had been built by Philip Astley in 1806, the same year in which John Scott had built the Adelphi. Astley's little theatre, constructed from the timbers of a French man-of-war, had proved unsuitable to the equestrian spectacles for which Astley was famous, and in 1813 it was bought by William Elliston. For six years, he had managed it profitably, but on becoming patentee of Drury Lane he had leased it to a succession of theatrical promoters. One after another they had foundered, and in 1826, when Elliston himself went bankrupt, the Olympic was acquired by John Scott. To judge from precedent, Madame's speculation had little to recommend it.

Situated only a few steps from Drury Lane, at the junction of Newcastle and Wych Street,[2] the theatre, in spite of its modest dimensions, held approximately thirteen hundred spectators when crowded. A contemporary describes it thus:

> The interior is of the horse-shoe form, but approaching to the semicircle. The proscenium is 25 feet wide; and the extent, from the front of the stage to the back of the pit, is 50 feet. The pit is 30 feet wide at the swell, and contains sixteen [rows of] seats, three of which are on the outside of the general enclosure, in a kind of lobby, under the boxes. There is one full tier of boxes; slips, or side-boxes, even with the gallery; and three private boxes on each side, elevated above the pit, but below the full circle. The latter contains four private boxes on each side, and five large central boxes, open at the back, and admitting a view of the stage from the lobby; immediately behind which is a small saloon. The gallery is small, having four rows of seats.[3]

Madame's ultimate goal was clear. She intended to civilize the little theatre, but she was equally determined to operate within the letter of the law. Within a few days she had obtained from the Lord Chamberlain a license allowing her to present "entertainments of music, dancing, bulettas, spectacle, pantomime and horsemanship, from Michaelmas . . . to Easter." [4] The terms were clear enough—with one important exception. Opinions sharply divided on the meaning of the word "burletta." Originally the word had signified a short musical piece in verse with continuous song or recitative. Subsequently it had been defined as a three-act piece with at least five songs in each act. But still more recently the term had been expanded to cover a broad spectrum of entertainments—vaudevilles, extravaganzas, burlesques, and comediettas. So difficult had it become to distinguish burletta from the legitimate drama that even the Lord Chamberlain's controller recognized the confusion.[5]

It was burlettas, above all, that were to make up the staple of repertory at the Olympic. Madame was hoping to offer the public short, light pieces, similar to the French *vaudevilles*, but purged of all vulgarity. Through them she could perhaps attract the type of audience which no longer attended the theatre. Since the violent Old Price riots in 1809, fashionable spectators had increasingly avoided the patent houses. Even in the dress boxes they might rub elbows with the ladies of the town, and

Sir Walter Scott complained that male theatregoers prosecuted "their debaucheries so openly that it would disgrace a bagnio." [6]

Only on rare occasions was the world of fashion lured away from the opera and back into the theatre. In 1826, P. F. Laporte presented a French company headed by Potier and Mlle. George in Tottenham Street. Audiences admired Potier's quiet style and mastery of stage business, and for a brief time the company attracted London society, but their repertory was conventional, the price of admission too high, and the theatre so

The Olympic Theatre.

dingy that attendance soon fell off. In 1830 Potier returned, and in the latter part of the same year another great French character actor, Bouffé, also appeared in London. Both had warm receptions, but in many respects their supporting companies left much to be desired. The actresses were generally inferior, the costuming haphazard, and the singing inadequate. While Madame did not expect to find an English equivalent to Potier or Bouffé, she did at least hope to set higher standards of production at the Olympic.

She was anxious to open the theatre as soon as possible, but there was much to be done and almost no time to do it in. She needed an acting company, a stage crew, and suitable scripts. Faced with the prospect of opening within a month, an experienced manager would have abandoned hope. Madame set to work.

She began by engaging Maria Foote, a popular soubrette, who agreed to perform for a limited number of nights before going on tour. Mrs. Glover, a mature and dependable comedienne, also agreed to appear, provided she was released to fulfill an engagement at the Tottenham Street Theatre when it reopened under its new lessee, George Macfarren. Madame also recruited William Fredericks and William Vining, two ex-members of Chapman's company, and, through Mr. Kenneth and "Honest" Smythson, the theatrical agents, she sought out unemployed "walking ladies" and "singing gentlemen." In one important respect, however, she broke with theatrical tradition. She had decided to do away with the actors' time-honored perquisite of benefit nights.[7] For generations it had been their prerogative on these occasions to devise the bill, dispose of the tickets, and pocket the receipts after the payment of house charges. Theoretically, a benefit could sizably supplement a performer's income, but it could also prove a cruel disappointment. More than one actor had found to his dismay that for all his efforts he had not covered his expenses. Benefits also tended to lead to bizzarre bills, with actors who were born to play Tony Lumpkin aspiring to Hamlet, and vice versa. Madame was not prepared to be so permissive, but prospective recruits were offered generous salaries, and within a short time she collected a company. Before long she had a technical crew as well.

It was no less important for her to find good new scripts. It would have been easy enough to swagger once more through *Giovanni in London* or *The Beggar's Opera*, but she had made up her mind to dispense with the shopworn repertory. Among the dramatists there was one, above all, that she was eager to win over to the Olympic. He was James Robinson Planché, the librettist for *Oberon*. He was diminutive in stature and something of a dandy, but his industry as a playwright was legendary, he was an authority on costume, and he had an intimate knowledge of the French theatre. Not least of all, he had a quality of innate elegance that recommended him to Madame. As one of his colleagues facetiously observed, "he wrote in white kid gloves." [8]

Planché agreed to provide her with a play and to function as her adviser, though Madame had already made up her mind on many matters. For decades it had been usual for managers to issue orders, and during the lean years at the patent houses the practice had grown to alarming proportions. Between May and July of 1829, so it was rumored, Charles Kemble had issued over eleven thousand free admissions to Covent Garden. Such a policy at the Olympic could only spell ruin. Consequently, Madame decided to abolish the free list, exempting only the press.

She also decided to do away with "puffing"—misleading promotion—a practice to which Elliston had been particularly addicted. The playbills of the printer Fairbrother had grown steadily more garish, with exclamation points and capital letters splashed across them in ever-increasing type size. Madame, like the Parisian managers, frowned on such expedients. A success needed no puffing, and no amount of artificial respiration could breathe life into a failure.

She wished to remodel the Olympic, but in the course of three weeks she could hardly hope to realize many improvements. In her mind's eye she envisioned a theatre as elegant and comfortable as the most tastefully appointed drawing room. In spite of the dust and grime in the diminutive house she recognized at once the type of audience and the type of entertainment to which it was best suited. It was to the boxes, primarily, that she proposed to cater. Admission prices were to be the same as those at the Tottenham Street Theatre and the Adelphi: 4 shillings for a box seat, 2 shillings for the pit, and 1 shilling for the gallery. She had no wish to encourage the patronage of the roaring boys or the Cyprians.[9] Hers was to be the theatre of the *beau monde*.

By some miracle the house was in order on January 3rd, 1831. In less than a month she had cast and rehearsed and provided sets and costumes for an opening bill of four short plays. On the morning of that day she timed the final rehearsal, astonished the company by presenting them with a week's salary, and went home to rest until evening. For days every available place had been booked, and by six-thirty long lines of emblazoned carriages stretched from Longacre to Wych Street. So great was the rush for seats that when the doors were finally opened even the boxes were invaded, and so crowded was the house that it was difficult to see exactly what Madame had accomplished. "When we afterwards got a view of it," Leigh Hunt wrote, "we found one of the prettiest interiors we are acquainted with, a perfect circle all but the stage, with the fronts of the boxes painted in medallions, and the whole presenting an atmosphere warm and cheerful." [10] John Wilson had painted a handsome new landscape drop, and as Madame stepped in front of the curtain and gazed around the house she had reason to feel satisfied. Lord Adolphus Fitzclarence, the natural son of William IV, led the applause, and the boxes had the glitter of an opening night at the King's Theatre. After a graceful speech of welcome, tumultuously applauded, the full company joined in the singing of "God Save the King" and the entertainment began.

The first of the four one-act plays presented that evening was W. H. Murray's *Mary Queen of Scots; or, the Escape from Loch Leven*. It was designed to show off the talents of Maria Foote who, in her shell-formed cap and pearl bodice, had been costumed to resemble the portraits of Mary. Still more authentic was the set, according to Matthew Mackintosh, a later member of the Olympic stage crew.

> With a full recollection of all that has been done since by Macready, Madame herself, and Mr. Charles Kean, I believe that no more elaborately perfect "set" was ever seen on a stage than that of Queen Mary's room in Loch Leven Castle, in this piece. Every single thing in it was in keeping with the period and with the other things, for which purpose the curiosity shops of London had been ransacked to procure the requisite furniture and properties. The tables, chairs, couches, &c., were all of genuine carved oak, and everything bore the arms or emblazonment of the Stuarts. The window curtains, table and chair cov-

ers, drinking goblets, candlesticks, knives and forks, nay even to the very carpet on the floor, were thus marked.[11]

This description has often been quoted, but it is almost certainly overstated. Mackintosh did not join Madame's company until 1832, and his observations, published over thirty years later, are often unreliable. Murray's play made little impact, and Planché's disparaging observations on the makeshift scenery at the start of the season make it plain that Madame was forced to make use of well-worn backdrops. Perhaps she did indeed freshen them up by a few judiciously selected properties, but there is little likelihood that she had either the time or the money to achieve quite the effect that Mackintosh describes. His account is worth quoting, however, because it suggests the attention to detail that characterized so many of her subsequent productions.

Of the remaining entertainments only one achieved any real success. Miss Foote was politely applauded in *The Little Jockey*, as was Mrs. Glover in *Clarissa Harlowe*, but the audience expressed enthusiasm only for *Olympic Revels*.

Planché had written the piece some years earlier, but he had not succeeded in interesting any manager in his "mythological, allegorical burletta." Finding that Madame Vestris needed a play for immediate production he offered it to her. The manuscript required some revisions, but since Planché was busy on various projects he entrusted the task to Charles Dance with whom he had previously collaborated.

Their joint *jeu d'esprit* is a retelling of the familiar legend. To punish Prometheus for creating men, Jupiter commissions Vulcan to create Pandora, "a lass of metal." He entrusts her with a mysterious casket, to be kept closed, and the admiring gods endow her with a variety of gifts. The jealous Juno, however, afflicts her with a fatal weakness—curiosity. Once united to Prometheus, Pandora gives way to temptation and opens the box. A host of fiends spring out, but Hope, found lurking at the bottom of the casket, intercedes for the couple and the piece closes with a general reconciliation.

Like Kane O'Hara's *Midas*, the burletta topicalizes life on Olympus. The gods play at whist. They discuss such diverse matters as railroads, various brands of snuff, and the new metropolitan police. The music is as eclectic. Jupiter and the gods thunder out their lines to stirring choruses from Auber's *Masaniello* and Weber's *Der Freischütz*; Mercury, Pandora, and a Swiss boy warble a medley of mountain airs, and Prometheus favors the audience with a Scottish ballad.

From the start the success of the piece was never in doubt, al-

Mr. Newcombe, Madame Vestris, and Mr. Beckwith in *Olympic Revels*. (*Shevelove Collection*)

though the physical production left much to be desired. The scenery "was limited to a few clouds," Planché writes, "the interior of a cottage and a well-used modern street, which was made a joke of in the bill to anticipate criticism." [12] In the costuming, however, Planché achieved an effective innovation. For decades it had been traditional to dress burlesques absurdly, but Planché insisted on dressing the actors as elegantly and as accurately as possible: "My suggestion to try the effect of persons picturesquely attired speaking absurd doggerel, fortunately took the fancy of the fair lessee, and the alteration was highly appreciated by the public." [13]

Clinching the success of the piece was Madame herself, in the role of Pandora. As she made her first appearance, rising through a trap door, she was received with a resounding applause. Her acting had a charm and ease that was far removed from the usual broad style of burlesque, and music-lovers noted with approval that even in the musical parodies she "never lost sight of Mozart or Rossini." [14] As the piece drew to a close she implored the audience to "fill with patrons all Pandora's boxes," but the plea was hardly necessary. Critics the following morning were enthusiastic. Within a few days a rash of poetic tributes appeared, acclaiming her as the tenth muse, and during the remainder of the season the house was packed at every performance.

Maria Foote's departure from the company had little effect on the season's success. It was her last engagement in London, for shortly after completing her provincial tour she married Lord Petersham, Josephine Bartolozzi's pursuer, and retired from the stage. The two pieces in which she had been appearing were promptly dropped from the repertory, and in their stead Madame substituted Auber's *Fra Diavolo* in which she and William Fredericks had appeared for Chapman. The substitution was only a stopgap, however. It was against her policy to offer entertainments which had already been seen elsewhere, and after three performances it was withdrawn. She was even more ruthless in dropping from the repertory, after only one performance, the unsuccessful novelty *The Castle of Steinberg*.

Although her first season was a short one, lasting for only twelve weeks, in its course she presented a total of fourteen productions. The majority were of little consequence. *The Chaste Salute*, an adaptation from Scribe, was well received, as was T. H. Bayly's *The Grenadier*. In the latter Madame found not one but three roles for herself, appearing in turn as the young heroine, a captain of the Grenadiers, and a Savoyard boy. Even so, she was compelled to divide the honors with her leading man —a pet monkey. Jou-la, as he was called, evidently captivated both the audience and critics, for Leigh Hunt approvingly noted: "Although exceedingly small, his figure is neat, his dress well conceived, his manner and air free, while his whole performance rather exceeds than falls short of expectation—in short, he is a very meritorious monkey." [15]

Reassured by her success, Madame could afford to mount her productions with increasing care. *Duke for a Day*, one of the final novelties, was no more substantial than her other offerings, but nonetheless she carefully rehearsed it, dressed it to perfec-

Madame Vestris in *The Grenadier*. (*Shevelove Collection*)

tion, and provided it with new scenery by William Gordon, a pupil of the great Clarkson Stanfield.

On the last night of the season, March 26, the lessee formally thanked the spectators for their patronage and gracefully took her leave of them until October: "As Fanny Bolton, the captain of the grenadiers, I salute the company in the pit [hand to forehead]; as Julian the Page [*Duke for a Day*] I pay my respectful duty to the boxes [bowing]; and as Pandora [*Olympic Revels*], I drop my curtsy to the gods." [16]

She could take justifiable satisfaction in what she had accomplished during her brief first season. In that time she had already effected various reforms. Critics had often complained of over-long theatrical bills. Leigh Hunt, for one, had pointed out that both the young and the old were virtually excluded from playgoing since performances often dragged on until the early hours of the morning. Reviewing the opening night at the Olympic, a critic on *The Morning Chronicle* renewed the complaint: "We are surely not singular in our opinion that the performances of the evening would have given unqualified pleasure had the entertainments been limited to three burlettas and those the three that were enacted last." [17] Madame agreed. Parisian theatre managers traditionally terminated performances by eleven, and within a week of the Olympic's opening she had inaugurated a similar policy.

She had also brought order to the Olympic both before and behind the curtain. She insisted on the strictest order in the auditorium. A new decorum also prevailed backstage. Under her management the Green Room was no longer a meeting place for the raffish world of the demimonde. During the palmier days of Garrick and Sheridan only visitors in full evening dress had been permitted, and each of the principal ladies had been attended by a page. At the Olympic she could hardly hope to revive such grandeur, but she made it a point to discourage casual visitors, making an exception only for literary men.

No less important were the reforms she effected in her productions. She did not share the casual views of Elliston who had slighted rehearsals and allowed his actors to skim through their parts in a perfunctory manner. She saw a play not as a vehicle for a leading actor but as an artistic unit. As Planché approvingly noted, she had the admirable habit of observing all performances and noting any imperfections. She had the additional virtue of insisting on keeping her productions fresh-looking and often redressed them during their run.

Despite her success, her company had been criticized as being, "with the exception of the stars . . . the very worst ever collected in a metropolitan theatre." [18] The comment was perhaps inevitable, since her company had been so hastily assembled. In the course of the season, however, she succeeded in effecting a few minor improvements. William Fredericks, who had been criticized for splitting the ears of the groundlings in *Mary, Queen of Scots*, in *Fra Diavolo* was praised for his non-melodramatic delivery. From the beginning to the end of her managerial career, Madame Vestris favored the easy, natural manner of the French school, though she realized it was not

Madame Vestris' Leg.

easy to achieve—particularly with an indifferent company. She had patience, however, and would have sympathized with Charles Kean's later observation: "One great point in a theatre is to have a company together for a good many years; they may not be people of very great talent, but they become so accustomed to each other, and get into such training that they harmonize." [19]

Her success made her once again the object of much attention. London wits quipped that the Garrick Club had invited her to become a member—provided she appeared in breeches. They found even more occasion for laughter in a case brought before the magistrate of the Marlborough Street Police Office. Mr. Papera, an Italian modeler, appeared in court to testify against a young journeyman "charged with stealing and disposing of, on his own account, and for his own use, the casts of several figures in plaster of Paris, the property of Mr. Papera." [20] Among them were casts of Madame's legs, "to a little above the knee, and including the foot." The original mold, so Mr. Papera explained, had been commissioned by a gentleman of large fortune, enraptured by Madame's performance as Giovanni. Only occasionally since then had he reproduced Madame's matchless limbs for the delectation of artists and connoisseurs. He had been shocked to find them exposed in various London shopwindows. When asked if the stolen legs had been sold under their value, Mr. Papera replied that "such a leg was always certain to fetch a high price in the market; and besides, the legs of this lady were in very great demand." The wits laughed and celebrated the incident with a torrent of bad verse. Among these effusions is a mock epic on the comparative anatomy of various actresses. After an invocation—"Legs and the Dames I sing," —the poet turns to the subject of Madame.

> Of all the ladies in theatric throng,
> "Who sought fame soon and had her favour long,"
> Vestris stands first—the first without debate—
> And does "most business," chiefly with the great.
> When she came out upon the Opera boards,
> She kept her ankles, "like a miser's hoards,
> Unsunn'd unseen:" but ah! thrice happy we
> That liv'd to mark the glories of her knee,
> That beauteous knee and calf's proportion'd size
> That oft drew tears from C[lage]tt's doating eyes.[21]

Madame was probably amused. In any case, it was good publicity. She had boosted her terms to £40 a night, but managers were not deterred. In May she appeared in Bath, and during the early summer she toured Dublin and the Midlands with Jou-la

as her costar. She returned to London late in July to perform at
Vauxhall and to prepare for her second season.

She acquired a new stage manager, James Vining, who could
double as her *jeune premier*. Gordon painted a new act drop,
and she engaged J. G. Crace to redecorate the theatre. Some
minor changes had already been effected. Earlier in the year she
had removed the gas from the dress-circle chandeliers and substituted wax candles.[22] The gas not only gave off an offensive
odor, it was dangerous as well. (An explosion at Covent Garden
in 1828 had caused the death of two men.)

Of more consequence, however, were the structural changes
which she commissioned Samuel Beazley to undertake. Following her instructions, he abolished the proscenium doors and substituted boxes in their place.[23] He also completely reconstructed
the stage:

> The stage itself was formed on a principle then quite novel,
> being elaborately yet simply built of component parts. Each
> four-feet in depth portion of it, measuring from the footlights,
> included six traps, all available for any piece that was played,
> and up which were sent all the properties for each scene, thus
> avoiding any awkward changes of this sort in sight of the audi-
> ence.[24]

The use of traps to speed the setting of a scene was an innovation on the English stage but a common practice in the French
theatre. Still another theatrical innovation of French origin was
the new green curtain which "instead of rolling down as customary, opens in the middle and draws up to the side of the
stage." [25]

But theatregoers in Wych Street on the evening of October
1, 1831, were far more interested in the transformations which
had taken place in the auditorium. Under Crace's direction, the
dingy little house had been metamorphosed into a "Temple of
Love," "a bower of Cupids and bouquets." Instead of the conventional red-and-gold decor of the nineteenth-century theatre,
white, blue, and gold dominated the color scheme. The effect,
according to the critic of *The Athenaeum*, was airy, light—
and French.

The ceiling is painted in imitation of an ornamented silk canopy, drawn tight by garlands of flowers, held by flying cupids —the chandelier being suspended, of course, from the center. The proscenium is divided by gilt beading into compartments, each containing a wreath of flowers. A border of flowers runs up each of the pilasters. . . . The lower tier of boxes is formed into panels in which are very prettily painted subjects selected from the works of the eminent artist Bartolozzi—a well-merited compliment suggested by the good taste of Madame Vestris to the talent of her grandfather. Rich arabesque scroll ornaments on a white ground, alternately with lozenge-shaped panels, containing emblematical figures, decorate the fronts of the upper tier. An ornamental gilt moulding runs round the top of the boxes, and the bottom of the facia is solid dead gold, relieved by burnished pateras and mouldings. The whole has a gay and pleasing effect and will present to view the elegance and finish of a drawing-room.[26]

Madame had engaged John Liston, the great comedian, at the unprecedented salary of £60 a week, to be the guest of honor in her drawing room. So great a favorite was he with audiences that he had only to walk on stage to set them laughing. His face, as Hazlitt put it, was a national calamity, so much had it contributed to the decline of legitimate comedy.[27] Madame had tried to persuade John Poole, the author of *Paul Pry*, to provide her with a novelty, but he had disappointed her, and on her opening bill she presented the comedian instead in *Talk of the Devil*, an adaptation from the French by her architect, Samuel Beazley.

To most of those in the audience on the evening of October 1 the substitution made no difference whatsoever. They had come to see Liston. While they waited impatiently for the performance to begin, the shirt-sleeved gods in the gallery joked noisily and passed the rum. They roared their approval when the curtain parted and their favorite came on as Dominique, an impoverished soldier. "Six months ago," he began, "who would have looked for such a change of circumstances? Yet here I am!" The audience roared again. But as the play went on, a change came over them. The actor was beating his head and chest in melodramatic fashion. The laughter became less certain.

Was it conceivable that he intended to be serious? In parts of Beazley's play it was certainly the author's intention, but the audience would have none of it. "If Liston was to break his leg on stage," observed Leigh Hunt, "it would be difficult to persuade them that it was not an excellent practical joke." [28] Madame Vestris had miscast him, but such was the comedian's popularity that it was a matter of small consequence. As one critic put it, he could "raise a piece of almost any weight, throw it over his shoulder, walk up and down and carry the audience with him." [29]

Madame had counted on Liston as the chief mainstay of her season and he did not disappoint her. *I'll Be Your Second*, a farcical comedy in which he appeared a week later, went off like a bottle of champagne. Madame had no intention, however, of pinning all her hopes on Liston. She had begun to build up a company that ultimately consisted of about forty performers. While a few of them, such as Mrs. Glover and William Vining, were stage veterans, the majority were relatively inexperienced. Nonetheless, she had ambitious plans.

During her second season she presented a dozen new productions. Of these, one in particular proved exceptionally interesting. For years Christmas pantomimes had been a staple of the London theatre, but Madame had rarely participated in them. The role of Columbine did not suit her talents.[30] It was virtually obligatory, however, for theatre managers to produce a holiday treat. In view of the success of *Olympic Revels*, she decided to offer Olympic playgoers another burletta on the same order but far more lavishly produced.

Once again turning to classical mythology, Planché and Dance decided to make use of the legend of Orpheus. The lessee was, of course, to play Orpheus, and the newly engaged Miss Forde, Eurydice. In short order the two playwrights produced a libretto stuffed with topical allusions and crackling with volleys of puns. The lyrics, as before, they fitted to popular ballads and tunes plundered from current operas.

Two other men also played key roles in the production and were to be closely associated with Madame Vestris for many years. One of them, Oscar Byrne, she had known as a solo dancer at the King's Theatre, and later as first dancer at Drury Lane. At her urging he agreed to choreograph the dances and supervise the crowd scenes, processions, and tableaux. The other was a new recruit whom she cast in the important role of Pluto. James Bland, the son of Mrs. Bland, the famous vocalist, had a sound knowledge of music, a resounding baritone, and an authoritative presence that justified his later title—King of Extravaganza.

The first performance of *Olympic Devils* took place on Boxing Night, December 26, 1831. It enjoyed a success even greater than that of its predecessor. Holiday audiences guffawed at the cascades of puns. They relished the parodies of standard plays such as *Othello* and *Pizarro,* and they were amused by the outrageous anachronisms. The production was also visually appealing, according to Planché.

> The Bacchanalian procession, arranged by Oscar Byrne, considering the size of the stage and the numbers employed, could not well have been surpassed at that time by the Patent Houses for picture and animation. A prominent feature in the tableau formed at the end of the march was a young Bacchante reclining listlessly on a leopard skin before the steps of the Temple. It was a study for Etty.[31]

Equally praised was Byrne's staging of the arrival of the drunken Silenus on an ass, and the engaging dance in which a lion and a panther waltzed, mountains rocked, and trees gracefully stirred their stumps.

The contributions of Mr. Rawlings, Madame's machinist, were also notable, the descent of Apollo in the car of the sun being particularly admired. He was perhaps a shade less successful in realizing the challenging stage direction: "The head of Orpheus is presently seen floating down the river." How he struggled to achieve this effect is described for us by a critic who witnessed a minor mishap during the performance he attended.

> The whole scene of the Bacchanalian orgies, ending with the tearing piece-meal of Orpheus, and the floating of his head

Madame Vestris as Orpheus in *Olympic Devils*.

down the Hebrus was so beautifully managed as almost to amount to a charming illusion. . . . The floating of the bard's head was managed in the same manner as the swimming of the wolves in *Mazeppa*, at Astley's, appearing through an aperture in the supposed water, which is gradually drawn across the stage. On the occasion alluded to the water was pulled along in so irregular a manner as to excite not only confusion, but alarm among the actors and the audience; and amid cries of "Take care! Here! There! Faster! Slower! Tighter! Looser! Pull! Let go!" etc. a voice exclaimed, "Damn it! You'll strangle her!!" Where now was the illusion? [32]

Despite these occasional minor blemishes, the production challenged comparison with the holiday amusements at the patent theatres—particularly since the Drury Lane pantomime, *Harlequin and Little Thumb*, featured a scene in which Harlequin transformed Paganini into Orpheus and his admirers into a pack of wild beasts. Madame's production, as far as one can judge, did not suffer by comparison.

The success of *Olympic Devils* led to rumors that she was considering leasing still another theatre, either the Coburg or the Pantheon, but she had troubles enough at her own. In addition to her busy production schedule, she was having problems with some members of her company. During her first season, after Maria Foote's departure, Madame had engaged as her replacement an attractive young soubrette, Miss Sydney. Before long gossip had it that Madame resented Miss Sydney's youth and beauty. In any case, the two women quarreled, and in March 1832 Miss Sydney brought action against Madame for two weeks' salary. Nonsuited by a judge who found that the young actress had violated the articles of her contract, she "indulged in a violent phillipic against Madame" [33] and left the company.

The lessee was also having problems with Liston. Like so many low comedians, he suffered from hypochondria. He resented innovation, and so individual were his talents that he was not easy to assimilate into a company. As Madame's productions moved increasingly in the direction of naturalism, he seemed more and more out of place. In addition, the spectators that he attracted to the Olympic were not of the sort that she wished to encourage.

No doubt Liston was aware of her feelings. His performances were often slipshod, and he is said to have sometimes "reeled through" them.[34] When Madame Vestris finally obtained from Poole his new comedy, *The Young Hopefuls*, it failed dismally, and so angered was the author by Liston's slipshod performance that he refused to write for him again. Fortunately, Madame was on good terms with other playwrights, and she found an effective vehicle for Liston and herself in T. H. Bayly's *My Eleventh Day*. As a comic Othello, Liston played the jealous husband in his broadest style. As his innocent young wife, who effects his cure by disguising herself as a dandy, Madame made an effective contrast to him. The role also gave her the chance to demonstrate her musical versatility, for in addition to rendering one song in French and another in English, she sang still another in Italian, in imitation of Pasta's bravura style.

Her energy was extraordinary, and at the close of her second season, prior to setting off on a summer tour, she appeared for a brief period at the Tottenham Street Theatre, rechristened the Queen's Theatre by George Macfarren, the new lessee. He had attractively redecorated the interior, and he featured a repertory much like Madame's, but he had neither her taste nor her drive, and shortly after her engagement he joined the ranks of theatrical bankrupts.

During her subsequent engagement in Liverpool, Madame was joined by her sister Josephine. Their reunion can hardly have been a happy one. Josephine had finally married Joshua Anderson, the tenor with whom Madame had feuded, and in the summer of 1831 the Andersons sailed for New York, the Mecca for so many English actors. But Anderson was poorly cast as a pilgrim, and on the voyage over he freely expressed his contempt for America. Not surprisingly, American playgoers reciprocated. At his debut they rioted and prevented his performing.[35] Two nights later he was again driven off by a shower of eggs. In Boston, audiences proved somewhat friendlier and the Andersons were allowed to appear, but on their return to New

York they found public opinion as hostile as before. For some months they stayed on. Josephine was permitted to play some of the roles her sister had made famous, but Anderson remained unforgiven. Though he had not been tarred and feathered, as some of the papers had reported, there was no disguising the fact that the trip had been a disaster.

Madame had little reason to sympathize with her brother-in-law, but she allowed him to sing the ballad of "Will Watch" at her Liverpool benefit and she was evidently anxious to remain on good terms with him. She drew the line, however, at offering him an engagement, and although he subsequently appeared at the Haymarket in July, 1831, his dismal theatrical career was coming to an end. He was already drifting into the raffish underworld of gamblers and gentlemen of the turf. Josephine's hopes for a career were also evaporating. So cold was her personality, and so limited were her talents, that managers showed little interest in her. As a sister, Madame was anxious to help Josephine as much as she could. As a manager, she sympathized with her colleagues.

She had already recruited a company for her third season, and two of them promised to be extraordinarily useful. One was Mary Ann Orger, a good-hearted, expressive character actress who could play down-to-earth roles without vulgarity. The other was Ben Webster. Madame had known him since the days when he had been an insignificant supporting player at Drury Lane, but he was rapidly developing into an all-around man of the theatre. He could knock together a farce, a melodrama, or a burletta. He had some musical talent, could dance, and play comedy and character parts.

It was with Webster in the lead that Madame Vestris on November 28, 1832, produced William Bernard's *The Conquering Game*. This one-act drama of an amorous episode in the life of Charles XII has no importance as a play, but nonetheless it has interested theatre historians, for it was in this production, so one of them asserts, that "the box set first appeared in England." [36]

While the play's engraved frontispiece, "from a drawing taken in the theatre," gives some credibility to the claim, not everyone agrees that it confirms the use of three-walled flats, a ceiling cloth, and real properties.[37] The playwright's directions for the scene in question read as follows:

> *Chamber at the Baroness' House, opening at the back, through glass doors, upon a Terrace in the Garden, distant view of the City of Stockholm by Moonlight. Closets right and left of this entrance. The room elegantly furnished in an antique style.—Pictures in heavy frames &c. Painting stand with the Picture of an aged Female half finished, U.E.R.H. Table with Chess Board &c.*
>
> The BARONESS *and* CATHERINE *discovered; the former seated in a large arm Chair, making lace, the other on a Sofa R.H., playing with a lap Dog, Candelabra on, with Candles.*

Scene 3 of *The Conquering Game* (1832).

72

Neither the sofa nor the candelabra are depicted in this illustration. In addition, it seems highly improbable that the "Pictures in heavy frames" were actual pictures since in the directions for the opening scene Bernard specifically calls for "suits of heavy armour painted on the scene." Another engraving of the same scene, from her 1837 revival of the play, corresponds far more closely to Bernard's scenic directions.[38]

While Madame Vestris in *The Conquering Game* may have made some modest advance beyond the level of realism in the famous production of *Les Trois Quartiers* (Paris, 1827), in which various pieces of furniture were painted on three-walled settings,[39] there is little reason to suppose that her production was in any sense revolutionary. Matthew Mackintosh, her ma-

Scene 3 of *The Conquering Game* (1837). (*Shevelove Collection*)

73

chinist at the Olympic from 1832–38, in his memoirs discusses a number of her productions but makes no allusion to *The Conquering Game*. Nor do the playbills draw attention to the scenery, usually an indication that the play was not provided with new sets. The critics also gave no indication that they found the production in any way novel. A brief observation in *The Athenaeum* perhaps sums up Madame's achievement: "The scene at the chateau of the baroness is nearly, if not quite, the most elegant and tasty room-scene we ever saw upon any stage." [40]

Whether a precise date for the introduction of the box set in England can ever be agreed upon seems dubious. Some scholars have argued for a date later than 1832. One has tentatively suggested that the two major components of the box set, the ceiling cloth, and the three-walled setting, may be found as early as 1829.[41] Men of the theatre had been theorizing on *decors fermés* since 1800 or earlier.[42] As a result, so it would seem, the box set developed through so gradual a process of evolution that no individual production can be singled out as marking a revolutionary break with the past. It is surely more than a coincidence that the various dates suggested, bracketing the years 1829–33, coincide precisely with the period during which Louis Daguerre and Nicephore Niepce experimented with "heliographic pictures." A review of Planché's *Promotion*, produced at the Olympic in February, 1833, implies that by that date, at least, sets of almost photographic realism were no longer uncommon. "We like the manner in which the stage is arranged. Its more perfect enclosure gives the appearance of a private chamber, infinitely better than the old contrivance of wings." [43]

Although Madame was eager to experiment, in some of her productions, notably the Christmas extravaganza for 1832, she continued to rely on the "old contrivances." Planché and Dance had by then perfected a formula that guaranteed success. Take a classical myth, sprinkle well with puns and topical allusions, add spectacle and music to taste—result: enthusiastic audiences. *The Paphian Bower* was no exception. To be sure, there were a few faultfinders. One complained that the doves on Venus's chariot showed a curious tendency to fly backwards. Another condemned Terpsichore for her thick legs, and one, taken aback by the brevity of the costumes, facetiously recommended "the intervention of the Society for the Suppression of Vice, or the pious intervention of his holiness the Bishop of London." [44] But these niggling objections were of small consequence when Bland played Adonis and Madame Vestris the Queen of Love.

Nevertheless, in spite of its success, the Queen of Love, like other managers, complained of hard times. The theatre was in an even more sickly condition than usual. Managers and playwrights, baffled by inconsistent legislation, had petitioned Parliament to appoint a committee to consider the current plight of the drama. The spirit of reform was in the air and politicians were at work upon an epoch-making bill designed to impose a rational framework upon the rickety political structure. In like spirit, for two months a committee headed by Edward Lytton Bulwer probed the laws affecting the drama. Among its members was Thomas Duncombe, who had been elected to Parliament in 1826. In their report, published on August 2, the committee concluded that only by freeing the theatres and regularizing licensing practises could the drama flourish.

Bulwer's bill urging such reforms was rejected in the House of Lords, but even if it had been passed, there were plenty of other problems plaguing the theatres. Among them, managers complained, were the rise of evangelicalism, recurrent waves of cholera, and the increasingly late dinner hour, to name but a few.[45] In addition, an age of great actors was coming to an end. Mrs. Siddons had died the year before, and Edmund Kean was failing rapidly.

Madame's productions during the spring of 1833 were on the whole undistinguished. The reigning attractions in London were the demonic Nicolo Paganini and the ethereal Marie Taglioni, who had created a sensation in the romantic ballet *La Sylphide*. No less an attraction was the soprano Maria Malibran, who drew such crowds that the Duke of Wellington counted himself lucky to find a seat among the fiddlers when she sang.

At the close of the Olympic season, Madame was anxious to

make some further appearances in London. The current lessee of Drury Lane was Alfred Bunn, a hot-tempered and bejeweled individual with whom she had little in common. More sympathetic by far was P. F. Laporte, the lessee of Covent Garden, whose consuming interest was in opera and ballet. Evidently he considered Madame a valuable attraction, and she joined his company in April.

She had hardly begun her engagement when a crisis developed. Appalled by the overhead at Covent Garden, Laporte pleaded with the actors to take a cut in salary. They refused. Madame Vestris then tactfully intervened. She offered them the use of the Olympic. Her terms were generous—£40 a week for the theatre, including the use of scenes, dresses, and stage properties. They accepted gratefully and for two months they appeared in Wych Street in their standard repertory, "to infinitely more advantage than in the wilderness of Covent Garden." [46] To the general astonishment Laporte, during their absence, attempted a brief season of German opera, but after its failure he abandoned Covent Garden altogether and Alfred Bunn, the lessee of Drury Lane, took over that theatre as well. Determined to get his money's worth from the two companies, he compelled them to work at both houses. Back and forth they shuttled, between the "Bunn shops." It was exhausting for the performers, though the lessee's ruthless policy resulted in some remarkable bills. At Madame's Covent Garden benefit on June 24 she appeared in *Masaniello,* Liston clowned his way through a farce, Malibran sang, and the evening concluded with Taglioni in *La Sylphide.*

Tired as she was, at the close of the season Madame migrated to the Haymarket for a month's engagement. Following that, she escaped to Brighton for a well-earned holiday. Her expenses, personal and professional, had been enormous. The bills at the Olympic were piling up, and still worse, she had begun a ruinous liaison with Lord Edward Thynne, a young nobleman even more spendthrift than herself. Spoiled, reckless, and indolent, he was up to his ears in debt. His wife bored him to distraction and he tolerated her only in the hope that he could lay his hands on her dowry. Evidently he strongly attracted Madame, for they began an intermittent affair which was to go on for nearly four years. Oddly enough, Thynne managed to remain on good terms with Duncombe. Still more oddly, Duncombe continued to be generous to Madame, presenting her with £3,000 in 1833 and with twice that amount during the following year.[47]

Some of this she undoubtedly squandered upon Lord Edward, but the Olympic was also a drain upon her purse. Her company was well paid and production costs were rising, but during her fourth season, thanks to Duncombe's generosity, she was able to offer the public thirteen new productions, approximately her annual quota. As usual, they had only one purpose —entertainment. Typical of these was Planché and Dance's *The Deep, Deep Sea* in which Madame, as Perseus, rescued Andromeda from a great American sea serpent who smoked cigars and spoke with a Kentucky accent. At the Olympic confectionery, as Planché observed, if one could not make a dinner, one could at least enjoy "a most agreeable refection consisting of jellies, cheese-cakes, custards, and such 'trifles light as air' served upon the best Dresden china, in the most elegant style." [48] Those with coarser palates might prefer the highly seasoned melodramas at the Surrey or the equestrian spectaculars at Astley's, but to Henry Crabb Robinson the choice was obvious. After a visit to the Olympic he noted in his diary: "These petites pieces are all that is left of the theatre that is endurable." [49] Many playgoers agreed with him. Visiting French companies with their "petites pieces" periodically turned up, even at the Olympic itself, during the summer season,[50] but Madame was offering the same fare painlessly Anglicized.

Four seasons at the little theatre in Wych Street had made her restless, however. She longed to try her powers on a more spacious stage, preferably one which was not restricted to burlettas, but occasionally she found a play which provided an outlet for her energies. Such a one was Planché's *The Court Beauties* (March 14, 1835). Based on an episode in Walpole's *Anecdotes of Painting*, it dramatized the rivalry between two Restoration artists—Sir Peter Lely and Sir Godfrey Kneller. The period was one for which Madame had a particular affinity and her production proved a triumph.

> The first scene was the Mall, in St. James's Park, beautifully reproduced from a print of the period of the play. The effect of this scene was much heightened by our making use of a passage, fully one hundred feet in length, which led from the back of the stage to Craven buildings, and by means of which the Mall was represented going away into perspective, with [a] wonderful appearance of reality. On wires hung between the trees were suspended numerous cages, with various kinds of singing birds—whose St. Giles' owners managed to make them sing, too, to perfection. On the rising of the curtain this scene used to call forth the most enthusiastic applause, and the demonstration certainly did not diminish when Mr. Hooper, looking the Merry Monarch to the life, came on, followed by his attendants, all in gorgeous and scrupulously correct costumes of the reign of Charles II. True to the life, the King was accompanied, moreover, by a number of genuine King Charles' spaniels.[51]

Not to be outdone, Madame herself, as the king's favorite page, led on a brace of magnificent buckhounds borrowed from the royal kennels at Windsor.

With the second scene, set in Hampton Court, she took even more pains. Through the intervention of Lord Adolphus Fitzclarence she obtained permission for her designers and technicians to study Lely's gallery of beauties. Against genuine seventeenth-century tapestries she hung eight vast gilded frames curtained with "the identical stuff, green with gold embroidery, which had for years covered the original portraits at Hampton Court." [52] In the climactic scene the curtains were drawn to reveal eight ladies posed in costumes identical to those in the Lely portraits.

Unfortunately, playgoers outside of London rarely had the opportunity to witness such a production, for when Madame toured she was restricted to appearing in stock plays or those Olympic burlettas which could be mounted without too much difficulty. Scenes in the provincial theatres were often half set, and simple backdrops were widely used. With the inauguration of the Manchester-Liverpool railway in 1830, the age of touring began, but while Madame was resigned to enduring the inadequacies of provincial theatres, she was determined to minimize the hardships of the road. Inevitably accompanied by a maid and a manservant, she made her forays into the midlands like a queen on a progress. She demanded the best in accommodations and hotelkeepers soon became accustomed to her communications: "Have the goodness to have ready for me a sitting-room, two best bed-rooms, one double, and a servant's room. A monkey will be sent . . . on Monday from hence directed to you, the guard will have the key of her box, pray have every care taken of him." [53] If Madame was a trifle vague as to Jou-la's gender, she was at least clear as to her requirements.

Each season she returned to the Olympic from these excursions to find a new set of problems confronting her. In the autumn of 1835 she was faced with the defection of her two leading playwrights. Planché had concluded a one-year agreement with Alfred Bunn to write exclusively for Drury Lane and Covent Garden,[54] and Charles Dance had deserted her because she had charged him £20 for introducing one of his songs. (*The Times* observed that in view of the quality of his lyrics she had behaved generously.) By default T. H. Bayly had risen to the rank of chief pastrycook in Madame's establishment. As a bold experiment she decided to produce *The Daughter,* his adaptation of Scribe's serious drama, *La Lectrice,* but the change of fare did not please her customers.

Madame was in need not only of playwrights, but of a good *jeune premier* as well. For the last few years James Vining had functioned as her leading man, but for all his goodwill he was hardly adequate. On stage, with his right hand extended and his left hand on his hip, he looked like a teapot. His clothes were wrong, and his manner suggested that he belonged behind a muslin counter rather than in a salon.

Suddenly Madame had an inspiration. During the summer Charles Mathews, the comedian, had died. Early in October his son undertook the direction of the Adelphi Theatre of which his father had been co-lessee. A few weeks of management had chastened him, but he still had hopes for a career in the theatre. He was a young man without professional stage experience but he was a gifted amateur actor. He had also written some successful farces since the abysmally unsuccessful *Pong Wong*. He might not be the young man she was looking for, but within a week of his leaving the Adelphi she had engaged him.

chapter 5

Enter Charles James Mathews

For £6 a week Madame acquired the services of a young man who bore one of the most famous names in the English theatre. Charles Mathews, his father, after years of struggle as an eccentric comedian, had become celebrated through his *At Homes*, one-man entertainments that gave him the occasion to show off his unequaled powers of mimicry. In spite of the fact that he was as thin as a rail, limped, and was afflicted with partial facial paralysis, his talents were Protean. He could impersonate a whole coachload of travelers, transforming himself into a loquacious Frenchman or a spry old Scotch lady with equal ease. He could just as easily have played the coach, and for years he delighted London and the provinces with his annual *At Homes*.

His son, Charles James Mathews, "came into the world with the pantomimes in a laughing season." [1] He was born in Liverpool on Boxing Night, December 26, 1803. At the time the elder Mathews was still a relatively unknown comedian and his wife, Anne, an obscure young actress. They had no wish to see their only child follow in their profession, but from childhood he showed a predilection for the stage. At the age of three, clad in diminutive canonicals, he preached a sermon to his elders.

Anne Mathews was delighted. A deeply religious woman, she construed it as the sure sign of a vocation, but Samuel De Wilde's lively watercolor of young Mathews as The Little Parson suggests a would-be actor far more than a would-be archbishop.[2]

The Little Parson received a polite education at a juvenile academy in Hackney, with music, dancing, fencing, and French. In later years he followed a more serious course of studies at the Merchant Taylors' School. Mr. and Mrs. Mathews wanted above all to bring up their son as a gentleman. Though they had many friends in their profession, they took pride in their more fashionable connections. Once in a while, however, they allowed young Charles a taste of backstage life. At the age of ten he watched a Covent Garden performance from the wings and for a few minutes was permitted to hold the prompter's book. The responsibility was overwhelming, and with all the gravity of a small child he subsequently admonished the veteran actor, John Fawcett, for a few trifling aberrations from the script. On still another occasion, in the course of a benefit at Covent Garden, he made his first appearance on stage—to tumultuous applause—dressed as a miniature doctor. It was a heady experience for a youngster, particularly an actor's son.

His parents, nonetheless, continued to hope that he would adopt a more respectable profession. It was during his schooling at Clapham, where he had as his fellow pupils the sons of Charles Kemble, Charles Mayne Young, and John Liston, that he first revealed an aptitude for drawing and mathematics. On the strength of this welcome development his parents urged him to make his career as an architect, and in May 1819 he was articled to Augustus Charles Pugin, the chief apostle of the Gothic style. The great architect was a man of considerable charm, but he took a casual view of his obligation to initiate students into the mysteries of ribbed vaulting and engaged shafts, and young Charles seems to have learned little from him. It was the elder Mathews who made a more substantial contribution to his son's education by commissioning him to design a modest Gothic library and picture gallery for his new house, Ivy Cottage, in Kentish town.

The French-born architect did, however, enlarge young Mathews's horizons by taking him on a trip to Paris. There he was exposed for the first time to the wonders of French Gothic and to the French theatre as well. His daytime visits to Notre Dame and the Sainte Chapelle may have been perfunctory, but he took full advantage of the evenings to study the leading French actors. Soon after his return to London he had the occasion to put these observations to use. At a private performance in the English Opera House on April 26, 1822, he impersonated the leading French comedian, Perlet, sang a song in the manner of M. Emile, and concluded the evening in his own person, playing Werther in a burlesque version of Goethe's romance. It was a tour de force in the true Mathews tradition. The actor in him had all but conquered when an unexpected proposal revived his drooping interest in architecture.

At the expiration of his articles to Pugin he was negotiating with John Nash for a place in his office when he received an astonishing offer. The theatre-loving Earl of Blessington, while en route from Italy to his enormous Irish estate, Mountjoy, stopped briefly in London and paid a call on his friend Charles Mathews. The library and picture gallery of Ivy Cottage caught his eye and he commented favorably upon them. Upon arriving at Mountjoy, he quarreled violently with his own architect and impetuously wrote to Mathews urging him to send his son to Ireland with all possible speed. Before the week was up the young man had arrived. He was slimly built, with the face of a witty faun, and he had a contagious vivacity and good humor. Captivated by his manner and enthusiasm, the Earl was soon immersed in vast schemes. Money was no deterrent—the course of a river could be diverted, or a hill leveled, if need be. Before long they had transformed a bare mountain face into a forest of saplings and were pondering plans for a castle suitable to this terrain. Torn between various possibilities, the Earl decided that it was imperative for them to consult Lady Blessington, who had remained behind in Naples.

Flattered as they were by the Earl's attentions to their son, Charles and Anne Mathews were not entirely happy. Lady Blessington's reputation was dubious, to say the least. It was common knowledge that she had been married off at fifteen to a brute of a husband, that she had deserted him, and that subsequently she had become the mistress of an army officer. Even more scandalous was the rumor that after the death of her first husband Lord Blessington had purchased her from her lover for the sum of £10,000. Whether the story was true or false, it gave the Mathewses pause, but after an effusive exchange of letters with the Blessingtons they consented to their son's departure, and in September 1823 the Earl and the architect set out for Italy.

The trip has been admirably described by Mathews and needs no detailed retelling. From Paris they rattled on to Geneva, accumulating a large entourage of Blessington friends and relations en route, and in a convoy of carriages lurched over the Alps to Milan. They reached Naples in late November. For young Mathews the trip had been a revelation. He responded enthusiastically to the wonders of Italian architecture by cramming his sketchbook with notes and drawings.[3] And at Naples he found himself in a society that was as dazzling as the sunlight-dappled bay. The Palazzo Belvedere combined the grandeurs of an Italian palace and the amenities of a stately home. The terraces overlooking the bay, the gardens, and the arcades delighted him, and his architect's eye rested with pleasure on the casual profusion of malachite and alabaster. The happy mingling of two cultures was perhaps nowhere more evident than in Lady Blessington's footmen who were uniformed like their London brethren but also sported flashing gold earrings.

If the setting was highly theatrical, the dramatis personae was hardly less so: the Earl, an impetuous hypochondriac of enormous wealth; the indolent Lady Blessington, a legendary beauty whose portrait had been painted by Lawrence while she was still in her teens; Miss Power, her sister, a fragile young Irish beauty; and Count D'Orsay, the prince of dandies, whom Mathews considered "the best fencer, dancer, swimmer, runner, dresser; the best shot, the best horseman, the best draughtsman of his age." [4]

The days sped by while the guests amused themselves. Sometimes they went sight-seeing. Sometimes they drifted idly about the bay in Byron's yacht, the *Bolivar*, which the Earl had bought the year before. The indolence of Lady Blessington and the hypochondria of the Earl gave Mathews and D'Orsay a good deal of time to themselves. (It was D'Orsay's observation that the Earl "could detect a current of air caused by the key being left crossways in the keyhole of a door.") Together they went on sketching expeditions or Mathews disappeared to explore on his own: "During the twelvemonth I remained a guest at the Palazzo Belvedere, I rummaged every corner of Naples and its environs, wandered on foot among the mountains with my sketchbook, and lived among the peasants, joining in their pursuits, dancing the tarentella under vine-covered pergolas by moonlight and picking up songs and stories in abundance." [5]

Occasions were not lacking when he could make use of his talents as an actor. To amuse the ailing Miss Power, he often played the role of a visiting doctor or impersonated the local priest. When Lady Blessington invited casual acquaintances to dine, he and D'Orsay sometimes disguised themselves, to the astonishment of the guests. The Earl, himself an actor of some talent, delighted in these impostures, and even Lady Blessington contributed to their diversions by making it mandatory on occasion to appear at the dinner table in masquerade.

After a year of sybaritic exile Mathews returned to England. The Earl was still pondering plans for a grandiose castle at Mountjoy, but Mathews was looking for an immediate commission. Soon after his return he was engaged to erect an inn, a bridge, and some miners' cottages in Wales. It was a sad letdown. As he put it: "Workmen's cottages and village ale-houses were not congenial to a mind filled with Italian images and panting with desire to execute works on Palladian grandeur." [6] He had not altogether forgotten the theatre, however, for in his idle moments he composed the lyrics of "Jenny Jones," and scribbled away at verses and burlettas. Upon his return to London he obtained a clerkship in John Nash's office, but once again his architectural ambitions were frustrated when his grandiose plans for a market at the bottom of Oxford Street failed to be accepted.

His disappointment revived his interest in the theatre, but in this field as well he found little encouragement. *Pong Wong*, the "Chinese extravaganza" designed for his father's friend, John Liston, proved a fiasco. Feeling that his career was at a standstill, he persuaded his father and mother to finance him on a second trip to the continent.

Accompanied by James D'Egville, son of the famous choreographer and a fellow pupil of Pugin, Mathews set off in April 1827 on the same route that he and the Earl had followed four years earlier—from Paris to Switzerland and Milan. Purportedly they were studying architecture, but they did not allow these studies to interfere in any way with their amusements. They attended the premiere of Bellini's first opera, *Il Pirata*. For eight pounds a month they rented a villa at Como, staffed by a boatman, cook, valet, and gardener, but soon after, bored by the lake and the "amazing quantity of mountain," they moved on to Venice where they spent the better part of the winter. Nominally students at the Accademia, they found ample time for other activities. Mathews's diary [7] abounds in references to the balls they attended, soirées at the ridotto, and nights that expired at Florian's in a haze of alcohol and cigar smoke. During the day they sketched, took time off for "smoking and gymnastics," and in the evening they returned to their rounds of pleasure. Though their finances were limited, they managed a trip down the Adriatic coast and gaped at the Roman amphitheatre in Pola rising in grandeur over the decaying provincial town.

After a fleeting visit to Greece they returned to Venice, but their diversions were interrupted when Mathews contracted smallpox. Fortunately his case was a slight one, and, upon recovering, he and D'Egville packed up their sketchbooks and moved on to Florence. It was easy to justify a visit to Tuscany as an essential part of their architectural education, and furthermore, the city had become the focal point for a large and fashionable group of English expatriates. The arrival of two personable young Englishmen did not go unnoticed, and they were at once welcomed into the circle of Lord Normanby and Lord Burghersh, leading members of the English colony. As in Venice, the temptation was constant to neglect their studies for frivolous amusements. Chief among these were the amateur theatricals to which both Lord Normanby and Lord Burghersh were addicted.[8] For years Lord Burghersh had produced plays and operas in his private theatre. The palazzo of Lord Normanby also boasted a private theatre, but it was of modest dimensions. At the urging of Lady Normanby, Mathews and D'Egville undertook the task of redecorating and enlarging it. In addition, they designed sets for it, and a drop curtain. Delighted with the results, the Normanbys launched an ambitious season of Shakespearian and modern plays. Not only English residents but English-speaking residents as well were impressed to fill out the casts. Among the roles which fell to Mathews were Tony Lumpkin in *She Stoops to Conquer*, Dogberry in *Much Ado About Nothing*, Launcelot Gobbo in *The Merchant of Venice*, and Falstaff in *Henry IV* (part I). The bustle of preparations amused them all, and Mathews records with pleasure "the agreeable rehearsals, the exciting performances, the brilliant suppers that wound up the night, in which the actors and the audience joined and talked over all the details of the evening." [9] Not to be outdone, Lord Burghersh staged a performance of *The School for Scandal* at his own palazzo. Lady Burghersh coquetted her way through the role of Lady Teazle, Lord Douro played Joseph Surface, and Mathews and D'Egville contributed their services as Sir Benjamin Backbite and Snake.

But Lord Normanby's theatricals evidently impressed Mathews far more. In contrast to Lord Burghersh's "turbulent republic," Lord Normanby's regime was marked by a "mild despotism." His production of *Henry IV* was in Mathews' opinion the most perfect of the plays presented at San Clementi, but he has recorded in somewhat more detail the preparations for *Romeo and Juliet*. Lord and Lady Normanby were determined to play the star-crossed lovers and equally determined that the sets and costumes should be as correct as possible. Like so many of his contemporaries, Lord Normanby had a passion for archaeological exactitude. The costumes for *Romeo and Juliet*, Mathews tells us, "were designed by Mr. Kirkup, an artist of high standing, from drawings made by him of the dresses of the period from reliable authorities in the Florentine gallery. The scenery was painted from sketches made in Verona by my friend D'Egville and myself, superintended and partly painted by us." [10] In the masquerade scene, he goes on to say, the stage was filled with pretty girls and handsome boys "all dressed from pictures."

Despite his admiration for Lord Normanby he felt an obligation to resume his architectural studies, and he and D'Egville re-

Charles James Mathews's pen-and-ink sketch for Lord Normanby's production of *The Iron Chest*. (*British Theatre Museum*)

luctantly left Florence for Rome. They remained there for a year, at the end of which time Mathews returned to London for a quick visit. Subsequently he and his parents made a brief stay with Lady Blessington and Count D'Orsay in Paris. (The Earl had unexpectedly died a few months earlier.) Young Charles was taken ill, but insisted on returning to Italy. At Venice he succumbed to malaria with rheumatic complications. The pain was excruciating and for three months he lost the use of his legs.

Not until the end of 1830 did he feel well enough to risk returning to London. Even then the trip was exhausting, and when he finally arrived at Ivy Cottage, he was carried into his parents' home by his devoted Italian manservant.

His recovery was painfully slow. He was still flirting with the notion of an architectural career and was elected District Supervisor of Bow, but his father's acquisition of a half-interest in the Adelphi once again turned his attention to the stage. Frederick Yates, co-lessee of the theatre, was an industrious actor-manager and an old friend of the elder Mathews, but he was troubled by the thought that Mathews, because of his commitments, would be on tour for much of the time. In an effort to mollify him, Mathews suggested that his son Charles might serve as his deputy. Yates flatly rejected the suggestion. One can hardly blame him. He had only one policy—to produce shows that brought in a three-figure return to the box office. During the 1830–31 season he had produced *The Black Vulture, Wreck Ashore,* and *The King of the Alps,* all of which had fulfilled this requirement. He was too seasoned a professional, too engrossed in the cutthroat rivalry of the theatrical world, to want the advice of an amateur from the Palazzo San Clementi.

In one respect, however, the amateur could claim a semiprofessional status. For some time he had been collaborating with Richard Peake on material for his father, though neither the nature nor the extent of this collaboration can be determined.[11] Mathews was reluctant to trade on his father's name and in consequence concealed his identity insofar as possible. In all likelihood he and Peake worked together on *The Adventures in Air, Earth and Water,* Mathews's *At Home* for 1821, though Ann Mathews makes no allusion to her son's contribution. The first play which can be definitely attributed to him is the ill-fated *Pong Wong* (1826), and very possibly he had a hand in *The Home Circuit,* his father's one-man entertainment for 1827.

On his return from Italy he once again began to scribble burlettas, and among his papers at Princeton is a fragmentary burlesque on the state of the English stage in 1831. Since the turn of the century, audiences had flocked to freakish entertainments.

They had swooned over Master Betty, the young Roscius, and laughed till they cried at the antics of "Romeo" Coates, the amateur of fashion. They had applauded a Newfoundland dog's heroic leap into a tankful of water and encored a thundering stud of horses clambering up the smoking ruins of a castle. Mlle. D'Jeck, playing the starring role in *The Elephant of Siam*, had packed the Adelphi to capacity and Drury Lane, not to be outdone, had enjoyed a similar success with *Hyder Ali, or, The Lions of Mysore*, featuring a cast largely recruited from the Paris Zoo.

The fragmentary burlesque is set in the Green Room of the East Grinstead Theatre and introduces us to Skyrocket, the stage manager, and Muddle, the doorkeeper. To the scandal of the latter, the stage manager defends the contemporary theatre: "If people want common sense, they can have that when they want by staying home—the uncommon is what they want and what we mean to give them." Aghast, the conservatively minded doorkeeper asks who is to perform the leading role in the play which is about to go into rehearsal. He is flabbergasted to learn that a lion is to be the principal tragedian, and the heroine is to be Mlle. D'Jeck, the elephant. Skyrocket assures him, however, that the minor parts can be played by two-legged actors, but all the male parts are to be played by women since the great London theatres have proved the male part of creation unnecessary. With the arrival of Vamp, the author of the new play, and two actors to impersonate a lion and a tiger, the rehearsal begins and the fragment concludes. In a postscript, however, the locale of the sketch is altered to read: "Scene 1: the painting-room and workshop of the Adelphi Theatre. Tompkins, Pitt, J. Evans and all the carpenters at work."

On October 24, 1831, the Lord Chamberlain licensed for performance John Buckstone's burlesque, *Hyder Ali, or, The Lions of Mysore*.[12] It begins at precisely the point at which the fragmentary manuscript comes to an end. Celebrating "the overthrow of the bipeds by the quadrupeds," it was well received and repeatedly performed at the Adelphi during the autumn of 1831. Perhaps the fragment was completed by Buckstone. Perhaps Mathews also had some share in it but preferred to disassociate himself from the finished work since he knew that his father felt it *infra dig* for legitimate actors to impersonate animals.

In any event, during a period of convalescence at Brighton, he began to write with some regularity, and in December, through John Liston, he submitted to Madame Vestris a one-act comedy, *Pyramus and Thisbe.* She offered him £25 for it, but for some reason it was not produced.[13] Subsequently, however, both this comedy and two others were successfully presented by David Morris at the Haymarket. Since it was hardly worth the trouble for Mathews to cultivate his own muse, he turned instead to the French vaudevilles, but even then adaptation was not always an easy matter. He was far from a prude, but many of the Parisian entertainments he found "very bad, most of them disgustingly obscene or blasphemous." [14] Like so many of his contemporaries he had a distaste for adultery as a comic theme, and his three Haymarket comedies—*The Court Jester, My Wife's Mother,* and *Pyramus and Thisbe*—are all innocuous, bustling in their action and brisk in their dialogue.

He was particularly anxious to succeed, for a series of foolhardy speculations had plunged his father into serious financial difficulties. Reluctantly, the elder Mathews and his wife moved from Ivy Cottage to Great Russell Street. Their new lodgings could not accommodate their superb collection of over four hundred theatrical pictures, and in hope of profitably exhibiting them, young Charles carefully catalogued them and arranged for their display at the Queen's Bazaar in Oxford Street. The results were dispiriting. While streams of visitors had been eager to visit Ivy Cottage, few took the trouble to go to Oxford Street. Adding to Mathews's gloom was his increasingly strained relationship with Yates. They quarreled over such matters as Yates' decision to include "a bath full of naked women" in *The Nymphs of the Harem* and Mathews complained heatedly of his partner's high-handed manner.

A lucrative offer to tour America left him with no alternative but to accept. He had toured there once before, in 1822. He had little affection for Cousin Jonathan and his health was worse than ever, but in spite of this in August 1834 he and his wife and their dog, Fop, set sail for New York.

Young Charles remained behind in Great Russell Street. No doubt he was concerned about his father's health and finances, but his diary gives little evidence of it. He escaped from London whenever he could on long visits to various ducal estates. When in town, he busied himself studying Spanish, German, and Italian. He painted regularly, and one of his canvases, "The Lake at Perugia," was accepted for exhibition at the Royal Academy. Frequently his evenings were spent at the theatre. In his diary he notes an invitation to Drury Lane from the Duke of Sutherland, and another to Covent Garden from the Duchess of Kent. On less exalted occasions he visited the minor theatres. On January 8, 1835, he notes without comment that he attended the premiere of *A Bottle of Champagne* at the Olympic.

In the course of these agreeable diversions a series of distraught letters trickled over from America. The trip to New York had been a tempestuous one. Mathews had survived it wonderfully, but Mrs. Mathews had been prostrate during most of the voyage. Matters had not improved after their arrival. Though Mrs. Mathews had recovered her strength, Mathews found the climate intolerable, fit only for butterflies and bears. New York and Philadelphia had acclaimed him, but only in Boston did he feel at home, and even there he felt ill most of the time.

The theatrical news from London was hardly calculated to cheer him. At the start of the season the patent houses had reduced their admission prices to the same level as those at the minor theatres, and as a result the Adelphi receipts had plummeted. But Mathews was too ill to care. He landed in Liverpool after a nineteen-day voyage, crippled by asthma, dropsy, and inflammation of the lungs. At the suggestion of his doctor he was removed to Plymouth to get the benefit of the sea air. The change did him little good, but it was at least closer to London, and periodically young Charles came down to cheer him up with songs and stories and airy visions of the plans he was submitting for the proposed reconstruction of the Houses of Parliament.

But Mathews was never to see London again, much less a realization of Charles's plans. On the morning of June 28, 1835, he died.

The comedian's estate had been decimated by litigation and debts, and young Charles and his mother were faced with the necessity of raising money as quickly as possible. His library was auctioned off at Sotheby's and his picture collection sold to the Garrick Club for £1,000, a bargain price considering the number of Hogarths and Zoffanys that it contained. There still remained, however, Mathews's most valuable asset—his half share in the Adelphi. Despite the reluctance of Yates, young Mathews was tempted to have a fling at management. In the course of the summer he had completed *Mandrin*, a "grand romantic melodrama burletta spectacle" adapted from the French, and he was anxious to see it produced. Yates, taking advantage of an offer from Drury Lane, decided to indulge the young man—temporarily—and discreetly withdrew.

The company assembled on September 14 and two weeks later the season began with a performance of Mathews's play. Dramatizing the escapades of a notorious French bandit, it was little more than a pastiche of *Fra Diavolo* and *The Brigand*, a farrago of kidnappings, hairbreadth escapes, and deadly ambushes. The production, however, was generally praised. The Louis XIV settings and costumes received favorable notice and two scenes in particular, one in a ballroom and one in a cave, were singled out for their effective staging.

For a month the play dominated the repertory, but it is dubious that Mathews took much satisfaction in its mild success. He could not help but be aware of the enormous disparity between his own taste and that of the Adelphi audiences. A few brief weeks of management convinced him that it would be best to dispose of his father's interest. Yates had reached the same conclusion. To the irritation of Mathews he had already begun independent negotiations with Ephraim Bond, lessee of the Queen's Theatre. Bond's reputation was notorious, and Mathews, suspecting that he would not honor existing contracts, broke off negotiations. Instead, the popular comedienne Louisa

Nisbett was appointed lessee and soon afterward Mathews disposed of his father's share in the Adelphi.

He had not given up his plans for a theatrical career, however. He needed more urgently than ever to enter an "immediately lucrative career." On November 15 he read his new farce, *The Hump-backed Lover*, to Madame Vestris. Two days later she engaged him. He was to make his debut on December 7. Mathews was delighted, for he felt that the size and "peculiar drawing-room nature" of the Olympic made it "most favorable to a novice." His self-estimate was a modest one. It was true that he had had no professional experience as an actor, but he had been preparing himself for the stage all his life. His family background, his architectural studies, his experiences as a playwright, his musical talents, even his social career, all contributed to make him, potentially at least, the ideal partner for Madame.

chapter 6

A Voyage to America

"Goodbye indeed! Why you haven't said 'How d'ye do?' yet!" These were the first words that Charles Mathews rattled off as he stepped briskly on stage. He was even more nervous than most beginners, for the Olympic was packed to the rafters with playgoers curious to see how he would acquit himself. The young man did not disappoint them. They detected at once something of the elder Mathews's vivacity of manner and crackling speech. The play itself was inconsequential, but it at least gave the young man the opportunity to play two roles—a high-spirited lover and his hunchbacked rival. Members of the audience expected no less from the son of Charles Mathews, the master of eccentric characterization. At the conclusion of *The Hump-backed Lover*, they applauded warmly, but the newcomer's real testing took place later on the same evening. Specifically for the occasion Leman Rede had written a two-act comedietta, *The Old and Young Stager*. John Liston had volunteered to do the honors and introduce the son of his longtime friend and colleague to the theatregoing public. The curtain rose revealing the two stagers in the stable yard, "the old coachman brushing up his hammercloth, and the natty young tiger cleaning his cabriolet." [1] The old stager was nearing retirement, the young stager was at the threshold of his career. As they stood side by side on the stage they made an admirable

Charles James Mathews in *The Old and Young Stager*.

contrast, the thickset, snub-nosed Liston and the slender, taut young man. If some of the duller spectators failed to grasp the applicability of the allusions as the older man initiated the younger into the mysteries of coaching, there was no possibility of mistaking the meaning of the old stager's last lines: "Passengers, we leave you here—as he carries on the stage, be his guard, he's my boy, and if he don't always handle the whip like an old hand, make allowances for the sake of his father." Overcome with emotion, Liston sank back exhausted, but he had successfully launched a new stager.

Young Mathews's friends were not all as enthusiastic as the audience. One wrote morosely: "You will, I suppose, soon forget all the valuable metaphysical knowledge I attempted to cram you with." [2] Another complained: "*Cher ami*, if you *would* act, why not act at home, like your poor father, which is a higher walk? And why Madame V——? And why a minor theatre?" [3] Fortunately, critics and playgoers overwhelmingly disagreed. Mathews had provided the Olympic with what it needed most—a gentlemanly young actor.

The good impression which he had made in *The Old and Young Stager* was confirmed by his subsequent performance in Bayly's *One Hour, or, The Carnival Ball*, in which he and Madame Vestris appeared together for the first time. Premiered on January 11, 1836, the piece lightheartedly dramatized the adventures of a group of English travelers in Naples. Madame had mounted the production with particular care. In *The Conquering Game* (1832) she had used only the simplest of properties to fill out the drawing-room set—a table, an easel, and a few chairs. In *One Hour*, she furnished a lady's sitting room which specifically called for "a large practicable clock . . . a cage with two birds, a glass globe with two gold and silver fish —a table with [a] workbox, guitar, [and] writing materials." The set may not have borne much resemblance to Lady Blessington's sitting room in the Palazzo Belvedere, but it at least suggested a milieu in which Mathews felt at home and in which he could show off his talents to advantage. The scene gave him the opportunity to deliver a much-applauded recitation in the character of a Neapolitan peasant. It also allowed him to play the guitar and to give Madame a singing lesson. The fact that he broke down halfway through the lesson in no way diminished the enthusiasm of the spectators, and in the final carnival scene he more than compensated for this momentary lapse by his spirited singing of a Neapolitan air. The play concluded with a tarantella danced by Mathews and Miss Fitzwalter. To ensure its success, Oscar Byrne, the choreographer, had disguised himself as a fisherman and stood on the side of the stage, beating time on a tambourine. He need not have worried. Mathews danced it, so one critic tells us,

> with an elegance, a force, a correctness sufficient to bring the ballet company from the Academie Royale over in a body to see and to envy him. We know not whether this execution of it would have cured him of the awful spider's bite, but we are inclined to suspect that the excitement of merely seeing him perform it so admirably would have cured us of the bite of a mad dog, had we been so afflicted.[4]

Madame Vestris and Charles James Mathews in the
finale of *One Hour*.

He had transformed the Olympic from "a close little theatre in Wych Street to a sunny spot in Naples, with the fresh air breathing from the bay." [5]

The success of this piece and of her subsequent season was such that Madame renewed her lease of the Olympic for five more years. In the course of six months she reportedly cleared some £5,000, and the grateful lessee showed her appreciation by doubling Mathews's salary. Inevitably her name began to be linked with his. By March of 1836 it was rumored that he was "likely to become a sleeping partner with the fair lessee." [6] By May their forthcoming marriage was reported. However exaggerated the stories were, their association was increasingly close, and at the end of the season they set off on a strenuous tour, appearing in various Olympic pieces before enthusiastic audiences in Dublin, Liverpool, Manchester, and Nottingham. In at least one respect the tour was unusual. Ordinarily, when leading actors provincialized they took with them their costumes, not their colleagues. Contrary to custom, Madame and Mathews were supported by a number of other members of the Olympic. With them were the diminutive Robert Keeley, a master of quiet drollery; John Brougham, famous for his Irish roles; Frank Matthews, a useful character actor; and "Gentleman" Hooper, a light comedian. Also pressed into service was Josephine Anderson. It was perhaps a slight exaggeration to advertise them as The Olympic Company, but if Madame could not hope to reproduce the original production of *One Hour* for provincial audiences, she could at least assure them of a good performance.

Evidently her touring group had a wide appeal, for when they returned to London they delighted boisterous audiences at the Surrey and had an equal success at the elegant St. James's. Built by John Braham, it had opened in December 1835. Since April it had been occupied by a French company headed by Mlle. Plessis. The French actors attracted fashionable audiences, and to avoid any conflict with the opera they performed on Mondays, Wednesdays, and Fridays. Their appeal was necessarily limited, but connoisseurs of acting were drawn to the St.

James's which was already becoming known as the "Théâtre Français a Londres." 7 Evidently Madame's company and the French visitors admirably complemented each other, for on a number of evenings they divided the bill between them.

At the close of the season, in August, Madame was ready for a holiday. She decided to make a trip up the Rhine, visit Paris, and on the way home stop off at Calais to visit Madame Bartolozzi who was living there in retirement. Mathews, on the other hand, could not afford a respite. He was hard up and he had promised his mother a quarterly annuity of £50. Occasionally he indulged himself with a few days in London, but except for these brief intervals he toured tirelessly—from Exeter to Cheltenham, to Leamington, Glasgow, and Leeds. Only in mid-September did he permit himself the luxury of a fortnight's holiday in Brighton.

The success of the previous season induced Madame to commission still further improvements at the Olympic, and in September 1836 she returned to inspect the results. Mr. Crace had installed a new chandelier and girandoles. Of more consequence, however, where Samuel Beazley's alterations. He had done away with the gallery and substituted a second tier of boxes. Liston, the darling of the gallery, was retiring at the end of the season, and Mathews, the young stager, was drawing an increasingly fashionable audience, just as she had hoped.

Fortunately, her company had remained virtually intact. Keeley was leaving for New York, the theatrical El Dorado, but Liston, Mathews, Bland, and Mrs. Orger were still with her, and to bolster the female contingent she had engaged Laura Honey, a singer and light comedienne from the Adelphi.

Preparations for the forthcoming season were marred only by a minor contretemps between the lessee and Mrs. Hooper, wife of the deputy manager and treasurer. For some reason the two women quarreled—in all probability about money. Madame promptly summoned Mr. Clarke, her lawyer, to consult him as to the most effective way of dismissing the Hoopers. Unfortunately in the course of their discussion she forgot to insert the plug into a tin pipe which ran from her dressing room to that of

Hooper, directly below. Overhearing their discussion, Hooper rushed upstairs and assaulted Clarke, much to the enjoyment of the company. It was a typical backstage fracas, brief as a summer storm, and the affair concluded with Hooper warning Madame "to put the cork in the spout" in the future.[8]

The 1836–37 season opened with Planché's *Court Favour.* Planché's contract with the two "Bunn shops" had expired and he was free once again to preside at the Olympic confectionery. The play was entirely a vehicle for Liston, providing him with a series of broad jokes based on that inexhaustible source of humor, his "inexpressibles," or breeches. A year earlier audiences had roared at the same jokes in Samuel Lover's *The Beau Ideal.* Madame was perhaps a trifle put out to find that despite the disappearance of the gallery, the laughter, at least when Liston was on stage, was as loud as ever. But if audiences relished their old favorite as much as before, they were also capable of appreciating the subtler comic style of Mathews. In *He Would Be an Actor*, his own adaptation of *Le Comédien D'Etampes*, he underwent a series of transformations—from an old man to a Welsh gardener to a Frenchwoman. It was an entertainment in the manner of his father's *At Homes*, characterized by fastidious attention to the niceties of accent, manner, and dress, and over the years it proved the most popular entertainment in the Olympic repertory. As Madame had hoped, she had found not only a promising young actor, but a useful playwright as well.

She was also cheered by the fact that Planché's energy remained undiminished. After completing *Court Favor*, he turned his attention to *The Two Figaros*, a clever pastiche of *The Barber of Seville* and *The Marriage of Figaro*, and following that he came to her with a proposal for a striking Christmas entertainment. Fifteen years earlier, while in Paris, he had witnessed an unforgettable performance by Potier as the grotesque hero of *Riquet à la Houppe.* Fired with enthusiasm he set to work on his own dramatization of Perrault's fairy tale, but London managers had shown little interest. Discouraged, he had laid his manuscript aside and had virtually forgotten it until Charles Dance reminded him that Madame expected a Christmas entertainment from them. For some years they had provided her with mythological burlettas. During their absence Samuel Lover had attempted to take their place by dramatizing the legend of Cupid and Psyche, but it had enjoyed only a mild success. Noting that "someone has been walking on our sky," Dance proposed a change of venue for their next entertainment. The remark recalled to Planché the forgotten manuscript and in short order it was dusted off, polished up, and submitted to Madame. The finished product left the lessee dubious. Perrault's tale was a variant on Beauty and the Beast but it had curious overtones. Audiences had no objections to a Beast, particularly if he wore Louis XIV costume, but how would they react to Planché's Prince Riquet—"hunchbacked, bow-legged, with a bump over one eye, and bald headed with the exception of one tuft of very red hair?" [9]

Planché and Dance were summoned to a solemn conclave with Mathews and Madame. Planché was at his most persuasive. The novelty of the piece would surely please and the extravaganza could easily be cast. Mathews, with his flair for the eccentric, would of course play Riquet, and Madame, as inevitably, would play the Princess Emeralda. There was a splendid part for Mr. Bland as the Duke, her father. Bland's earnest manner and imposing presence would admirably bring out the burlesque elements in the story. There was even a part in it for Josephine Anderson, with not too many lines, but one song.

Audiences proved Planché right by warmly receiving *Riquet with the Tuft,* and if Mathews did not bring to the role the same pathos it had had when played by Potier, he invested it instead with captivating energy. Though Planché is perhaps guilty of overstatement in claiming that this piece marked a turning point in the history of extravaganza, it did mark a turning point in his career, an abandonment of the world of the gods in favor of the fairy-tale world of Perrault and the Countess D'Aulnoy. Stylistically also it marked a break with his previous burlettas. Much of his dialogue is in prose rather than couplets. What verses there are, however, sparkle with wit. The hunchbacked Riquet's *apologia* might have been written by W. S. Gilbert after seeing *Richard III:*

I'm a strange-looking person I own,
  But contentment for ever my guest is;
I'm by habit an optimist grown,
  And fancy that all for the best is.
Each man has of troubles his pack,
  And some round their aching hearts wear it;
My burden is placed on my back,
  Where I'm much better able to bear it.

Again tho' I'm blind of one eye,
  And have but one ear that of use is,
I but half the world's wickedness spy,
  And am deaf to one half its abuses;
And tho' with this odd pair of pegs,
  My motions, I own, serpentine are;
Many folks blessed with handsomer legs,
  Have ways much more crooked than mine are! [10]

In his fairy-tale extravaganzas, rather than his mythological burlesques, Planché was pointing the way toward the Savoy operas.

The Two Figaros and *Riquet with the Tuft* remained on the
Olympic's bill of fare for much of the season, but despite their
success Madame's troubles were increasing. Her taste was generally unerring, but in practical matters her judgment left much
to be desired. As a manager she was incorrigibly extravagant.
Her order sheets headed "Please send to Madame Vestris" were
dashing but invited exploitation. A further dispute with Edward
Hooper, her treasurer, led to his resignation. She also quarreled
with her boxkeeper, James Stride.[11] Following the usual managerial practice, Madame, in return for a weekly fee, had allowed
him to accept tips from playgoers. He had fallen behind in his
payments, however, and when Madame took him to court, he
too left the Olympic. The unpleasantness had at least one bene-
ficial result—from then on tipping was forbidden. Her new
boxkeeper was a salaried employee, and when he tried to revive
the practice of tipping he was publicly reprimanded by her new
treasurer, Charles Peake.

But these professional difficulties were trivial compared to
those that beset her in private life. She had been foolish enough
to authorize Lord Edward Thynne to raise money for her. Still
more foolishly, she had placed in the hands of Joshua Anderson,

her brother-in-law, a number of signed blank acceptances for loans. To her dismay she discovered that the two men had negotiated with the most rapacious moneylenders in London. There was little reason to be surprised. During the preceding two years Thynne had grown steadily more reckless. Despite the fact that he had received £30,000 from his father to pay off his creditors, he had sunk even more deeply into debt. He had permanently separated from his wife and had succeeded in alienating most of his friends. He had attempted to block the reelection of Thomas Duncombe by denouncing him as a radical. He had even quarreled with his agent, the easygoing Charles Harris. They shared an enthusiasm for the hunt and on occasion they had exchanged prize retrievers. But all that had changed. They were bickering over some disputed silverware. Lord Edward's situation was common gossip—so common, in fact, that it had already provoked a sheaf of satirical verses.

> I don't mean myself or my talents to flatter,
> But I've swindled my tailor and I've swindled my hatter;
> I've swindled my carriages, horses and plate,
> I've swindled the small and I've swindled the great.[12]

Even Madame had had enough. On February 24, 1837, she successfully applied for an injunction to restrain Anderson from negotiating any further bills of exchange. Thynne, Anderson, Harris, and perhaps even Charles Molloy Westmacott, the blackmailing editor of *The Age*, had all to some extent profited by her folly. Madame obviously needed to raise money as quickly as possible, but Lent was beginning and the Olympic was not licensed to perform on Wednesdays and Fridays during that period. She could not afford to be idle on those evenings, so twice weekly she and her company trouped up to Tottenham Street to the Queen's Theatre where performances were not prohibited.

The situation was a preposterous one. Thomas Duncombe was attempting to bring pressure on other members of Parliament to regularize such matters. He was also attempting to broaden the privileges of minor theatres, and it was perhaps through his influence, or through that of Lord Fitzclarence, that Madame Vestris obtained an audience with William IV. According to contemporary reports, it was partly as a result of this interview that the minor theatres were licensed to perform for an additional two months.[13]

Under the circumstances it was hardly surprising that the Olympic season was undistinguished. The only novelty that caused a ripple of interest was Oxenford's *The Rape of the Lock*. Doubtless it was a relief to her to escape from the ugly world of bailiffs and lawyers to Hampton Court in the reign of Queen Anne. It was an age for which she had a strong affinity, and though the threat of imminent bankruptcy cast a shadow over her private life, she did not allow it to blight the Olympic production. As Belinda she looked as radiant as ever, surrounded by attendant sylphs in her perfectly appointed boudoir.

But soon afterward the storm broke. On April 19, in a letter to *The Times*, she announced her bankruptcy, categorically denying that this could be attributed to personal extravagance or theatrical mismanagement. On April 25 she made public a second letter, and one week later she appeared in bankruptcy court.[14] The role was a new one for her. So great was the crush at the door that the commissioner had difficulty elbowing his way in, and many of her creditors were unable to force an entrance through the crowd. Those inside listened with hushed attention to Madame's evidence and to a tangled discussion of discounted bills and blank acceptances. When she had completed her testimony and departed, the courtroom promptly emptied, leaving only a gaggle of lawyers to unravel her affairs as best they could. Her debts were not as formidable as she had feared, but even so they amounted to nearly £1,400. She was scheduled to appear in court once again, but on June 5 her creditors agreed to settle for 5 shillings in the pound, the initial payment to be financed by an auction of her effects.[15]

The next few weeks were intensely active. She arranged to move from Belgrave Square to more prosaic lodgings in the Notting Hill district,[16] and she put the final touches on the last production of the season, Planché's *A Peculiar Position*. As usual, he had found his inspiration in France, and it was in this trifling vaudeville of a grocer mistaken for a count that John Liston, on June 4, 1837, quietly took his leave of a public that had idolized him for over thirty years. Perhaps his farewell was a trifle too sedate, for in the course of the following month he refused to take part in any of the benefits arranged for Madame—one at Drury Lane, one at Covent Garden, and one at the English Opera House. On the other hand, perhaps he

Madame Vestris and Charles James Mathews in
The Rape of the Lock.

had really left the stage for good. In any case, she was too busy to trouble herself over his refusal.

The auction of her effects took place on June 22–23 in Belgrave Square. Much of her furniture was French, but the accessories were largely English. Only two days before the auction took place the young Princess Victoria had been roused from sleep and told that her uncle, William IV, was dead. The eighteen-year-old queen-to-be evidently admired the actress, for a few weeks earlier she had attended the Olympic and attempted two pen-and-ink sketches of Mathews and Madame. The two women had little in common, but the young princess would not have felt ill at ease in the Belgrave Square drawing room. It was adorned with five cases of stuffed birds, one stuffed otter, and various engravings by Sir David Wilkie. It also boasted "an expensive striking mantel clock, in an uncommonly rich gilt ormolu case, the subject Mazeppa, on a stand, which conceals a powerful musical movement." [17] From attic to pantry, her effects were those of an eminent Victorian.

After the last lot had gone under the hammer—three japanned coal scuttles—she set out on a tour of Ireland, Scotland, and the Midlands. She performed even in such relatively small towns as Leamington and Stratford-upon-Avon. The summer came to an end with a brief engagement at the Haymarket and a fortnight in Brighton before the reopening of the Olympic.

Replacing Liston, as the new season began, was William Farren, an actor who specialized in crotchety character parts. Mrs. Orger was again at hand, and Robert Keeley had returned from a profitable tour to America. In view of her bankruptcy, Madame's productions were necessarily modest. Contrary to her usual practice, she produced two plays by Mathews which had already been seen elsewhere—*Truth* and *Hugo Bambino* (formerly entitled *The Court Jester*). Among the others only one attracted some attention—the anonymous burletta, *Carlo; or, The Watch Dog*. Like Bayly's *The Daughter*, it marked one of Madame's rare excursions into pathos. Its characters—an idiot boy, a countess, and a dying priest—and its plot devices—a secret panel and a hidden sword—brought to mind the Adelphi rather than Wych Street. Still more of a surprise was the casting of Mathews as the idiot boy. The reaction of the Olympic's patrons was predictable. Although *The Age* asserted that Mathews had never been seen to greater advantage, *The Satirist* doubted that any audience "could interest itself in the revolting characteristics of an idiot," [18] and the play was withdrawn almost immediately.

In the course of the season Stephen Price, the impresario of the Park Theatre in New York, approached Madame and

Mathews with a proposition. He offered them a year's tour in America with a guarantee of £20,000. The proposal was a dazzling one. Edmund Kean, Ellen Tree, the Keeleys, and Mlle. Celeste had all reaped a golden harvest there. Though Madame recalled only too well the dismal experience of the Andersons, and Mathews was equally mindful of his parents' dislike of America, the offer was irresistible.

Price's proposal, as might be expected, caused much discussion and exposed both the lessee and Mathews to considerable comment in the press. As a result, scavenging journalists promptly revived the rumor that Madame was having an affair with her leading man.

The story was particularly distressing to Anne Mathews. Her son was still living with her, but she fretted herself into sick headaches worrying about him. In a letter to Charles written the day after the auction at Belgrave Square, she alludes at some length to the alarming subject of his relations with Madame. Evidently she had already referred to the matter in a previous letter, and she was disturbed by the possibility that he might have misunderstood her words.

> I think I said I "loved her for what I found her"—by this I meant that I found her so engaging, so womanly & domestic —so full of feeling, & withal so indisputably & disinterestedly attached to you—that I yielded my heart involuntarily to her . . . for indeed I really feel a love for the sweet creature, as fervent as my admiration for her public talents has been—I think she has been most cruelly sinned against and that her innate good & amiable qualities have never before now had means and power of being exercised and appreciated.[19]

The two women obviously disliked each other. Anne Mathews—evangelistic, conventional, and possessive—had little in common with the "dear Lizzy" she so mistrusted. Both preserved the amenities, however, and Charles steered his course skillfully between them.

Madame's affair with Lord Edward was a thing of the past and doubtless she found pleasure in the company of her personable young colleague. The journalists, however, were not content to let it go at that. By April 1838 it was reported that they were married and that Madame was already enceinte. "Pigeons begin to pair; Mrs. C. Mathews is seen to stop at a ready-made Baby Linen warehouse; and Charles is exceedingly anxious and attentive." [20] A week later the editor denied the truth of this report but compensated for this disappointment by providing his readers with a fictional account of their wedding night.

While Madame had not yet committed herself to matrimony, she had at least committed herself to the American tour, and Planché's Easter entertainment, *The Drama's Levee, or, A Peep at the Past*, celebrates this decision. With Madame Vestris, Charles Mathews, Mrs. Orger, and Josephine Anderson in the leads, this *pièce d'occasion* is one of his wittiest productions. Like his earlier *Success*, it burlesques the current state of the theatre. The Drama is plagued by two quarreling sons, one legitimate and one illegitimate, and vexed by two old friends, Praise and Censure. After a short scene in which various characters from current entertainments pass in review, she complains bitterly of the exodus of talent to America. Finally, as one critic describes it:

> The curtain of a mock stage is then withdrawn and Madame Vestris discovered asleep . . . the scene represents Liverpool, a packet ready to sail. . . . [a] Sea Serpent arrives to convoy the lady to New York, which she exhibits a great reluctance to visit: the spirits of her departed characters, Venus, Psyche, Pandora, &c. rise, accompanied by divers mythological and allegorical personages.—Madame parodizes Richard's dream, rushes forward, makes a poetical farewell, and the piece concludes.[21]

Planché's burletta was not without its ominous undertones, but no such gloom overclouded the last production of the season, Mathews' *Patter versus Clatter*. Changing his identity and his accent with dizzying speed, Mathews rattled off comic songs at a breakneck pace and all but buried his fellow actors under a torrent of language that left his audience limp with laughter.

On May 31 the Olympic gave its final performance of the season. The company presented Madame with a handsome bracelet and in an unusually moving farewell she explained to the crowded house: "Offers of so liberal a nature have been made to me from America that no one who labours for ultimate independence would be justified in declining them." [22] After assuring them that the theatre would be conducted as before, she concluded, "And now that I have told you what you have to expect, promise me that when the cat's away you will come and see the mice play."

Planché agreed to act as her deputy manager, and as her replacement she engaged Louisa Nisbett, who had recently had an enormous success in Sheridan Knowles's *The Love Chase*. Mathews and Madame were booked to sail on *The Great Western* in July, but they managed to find the time to visit Madame Bartolozzi in Calais [23] and play a short engagement at the Haymarket.

On the morning of July 18, 1838, one week before sailing, they were married in the parish church of Kensington. According to one account, they left Madame's cottage in Notting Hill

a few minutes before nine o'clock, and walking to the church, entered by different doors, both of which were immediately closed, the only persons within the edifice besides the principals being the officiating minister, Mr. Brothers, the clerk, who was also "papa," and his two sisters, the two Misses Brothers, who officiated as bride's maids. The secret, however, by some means soon became known, and numbers of persons hastened to the church to obtain a sight of the celebrated comedians, but ere they reached it, the nuptial knot was tied, and the happy pair had taken their departure in the same secret manner in which they had come; without even the ringers announcing that a wedding had taken place.[24]

The account appears to be an accurate one. Ann Mathews was conspicuously absent, but the couple did at least have one friend present as a witness—Charles Peake, the Olympic's treasurer.

As might be expected, the marriage aroused much comment. Most considered it a marriage of convenience between a fading beauty and an ambitious young actor. Others claimed that it was a purification ceremony—a necessary preliminary to their American tour. In any event, it touched off a round of Green Room jokes about Madame and her "young tiger."

"They say," said [Mrs.] Humby, with her quaint air of assumed simplicity, "that before accepting him, Vestris made a full confession to him of all her lovers! What a touching confidence!" she added archly. "What needless trouble!!" said [Mrs.] Orger dryly. "What a wonderful memory!!!" wound up [Mrs.] Glover triumphantly.[25]

Others recalled with amusement the title of a recent Olympic burletta, *You Can't Marry Your Grandmother*. Equally apropos were two other Olympic titles of recent vintage—*What Have I Done?* and *A Hasty Conclusion*.

After a short honeymoon in Bristol, the couple set sail from Liverpool. They embarked on *The Great Western* with high hopes, but their troubles began on the voyage over, one journalist reported.

It is most positively stated that Madame Vestris's conduct on board *The Great Western*, on her voyage to New York, was of a character repulsive and unfriendly; and that on the occasion of Mr. Mathews joining the festivities on board, with a judicious acquiescence to sing a song, was rebuked with the words, "You had better get on the table and spout to them next," which being overheard by the company created the first feeling of objection towards them as public characters.[26]

Whether the story was true or not, their arrival in New York in mid-August was inauspicious. The city was sweltering and in the grip of a depression. The couple were to give their first performance at the Park Theatre on September 17. Ordinarily, they might have stayed on in New York, but the heat was such that they left at once, traveling up the Hudson to Poughkeepsie and going on from there to Mountain House in the Catskills. Mathews's account of their arrival is a vivid one.

. . . after a long steamboat run [we] were bumped and jolted up a half-made road of miles, in a half-made carriage crammed full of people, to the monster hotel at the top, where we arrived, with aching bones, just at nightfall, in search of cool and repose. Sounds of revelry met our ears as we approached, and on reaching the house, tired to death with our fatiguing journey, and covered with dust from head to foot, we had to make our way through a blaze of light and a host of elegantly-dressed men and women, who abandoned the illuminated ball-room and lined the piazzas and corridors, to inspect the new arrivals. Through this bevy of strangers we sneaked as quickly as we could, in search of a room. A room! What an idea! The whole place was brimful and over-full, and every bed doubly occupied. Sitting-rooms were unknown; the public saloons were the only resorts for meals and conversation, and repose and quiet were things never even inquired for. After writing our names in the book, for public inspection, the whole party was in a state of tumult, and "The Mathooses!" travelled from mouth to mouth with electrical speed. A small bedroom was given up by one of the officials of the house. It was divided by a scanty Venetian blind from the public corridor, or piazza as they called it; and we were allowed, on the plea of ill-health, to have a cup of tea in it alone. This, it appeared, gave great offense; and there is no doubt we were greatly to blame in not at once putting on our ball dresses and joining the dancers.[27]

The following morning they fled by a back staircase and returned to the quiet hotel in Poughkeepsie where they spent the remainder of the month.

By the time they returned to New York, highly colored accounts of their Catskills visit had circulated widely. They had arrived with a valet, two lady's maids, a liveried coachman, and two footmen. Madame had not deigned to come down to meals but had sent her maid in her place. As one reporter put it: "If she had slapped the faces of the ladies at the old Catskill Mountain House they could not have been more insulted." [28] In some versions, ex-governor Marcy had fallen victim to the charms of Madame's maid, mistaking her for her mistress. In others, the events had occurred not at Mountain House but in Saratoga. In either case, they had insulted the citizenry. Journalists retaliated by raking up Madame's scandalous past and by spreading the rumor that she and Mathews were not, in fact, legally married.

In view of the experiences of the Andersons, Madame and Mathews had reason to be alarmed. Their first glimpse of the audience at the Park Theatre on the night of September 17 heightened their agitation. Mathews found the house "crammed to suffocation, and—alarming symptom—entirely men."

Unfortunately, both he and Madame were unaware of the fact that it was rare to see a woman in the pit of the Park Theatre.

The evening began with the first scene from *The Drama's Levee*, a poor choice considering its tone and its topicality. Mathews and Vestris began the performance with some trepidation, but the audience's applause reassured them, and by the time it concluded they had recovered their confidence. Their still more cordial reception in *One Hour* and *The Loan of a Lover* led them to hope that perhaps the incident at Mountain House had been forgotten. The next morning they found the notices favorable. On the second night, however, receipts fell off sharply, and during the remainder of their two-week engagement they played to almost empty houses.

Disheartened, they went to Philadelphia where they were to perform for thirty-six nights at the Chestnut Street Theatre. Despite a sheaf of good notices business again fell short of expectations, and their engagement was suspended after twelve performances. The news so alarmed Thomas Ward, the Baltimore theatre manager, that he in turn canceled his agreement with them, and the discouraged couple returned to New York. Any notion of extending their tour had been abandoned, but they agreed to appear at the Park for a final two weeks. To some extent the engagement restored their confidence. Business gradually picked up, and at their final performance on November 13 a crowded house received them with cheers and applause. There was no disguising the fact, however, that the trip had proved a bitter disappointment.

Their failure aroused much discussion in the theatrical world, but it was not totally unexpected. On the eve of their departure for America one anonymous journalist had gloomily predicted: "Jonathan expects a young beauty and is little prepared for a lady rising 44." [29] Another had foreseen failure for still another reason:

Madame Vestris has, from being accustomed to illustrate the muses of Planché, Peake, the Dances, and other "Shining

Lights," been rendered totally unfit for characters in the regular drama; and it is this circumstance that induces us to believe that her appearance among the great American people will not create the sensation which is so generally expected.[30]

Without a doubt there was some truth to both these observations. Madame was rising forty-two rather than forty-four, but she had gained weight and her lavish use of blanching cream gave her an enameled look. As to her repertory, it had indubitably disappointed many. Some had expected to see her *en travestie*. Others no doubt had hoped that she would appear in "the regular drama." Even the novelties in which she appeared were not really novel. Some had been performed by the Keeleys. Others, such as *One Hour* and *The Ladder of Love* had already been seen in New York's New Olympic Theatre, named after its London counterpart. In addition, despite the fact that she and Mathews were appearing in plays selected from the Olympic repertory, they were not appearing in Olympic productions. In contrast to Madame, Edmund Simpson, the manager of the Park, was easygoing in the extreme. When George Vandenhoff, the Shakespearian actor, arrived to begin an engagement, he was astonished by Simpson's casual question: "Where is your Beatrice and your Lady Macbeth?"[31] During their first fortnight at the Park, Mathews and Vestris were miserably supported, though on their return Simpson strengthened the company by engaging Charlotte Cushman and Henry Placide. Critics also noted with satisfaction that Madame had apparently altered things for the better in the productions in which she was appearing. "In the furniture of the rooms, in the dresses, and in the perfect propriety of all the stage arrangements, there is a most perceptible improvement on the nights of her performance. We hope the stage manager will take a lesson from her and exercise a little of the same propriety upon other occasions."[32]

But of all the explanations subsequently advanced to account for their failure, perhaps the most interesting is the suggestion that Mathews and Vestris failed because of their style.[33] American critics repeatedly described their acting as "true to nature," and writing of Madame one playgoer observed: "The style of her acting is such that persons who wish to see something beyond nature had better not witness her performances—such persons can see just such acting every day in a lady's parlor without paying a dollar, if they have only the happiness of being introduced into good society." [34] The comment would explain the fact that Madame attracted comparatively few spectators to the Park. As one critic put it: "The public taste has been vitiated by highly seasoned dishes, so that when superior food is presented, without the aid of piquant sauces . . . we turn from it with indifference." [35]

Whatever the cause or causes, the fact remained that the tour had been a failure. They were booked to return on *The Great Western* but Madame was indisposed. (It was rumored that she had suffered a miscarriage, but such rumors had periodically circulated about her. In 1835, after recovering from a short indisposition, she was described as looking "Thynner.") Within a few days, however, they set sail, arriving in Liverpool in the latter part of December. Their earnings in America had amounted to only £1,750, a far cry from the £20,000 they had hoped to realize. Furthermore, the season at the Olympic had gone badly. Louisa Nisbett, for all her charm, had disappointed expectations. In *The Idol's Birthday*, a pendant to *The Rape of the Lock*, she had looked delightful in her spreading train and little black velvet hat, but the play cried out for the talents of Madame. William Farren, as well, had proved a disappointment, brilliant though he was in *The Court of Old Fritz* as Frederick the Great. By Christmas the Olympic was £3,400 in debt and theatrical journalists were gloomily predicting the worst: "Wanted: a few clever men to manage a property on the verge of ruin. Apply in Wych Street." [36]

Under the circumstances Planché decided to defer the Christmas entertainment, *Bluebeard*, until the return of the lessees. As a substitute he presented Dance's *The Burlington Arcade*, produced with all the attention to detail that had characterized Madame's regime. Under the direction of Telbin, the scenic designer, the famous arcade was reproduced with extraordinary accuracy. Wigs adorned the hairdresser's window, flowers decked the florist's shop, and in the rooms above people could be seen passing to and fro. One critic describes it thus:

> There also sat, in his armchair, the portly beadle, armed with switch and mace, making war on the dirty little boys, the ragged men, the elevated umbrellas, and the clanking pattens— there as the twilight fell, the long array of gas lamps—
> Touched by the lamplighter's Promethean art,
> Start into light and make the lighter start.
> It was the perfect metropolitan nature—with the exception of the usual crowds of customers, passengers, and loiterers who were rather thinly represented.[37]

Five years earlier such a scene would have attracted much attention. By 1838 Olympic audiences were accustomed to effects of this kind.

On December 26, as Captain Patter, Mathews was welcomed back enthusiastically. One week later Madame returned to the Olympic as Bluebeard's last wife. The warmth of her reception almost justified the trip to America. She made her entrance to the tune of "Home Sweet Home" as cheering spectators waved their handkerchiefs and tossed bouquets on stage. The evening belonged to Madame, though spectators were amused by the chorus of Bluebeard's wives and dazzled by Planché's fifteenth-century costumes.

With the return of the lessees, business picked up at once. The plays in which they appeared were trifling, but of the sort that Olympic customers preferred. Planché's *Faint Heart Ne'er Won Fair Lady*, a salon version of *Ernani*, gave them the opportunity to parade in costumes of the period of Velazquez, and Charles Dance's *Izaak Walton*, if it did nothing else, permitted Madame to appear as the poetical milkmaid, singing "Come Live With Me" before a delightful setting of meadows by a river.

But the most dramatic event at the Olympic during the spring of 1839 occurred offstage. One day in early March a gentleman named Lancaster, while strolling in the vicinity of Lincoln's Inn Fields, overheard two roughly dressed men referring to "Charley" and "Madame" in what seemed to him a menacing manner. Following them at a distance, he observed that one of them had inadvertently dropped a letter. A quick glance at its contents alarmed him still more.

Dear Jack

Now mind what i say I will have no corpseing work so take care and do nothink of the species. Do something as will tattow her d—— countenance and disfigger it with everlasting pepper. Better her than him this time 'cause if she's prevented from practising her playhouse won't pay and he will suffer in his pockets for daring to speak again a free country. Dam him we'll serve him out another way another time. You had better send the thing at the parcels delivery and address it to her at the stage door in Craven buildings mind I won't have no shot or shells only gunpowder. That ull be enough to throw her into fits and blind her, so remember your loving
B. F. Zatchell [38]

By the time he had finished reading the letter, the men had disappeared up a side street. Highly alarmed, Mr. Lancaster hastened to the Olympic to forewarn Madame. The warning was not in vain. Soon afterward an unknown messenger delivered a parcel for the lessee. It was a mahogany box, about the size of a tea caddy, and inscribed *Open Sesame*. Mr. Strachan, the Olympic machinist, who had recently replaced Matthew Mackintosh, gingerly examined the box, then, in a burst of courage, he dashed his heel through the lid. Fortunately there was no explosion, but the box was found to contain gunpowder and a crude detonating device.

For a week theatrical London discussed the infernal machine. Was it a plot by two disgruntled American seamen or was the whole incident a hoax? The incident smacked of melodrama, though even Adelphi audiences might have balked at Zatchell's letter. A reward of £100 failed to provide the slightest clue to the identity of the messenger. Similarly, Zatchell, Jack, and even Mr. Lancaster mysteriously disappeared. Londoners were understandably skeptical, and a reporter on *The Weekly Dispatch* dismissed the incident under the headline "Venus Preserved; or, A Plot Discovered." But the definitive quip was Theodore Hook's. In answer to Planché's remark that "there was a quantity of gunpowder found at the bottom of the infernal machine sent to Vestris," Hook jocosely replied, "My opinion is that if the truth were known Madame herself was at the bottom of it." [39]

The season at the Olympic concluded with Charles Dance's *A Dream of the Future*, which required the actors to age forty years. Madame's transformation, we are told, was "shockingly faithful and unlovely." [40] Business had improved since their return, but Mathews and Madame had not recouped their losses. Suddenly, however, a golden opportunity presented itself. After two seasons of management, Macready was giving up Covent Garden. Madame was eager to take up the challenge.

She had succeeded in civilizing the illegitimate drama at the Olympic. She had banished the gross and the sensational from the little theatre in Wych Street and succeeded in reproducing on its stage the appearance and manners of contemporary life. At Covent Garden she would have the opportunity to apply these same principles to the legitimate drama.

By the end of May, 1839, matters had been settled. The Duke of Bedford and the shareholders agreed to minimal terms, but even so "the total charge upon the building stood at about £5000 per annum (consisting of ground rent, rates and taxes, salaries of treasurer and firemen, and provision for gradual repayment of outstanding debts)." [41] Undeterred by the failure of the three most recent lessees, Madame optimistically announced her plans for the coming season. She assured her admirers that "Mr. Mathews will not play Macbeth and I have positively refused Queen Katharine." [42] Even had they chosen to do so it would have proved difficult. Macready, Helen Faucit, and Mrs. Warner were all leaving Covent Garden, depleting its ranks of serious actors. But their defection was not alarming. Madame was planning to stress traditional and modern comedy, and with this in view she reengaged a number of key actors from the Olympic—William Farren, John Brougham, James Bland, James Vining, Robert Keeley, Mrs. Nisbett, and Mrs. Orger. Others from the Covent Garden company agreed to stay on, among them John Harley and George Bartley, the veteran comedians, Mrs. Humby, the character actress, and James R. Anderson, a personable young leading man. Madame also tried to coax

Liston out of retirement, and in his silkiest manner Mathews threw out his lures:

> You may consider yourself King of Covent Garden; act when you please, what you please, and as long as you please; stop when you please, take what money you please, do what you please, and say what you please, and be sure that do whatever you please, you cannot fail to please. More than this I cannot add, except that you shall be allowed to sweeten your own tea, and when you are too late for rehearsals, you shall beat the prompter.[43]

It was hard to resist such blandishments, but Liston had resisted Macready's similar pleas a year earlier, and he again refused to return to the stage.

The problem of collecting a company was complicated by the fact that during the month of June the new lessees were touring the Midlands. From Manchester and Birmingham they deluged Planché with questions. Would Ellen Tree be available on her return from America? Was it true that Louisa Nisbett was seceding to Bunn at Drury Lane? Early in July, Mathews returned to London to straighten out some of these problems. In the course of his visit he found time to attend at least two of Macready's best-known productions. How he reacted to the eminent tragedian's interpretations of Henry V and Richelieu is not known, but he was evidently impressed by Stanfield's spectacular settings, for he recorded his impressions of them in his sketchbook.[44] One might expect that these visits would have chastened him. If Macready, buttressed by Bulwer and Shakespeare, had failed, who could hope to succeed? But Mathews, like all actors, was congenitally an optimist.

On July 16 a host of Macready's admirers convened at a banquet. In speeches almost as long and as indigestible as the dinner, they paid tribute to him and celebrated his escape from the frustrations of management. Two days later Mathews and Madame took possession of Covent Garden. It is unlikely that they marked the occasion with a fervent prayer, as Macready had done two years earlier, but they would have been well advised to do so.

chapter 7

Covent Garden

A month before the season began, Madame and her husband spent a few days by the sea. Both were engrossed in their own careers, but they were finding that they had more in common than the life of the theatre. Both were spoiled and extravagant. Both were also fundamentally reserved, but as time passed they were learning to trust one another. It was hardly a secret that Madame had treated her admirers much as she did her pet spaniels, Biche and Fidele. Only Lord Edward Thynne had aroused stronger emotions in her, but he had vanished from her life. In Mathews she found a man who had wit, vivacity, good manners, and, above all, a kind heart. He in turn was discovering in her an unsuspected generosity of spirit and depth of feeling.

As they paced the sands at Yarmouth much of their conversation necessarily turned on the problems that they faced. For over a decade the lessees of Drury Lane and Covent Garden had failed to show a profit. Macready had engaged a strong company. His productions had been painstakingly rehearsed, and staged to achieve a maximum unity of effect. Audiences had flocked to see *The Tempest* and *Henry V* and Bulwer's *Richelieu* and *The Lady of Lyons*, but Macready, in his obstinate fashion, had attempted to foist off on them a number of dull old pieces which played to empty benches. He was leaving Covent Garden a poorer man, if not a wiser one.

Alfred Bunn's career at Drury Lane had proved even more disastrous. Convinced that the legitimate drama spelled ruin, he had featured such attractions as opera, tightrope walkers, and Ducrow's stud of horses. Van Amburgh and his lions had created a momentary sensation, and much to Macready's disgust the Queen had repeatedly patronized their performances, but even so, these sensational attractions had not turned the trick. Receipts at Drury Lane during the 1835–36 season had totaled over £57,000. Three years later they had dwindled to £28,000, leaving the lessee £15,000 out of pocket for that season alone.

Nonetheless, Mathews and Madame went ahead with their plans. Together they assembled a company and together they began to plan their repertory. Understandably, they proposed to feature comedy, but they realized that they had an obligation to produce some serious drama as well. While the company that they had assembled was unsuited to play the standard tragedies of Shakespeare and Otway, it might well do justice to a modern tragedy.

At Covent Garden, freed from the restrictions imposed on the minor houses, Madame hoped to offer new five-act plays presented with the same attention to detail that had characterized the Olympic productions. It was scarcely an easy matter, however, to develop a modern repertory. Macready's literary friends, Dickens and Browning, eager as they were for success in the theatre, had proved inept as dramatists. Writers with a more practical sense of the theatre, on the other hand, found much to discourage them. The monopoly exercised by the patent houses, the caprices of the Lord Chamberlain, the greater economic rewards of novel writing—were only a few of the deterrents. Provincial managers pirated their plays and then murdered them, and James Sheridan Knowles, the most successful playwright of the age, complained that he could scarcely scratch out a living with his pen.

The new lessees of Covent Garden could always turn to cheerful hacks such as W. T. Moncrieff and Edward Fitzball who were ready on twenty-four hours notice to provide managers with a five-act play, but they did not propose to offer Covent Garden patrons such fare. They had paid the Olympic authors generously, and they were prepared to be even more generous under the present circumstances. Above all, they wanted a play from Knowles. He was best known for *Virginius* and *The Hunchback*, two effective costume dramas, but he was also capable of writing in a lighter vein, and in *The Love Chase* had provided an effective vehicle for Mrs. Nisbett. It was clearly with this kind of play in mind that Madame Vestris wrote to Knowles, offering him generous terms and volunteering to do anything he proposed "except burn down the theatre." [1] At the moment he was unprovided with a comedy, but he agreed to furnish her with a "very strong play," admirably suited to the talents of Ellen Tree. [2]

It was at least a beginning. They could make use of some items in the traditional repertory, and they were hopeful that some of the Olympic productions might bear transplanting to Covent Garden. There was some doubt, however, that a theatre seating three thousand people was the proper arena for lightweight pieces by playwrights such as Planché. At the Olympic his kid-glove elegance had been an asset. At Covent Garden it might prove a drawback. As his hardworking colleague, Edward Fitzball, put it:

> Planché is a practical author and one of our cleverest; a little too cautious *perhaps;* he would braid the sunbeams so carefully as not to burn his fingers. In the general parlance of theatrical business a practical author means a play-writer who looks beyond his steel pen and quire of foolscap to the O.P. and to the P.S. It is not *quite* essential, as our friend Dickens has it, that he should write for the wash-tub; but it is *absolutely* necessary that he should know there is such a commodity as a washing-tub in the theatre where he may be engaged to write. [3]

Fitzball's observation had a measure of truth. Planché preferred not to dip his fingers in the suds. He was well aware, however, that there was such a commodity as a washtub, and he was a thoroughly professional man of the theatre. Although he had been engaged as "superintendent of the decorative department" at Covent Garden, he volunteered to help Mathews as a

reader, and together they began sifting through piles of manu-
scripts, among them three five-act comedies on cricket by an
addled clergyman.

While they went on with their dispiriting search, Madame
was making preparations. Naturally enough, she had retained
many of the Covent Garden staff and backstage crew. George
Bartley would continue as stage manager, Henry Bishop as musical director, the Grieves as scene painters, and Mr. Sloman as
chief machinist. But she had also retained various key members
of the Olympic company. James Tully would serve as chorus
master, Oscar Byrne would superintend the ballet, and Miss
Glover the costumes. She also brought with her E. W. Bradwell, her machinist-decorator and general factotum. He could
rise to any occasion, fill any need. Some years earlier, having
been sent to see the elephant at the Exeter Exchange, he was
asked if he could construct a model of the animal for a forthcoming extravaganza. "I should be very sorry if I couldn't make
something better than that!" had been his answer.[4]

The wardrobe, machinery, and scenery of the Olympic having been auctioned off for 5,850 guineas,[5] Madame was provided with some working capital and was able to effect a
number of necessary changes. Under the direction of the invalu-
able Bradwell, Covent Garden was thoroughly cleaned, re-
painted, and repapered. Insofar as it was possible, she wanted to
recreate the Olympic ambience. Most of the gas fixtures were
replaced by wax candles, and color schemes throughout the theatre were freshened and lightened. As at the Olympic, the shilling gallery was to be abolished to discourage the raffish element, and more genteel playgoers were to be encouraged. The
boxes were redecorated and prospective patrons of the dress circle were promised a separate entrance and gilt chairs instead of
hard benches. Furthermore, they could reserve their seats for
the whole evening. Even the actors benefited, for the Green
Room was refurnished in a manner that would have gladdened
the heart of any peacock. As one of her company describes it:

> [It] was a withdrawing-room, carpeted and papered elegantly;
> with a handsome chandelier in the centre, several globe lights at
> the sides, a comfortable divan, covered in figured damask, run-

ning around the whole room, large pier and mantel-glasses on the walls, and a full-length movable swing-glass so that on entering from his dressing-room an actor could see himself from head to foot at one view, and get back, front, and side views by reflection all around.[6]

To open the season Madame Vestris selected *Love's Labour's Lost*. The choice was a peculiar one, but far from capricious. She was sensitive to the type of charge that Macready had jotted angrily in his diary: "It is not a fitting spectacle—the national drama in the hands of Mrs. Vestris and Mr. Charles Mathews!" [7] Since she could not produce a Shakespearian tragedy or history, why not revive a long-forgotten comedy? It had all the advantages of novelty and she could make her obeisance to Shakespeare at a minimal risk.

On the evening of the premiere, September 30, a hostile crowd, angered by the abolition of the shilling gallery, swarmed into the lobby. They were finally admitted to a lower gallery at the traditional price, but they were still in a sullen mood when Madame stepped before the curtain to make her opening address, and they occasionally interrupted her with hisses. After assuring the audience that she and her husband would uphold the standards to be expected at a national theatre, she went on:

> We commence by presenting to you a long-neglected play of England's immortal bard—his works and those of the higher class of Dramatic Authors, ancient and modern, will usually hold the first place in our evening's entertainments and this course will be adhered to as long as it is your pleasure to afford us adequate encouragement.
>
> In respect to afterpieces our doors and purses will be alike open to all writers of merit. We have been told in sober sadness that pieces written for a small theatre cannot be heard in a large one, but we have procured performers as large as life and we mean to try the question. One of our Olympic writers indeed is the author of our new farce tonight, but we have taken every possible precaution to ensure him a hearing by warning him to get a particularly large pen, to dip it in the very blackest ink, and to write in unusually loud English.
>
> In conclusion I beg to hope that as you have often been pleased to admit that I have done great things in a small theatre

' so you will not now find cause to complain that I have done small things in a great one and that as the production of a Shakespearian play has been to us a labour of love so you will not give us cause to complain that our *Love's Labour's Lost*.[8]

Madame's hopes were not entirely realized, however. When Hazlitt wrote of *Love's Labour's Lost* "If we were to part with any of the author's comedies, it should be this," [9] he spoke for most of his contemporaries. The pedantic affectations of the court of Navarre had few attractions for Victorian playgoers. Despite prodigious cuts, particularly in the scenes between Don Armado and Moth, the quibbles and wordplay left spectators yawning, and only with Berowne's apostrophes to love did the play flare briefly into life. Nor did the casting help. As Don Armado, J. P. Harley failed to convey the quixotic quality of the fantastical Spaniard, Anderson played Berowne ponderously, and Mrs. Nisbett and Madame Vestris, as the Princess of France and Rosaline, lacked their usual animation. Only Keeley, as the dull-witted Costard, aroused some enthusiasm.

If Madame's labors proved largely lost, Planché and Thomas Grieve, the scenic designer, had not wasted their time. Between them, so one critic tells us, they recreated the vanished elegance of the court of Navarre.

> The rising of the curtain on *Love's Labour's Lost* displayed a scene of surpassing grandeur—the stage representing the terraced portico of the palace of the King of Navarre, approached by a broad flight of steps, leading to spacious gardens laid out in the old French taste, forming a beautiful background; the ascent of the King, his lords and officers of the court, in picturesque and appropriate costumes, completed the magnificence of the tableau, and prepared the audience for the characteristic splendour and finished elegance of the succeeding scenes.[10]

The pageant of the Nine Worthies and the concluding procession of Summer and Winter came too late in the evening to overcome the boredom of the audience. Superbly mounted as it was, the play sagged under the weight of recondite allusions and obscure jests, and after nine performances it was withdrawn. If Madame Vestris wished to produce comedies, so one reviewer observed, she would be better advised to turn her attention to the eighteenth century.

The suggestion was not wasted, for in the course of the autumn she revived *The School for Scandal* and *The Rivals*. As might be expected, both productions were characterized by fastidious attention to dress and setting and inevitably they were compared with Webster's productions at the Haymarket. In terms of decor, Madame's were clearly superior. Ben Webster made no pretensions to antiquarianism. He was content to slap together a revival with whatever costumes and backdrops he had at hand. A strong cast was, to him, the all-important necessity. But Madame's productions even in this respect were formidable. If Mrs. Glover, at the Haymarket, excelled as Mrs. Malaprop, William Farren, at Covent Garden, was inimitable as the crusty Sir Anthony. Tyrone Power, as Sir Lucius O'Trigger, had his ardent admirers. John Brougham, in the same role, was no less warmly applauded. Perhaps the weakest performances were those of Madame herself, for though she was far too mature for Lydia Languish, and far too worldly for Lady Teazle, she still insisted upon playing Sheridan's ingenues.

Also of interest were the rival versions of *The Beggar's Opera* at Covent Garden and Drury Lane. At the latter theatre William J. Hammond, a light comedian, had succeeded Bunn as the lessee. The rent had been reduced to £5,000 a year, approximately the same amount that Mathews and Madame were paying at Covent Garden. The speculation was a rash one, but Hammond induced Macready, Phelps, and Mrs. Warner to join his company, and for a few months he attempted to do battle with Madame. Both versions of Gay's opera were in period costume. Hammond, in addition, clapped bagwigs and embroidered coats on members of the orchestra, but Madame's version, it was generally agreed, was by far the better one. She and Planché had carefully recreated Gay's London, and her company had been drilled by Oscar Byrne until they were completely at ease in their eighteenth-century dress. The results of such discipline were striking. Hammond's actors looked like refugees from Monmouth Street, the headquarters for theatrical costumers.

Madame's looked as if they had walked out of Hogarth's prints. The same careful attention to detail marked her revival of Arne's *Artaxerxes*. Once again appearing as the Persian prince, Madame warbled "In Infancy" before settings of Persepolis inspired by Sir Robert Porter's archaeological studies.

But she had not yet found a modern play to which she could apply her theories of production. Furthermore, she had not yet found a proper outlet for the talents of Mathews. In the vast reaches of Covent Garden he seemed somehow lost. She had

Madame Vestris and William Harrison in *Artaxerxes*.

been unable to cast him in *Love's Labour's Lost*. They had inaugurated a short-lived series of "Olympic Nights" but the champagne entertainments lost their bubble at Covent Garden. He had failed to distinguish himself as Charles Surface in *The School for Scandal*. As Perez in Fletcher's *Rule a Wife and Have a Wife* he proved no more successful. In traditional comedy he appeared uneasy. In a modern comedy, if they could ever find one, he would probably appear to advantage.

During the first few weeks of the season Madame was primarily concerned, however, with Sheridan Knowles's *Love*, which had its first performance on November 9. Ellen Tree had joined the company for a limited engagement and in her role as a medieval countess enamored of a serf she had ample opportunity to demonstrate her gift for pathos, but beyond that the piece had little to recommend it. The "very strong" play so eagerly anticipated had turned out to be merely another pallid costume drama. But Ellen Tree had her admirers, and sensation-hungry playgoers enjoyed an effectively staged storm scene in which a massive oak was realistically splintered by lightning.

For ten weeks, until Ellen Tree left the company to go on tour, the play drew good houses. Mathews and Madame needed a more lasting success, however. They had six hundred and eighty-four employees on the Covent Garden payroll—one hundred and sixteen in the wardrobe department and one hundred and ninety-nine in the scenic division. They had a company of eighty and eighty-nine supernumeraries. Aghast at these obligations, Mathews wrote:

> I was initiated for the first time in my life into all the mysteries of the money-lending art, and the concoction of those fatal instruments of destruction called bills of exchange. Duns, brokers, and sheriffs' officers soon entered upon the scene, and I, who had never known what pecuniary difficulty meant, and had never had a debt in my life before, was gradually drawn into the inextricable vortex of involvement—a web which, once thrown over a man, can seldom be thrown off again.[11]

In addition, their daily routine was a punishing one. They rehearsed from ten to five, went home for dinner, then returned to the theatre for the evening performance. Every moment counted. Even during their carriage rides to and from the theatre they were busy memorizing new roles. Occasionally Madame succumbed to sheer exhaustion, but even then she fretted over details, firing off letters from her sickbed on such matters as the proper draping of her new turban.

Fortunately, she had a reliable staff and backstage crew. Many of those on the roster had been with her at the Olympic, and Planché, her "superintendent," she looked upon almost as an alter ego. She could entrust to them such matters as the Christmas pantomime which, by tradition, was as conventional as Christmas pudding. *Harlequin and the Merry Devil of Edmonton; or, The Great Bed of Ware*, proved no exception. Stuffed with songs, comic business, and topical allusions, it featured "a grand moving panorama of the Clyde" by Grieve, and culminated with a scene in which a vast number of baskets filled with eggs were transformed into cradles filled with babies. Madame's staff could also cope with routine productions of standard plays. It was virtually obligatory for Covent Garden to offer the public at least a taste of Shakespearian tragedy. Madame met the requirement by engaging a Mr. Moore, an obscure provincial actor, to play the lead in *Hamlet*. The results were dispiriting. While Mr. Moore had all the mannerisms of Macready, two performances were enough to prove that he had none of his genius.

His failure made it all the more imperative to find a good modern tragedy. Madame's hopes were momentarily raised when Leigh Hunt submitted to her his poetic drama, *A Legend of Florence*. A variant on *Romeo and Juliet*, it was well suited to the talents of Ellen Tree who was returning to Covent Garden for another interim engagement. In January 1840 the play went into rehearsal and Hunt was enthusiastic in his praise of Madame for her generosity and for the attention which she lavished on the forthcoming production. It opened on February 7 to polite but tepid reviews. The parallels to *Romeo and Juliet* were all too obvious, but where Shakespeare's treatment was passionate and full-blooded, Hunt's was languid and anemic, and after only a few performances it vanished from the repertory.

Madame was discovering, as Macready had, that audiences had little taste for the thin gruel of the poetic dramatists. As a change of fare she offered them the roast-beef patriotism of Planché's *The Fortunate Isles*. Inspired by the seventeenth-century masques, Planché's pageant was designed as a compliment to Victoria and Albert on the occasion of their marriage. Mathews and Vestris had reason to feel grateful to the young queen. While her theatrical taste left something to be desired, she had been generous in patronizing Covent Garden and had dutifully endured both *Love* and *The Legend of Florence*. Planché's pageant, which suggests a collaboration between Inigo Jones and Mr. Puff, was produced on February 12, 1840, two days after the royal marriage. As The Spirit of Liberty, Madame presided over a panorama of British history—the signing of the Magna Carta, the destruction of the Spanish Armada, and Charles II's landing at Dover. The pageant concluded, one critic tells us, with a tribute to the royal couple: "The [final] scene represents the ocean out of which rises the 'star of Brunswick,' a beautiful piece of mechanism, which opens as it enlarges, and discovers the word 'Victoria' in brilliant letters, surrounded by smaller revolving stars. A hymeneal altar rises, heraldic cupids fly about the air, and amidst this excellent effect the curtain drops." [12]

Another feature of the season was the return of Charles Kemble to Covent Garden for a limited number of performances. He was sixty-five, frail and deaf, but he was a favorite of the queen and of sentimentally minded audiences. He gave his first performance on March 24, playing Don Felix in Mrs. Centlivre's comedy *The Wonder*. It was the role in which Garrick had taken his farewell of the stage. The Queen was present, and when the old actor made his entrance, the house rose in tribute. Somehow, as if by magic, he threw off the years. His voice took on resonance and his step new elasticity. Two days later he undertook the still more challenging role of Mercutio. Physically he was better suited to play Capulet, but once again he triumphed over his limitations. Recalling his earlier performances, reviewers were not entirely enthusiastic, but Mathews was deeply impressed. Rushing into the Garrick Club he exclaimed to one of his friends, "I've had such an escape! I was going to play Mercutio myself, and I've just seen Charles Kemble play it! What an escape I've had!" [13] In the course of the spring Kemble also appeared as Charles Surface, Benedick, and Hamlet, performing gratuitously on a number of occasions. The Queen's continuing patronage and the public's curiosity brought a welcome transfusion to the box office. As Alfred Bunn sourly commented, it was a great piece of luck for Madame—the sort of luck *he* had never enjoyed!

Bunn's successor at Drury Lane, W. J. Hammond, gave up the ghost after a five-months' season. The London theatre world gloomily predicted the same fate for Mathews and Madame, but they failed to take into account the indefatigable Planché. At Easter time he was ready with a new extravaganza, *The Sleeping Beauty*. In subject matter it was typical of the Olympic entertainments, but in scale it was eminently suited to Covent Garden. At the bidding of Mr. Bradwell, so one critic tells us, the stage dutifully opened to "swallow a forest, disgorge a palace, or give passage to some demon of the upper or nether regions." [14] For the climax Bradwell devised a still more spectacular effect—seven fairies, waving colored lights, ascended to the top of the proscenium. Throughout the rehearsals they rose effortlessly, in a machine of his own devising, but on the opening night, the same critic reported, "some malicious imp, envious of the success of the cunning sprite whom mortals call Bradwell, locked the wheels of the 'Patent Safety Fly' which was to have been launched on this occasion, so that the aerial omnibus with its fairy freight could not ascend." [15] In their many subsequent performances, however, the fairies in their "Patent Safety Fly" levitated faultlessly and to infinite applause.

The lessees, for the moment at least, had been reprieved. A successful revival of *The Merry Wives of Windsor* gave them a further stay. The version was, of course, the Reynolds-Bishop adaptation in which Madame had so often appeared. It was costumed in Tudor dress, but Madame drew the line at the bare stage of the Elizabethans. The Grieves's settings of Windsor were opulently realistic and the last scene at Herne's oak evidently resembled the finale of *The Sleeping Beauty*. Bartley was criticized for playing Falstaff in too vulgar and farcical a manner, but the cast was on the whole a strong one. Madame and Mrs. Nisbett delighted audiences as the Merry Wives, and Mathews, in the modest role of Slender, gave an easy, attractive performance.

The season came to a close on May 29. They had not found any worthy new plays, nor had they turned up any particularly promising young actors. Mrs. Nisbett's sister, Miss Mordaunt, had made so disastrous a debut as Juliet that after only three performances she retired from the stage. George Vandenhoff had played Mercutio in leaden fashion and James Anderson as Romeo was equally bad. He attitudinized, he roared, and he blubbered. It was understandable, therefore, that Madame in her curtain speech pleaded for the establishment of a national school of acting. Without it, she argued, the theatre might soon find itself in the position of the Irishman who vowed not to go into the water until he had learned to swim.

She was prepared, however, to give a few swimming lessons, for she reengaged not only Vandenhoff and Anderson, but Mr. Moore as well. The season had not been a particularly distinguished one, but morale was high, and when Mathews and Madame returned from their summer tour the company presented them with a declaration of allegiance and support.

Their second season began with a new tragedy by Sheridan Knowles—*John of Procida*. Madame had hoped for a comedy and only reluctantly agreed to produce it. Cast in the leads were Ellen Tree, Mr. Moore, and James Anderson. Its premiere was attended by Macready. Much to his irritation he was forced to pay for his ticket and passed into the theatre unrecognized. He found the play dull, but Mr. Anderson much improved. Madame, in all likelihood, had taken him firmly in hand. But Macready's low opinion of the play was shared by both critics and the public and in short order it was withdrawn.

In its place she substituted Fletcher and Massinger's *The Spanish Curate* and Colley Cibber's *The Double Gallant*. Like most of her contemporaries she avoided the Restoration playwrights. Even *The Beggar's Opera* she found uncomfortable, and despite her success with it, bowdlerized Macheath's scenes with his doxies. Necessarily, these revivals were not always newly mounted. Her production of Cibber's comedy was evidently staged with stock costumes and settings, and her revival of *The Spanish Curate* seems to have been equally casual. "The dresses were of various countries, we did not observe a new scene, and the arrangement of a Spanish court of justice was such as a strolling barn [troupe] might have given us," [16] wrote one miffed reviewer.

On some revivals, particularly those in which Madame appeared, she was prepared to lavish more money and attention. The acclaim which had greeted *The Merry Wives of Windsor* persuaded her to undertake a major production of *A Midsummer Night's Dream*. Not since the closing of the theatres in 1642 had audiences seen Shakespeare's play in its original form. During the Restoration it had been metamorphosed into an opera, concluding with a hymeneal dance in a Chinese garden. Since that time it had been repeatedly "improved," most recently by Reynolds and Bishop. The production by Vestris and Planché returned to the original text of the play, although lavish cuts were necessary to accommodate Mendelssohn's incidental music and various other interpolations from Beethoven and Weber. Vestris and Planché knew Victorian playgoers too well to suppose that such cutting would offend their sensibilities. Nor did they propose to tax the spectators' imagination. The play was close in subject matter to the fairy extravaganzas and would allow them to draw on all the backstage resources of Covent Garden. "If Planché can devise a striking effect for the last scene," George Bartley predicted, "the play will run for sixty nights." [17] Oberon's concluding lines gave Planché the inspiration he was looking for.

> Through this house give glimmering light
>   By the dead and drowsy fire;
> Every elf and fairy sprite,
>   Hop as light from brier to brier;
> And this ditty, after me,
>   Sing and dance it trippingly.

Fortunately it was the sort of effect that Bradwell had already perfected in *The Sleeping Beauty*.

The play's reception on November 16, 1840, justified Bartley's prediction. Madame Vestris, as Oberon, was warmly welcomed and bursts of applause greeted every scene, from the opening view of Athens to the concluding vision of "countless fairies ascending and descending and waving torches of various colored lights." [18] As a production it anticipated Charles Kean's later revivals of Shakespeare, striking a somewhat uneasy balance between historical accuracy and Victorian convention. Demetrius and Lysander in their straw basket-hats might have satisfied the most demanding historian of costume. The fairies in their white silk stocking would not have offended Mrs. Grundy.

In spite of the public's enthusiasm, a number of the critics had reservations. Some felt that it had been overproduced. "An occasional preference of the suggestive to the actual would be more in keeping with the fairy texture of the drama," [19] suggested one. *The Times* deplored the cult of the scenic designer and, unkindest cut of all, *The Examiner* breezily proposed that the text might as well be totally discarded in favor of unadulterated spectacle. Madame was not without her champions, however, among them an enthusiastic undergraduate who was to make a reputation for himself as a Shakespearian scholar. In a long letter to *The Cambridge Advertiser*, J. O. Halliwell vigorously defended the production as the first successful performance of the play since the time of Shakespeare.[20] Such a response was gratifying, but audiences had already returned their verdict. They crowded the theatre nightly and continued to do so for months.

It was fortunate that they did, for the season's new productions were few and undistinguished. The Christmas pantomime proved a comparative failure, and as a result Mathews and Madame were looking for new plays even more eagerly than usual. On February 1, 1841, an inconspicuous item in *The Theatrical Observer* noted: "A comedy in five acts by Mr. Lee Moreton has been accepted by Madame Vestris and is to be read in the Green Room for the first time on Tuesday."

The young author's real name was Dion Boucicault. Two years earlier he had made his theatrical debut in Brighton as a swaggering teen-aged Sir Giles Overreach, but neither this nor his subsequent provincial performances had attracted attention. Brighton had also seen a production of his drama, *The Legend of the Devil's Dyke,* but this too had failed to impress playgoers. In January 1841 he was hopefully scribbling away in the garret of a dingy lodging house in Villiers Street. He had submitted a one-act farce to Covent Garden and one afternoon called at the theatre to get an opinion on his manuscript. He was ushered into Mathews's office by a stage doorman who mistook him for Maddison Morton, the well-known farce writer. In his most disarming manner Mathews regretfully declined his play and explained to the young author that what was wanted above all was a good five-act comedy of modern life. A month later Boucicault returned—with a manuscript.

So impressed were Madame and Mathews by the young playwright's work that they accepted it at once and arranged for a formal reading. On the morning of Tuesday, February 5, the company gathered in the Green Room. Placed at a central table, by tradition, were three chairs—one for the prompter, one for the stage manager, and one for the author. Boucicault nervously took his place and the reading began. At its conclusion, Madame rose and embraced him. The usual flurry of compliments followed, but the author's work had just begun. The play's original title, *Country Matches,* was not much admired, nor was its alternate title, *Out of Town.* In the course of rehearsals they settled on a new title, *London Assurance,* and the real playwriting began. The play was still only a crude sketch, but the enthusiastic Boucicault was eager to oblige and "scene after scene was re-written at the prompt-table and handed wet to the company." [21]

Despite its inchoate state Madame had such confidence in the play that she was anxious to present it to maximum advantage. In December 1840 Bulwer's modern comedy, *Money,* with Macready in the lead, had triumphed at the Haymarket. Over the objections of Webster, Macready had taken extraordinary pains with the production. He made the unprecedented suggestion that outside actors be engaged to play certain roles and even proposed to pay their salaries by performing gratuitously on some evenings. He persuaded Count D'Orsay to approve the fit of the gentlemen's clothes and to vouch for the accuracy of the club scenes. In addition, the supernumeraries playing menial roles were drilled by Bulwer's manservant in the fine points of domestic service.

Madame did not propose to be outdone. She cast the forthcoming play as strongly as possible, contenting herself with the somewhat colorless role of Grace Harkaway. It gave her a freer hand in overseeing details. When the young author suggested that a real carpet might perhaps be used in the drawing room, the stage manager grumbled, "He will be asking for real flowers and real sunlight in the garden." [22] Madame was doubtless amused. He had plainly not had the advantage of seeing her productions at the Olympic.

She could not provide real sunlight, but everything else was to be as real as possible. Bulwer's *Money* had achieved only a limited realism which she was determined to surpass. Webster's sets were traditionally inconsequential and the costuming in his productions usually erratic. Stage fops and heavy fathers, in particular, more often than not appeared in costumes as bizarre as they were out of date. Madame would have none of this. William Farren, cast as Sir Harcourt Courtly, an aging Adonis, was so associated with eighteenth-century comedy that audiences automatically expected to see him in a bagwig, knee breeches, and diamond shoe buckles. For this production he went to Stultz, the leading tailor, and ordered modern clothes that would not have raised an eyebrow at White's or Crockford's. For Dazzle, the young man-about-town, Mathews selected an equally appropriate wardrobe. His frock coat fitted him like a glove and his patent-leather boots shone like mirrors—he was, in short, the model of a would-be gentleman.

The interest aroused by the play was heightened by a quarrel between Mathews and Macready. During a Green Room conversation Boucicault indiscreetly alluded to some negotiations he had had with Macready. The eminent tragedian allegedly had agreed to produce a play of his entitled *Woman* provided he revised it to Macready's specifications. As a result, Boucicault had withdrawn his play. Mathews and Madame, who had heard rumors that Macready was negotiating for Drury Lane, were not disposed to discourage the story. When it reached Macready he responded with a spate of angry notes categorically denying the story. He also went to the trouble of seeking out the young playwright. Somewhat lamely Boucicault explained that he had given his manuscript to a Mr. Ronyon Jones who had returned it to him and reported Macready's reaction. The explanation satisfied no one. Mr. Jones never materialized to substantiate it, Macready went sulking, and Mathews and Vestris from then on viewed the young playwright with some mistrust.[23]

The incident soured the already uneasy relationship between Macready and the Mathewses, but it did not diminish interest in the play. Nor did the rumor that the forthcoming comedy was in large part the work of John Brougham, the popular Irish actor in Madame's company. As gossip had it, not only could he claim coauthorship, but he had also conceived the character of Dazzle for himself. In his own account of the play Boucicault makes no mention of this, but many of his contemporaries substantiate the story. Perhaps the best account of the affair is to be found in the memoirs of Lester Wallack, who was a friend not only of Boucicault and Brougham, but of Mathews as well.

> There is very little doubt that Brougham first suggested the idea; and there is no doubt that he intended the part of Dazzle for himself. Charles Mathews was the original Dazzle. So far as I know, Mr. Brougham, for a certain sum of money, conceded to Mr. Boucicault his entire rights in the comedy . . . [but] there is no question that the success of the whole thing was due to Mr. Boucicault, to his tact and cleverness and to the brilliancy of his dialogue.[24]

The play had its premiere on March 4, 1841. The first act aroused little enthusiasm, but the second-act setting for Oak Hall drew a round of applause, and by the end of the act the audience's interest had been thoroughly aroused. Lady Gay's entrance clinched its success. A Victorian Hippolyta, "she darted in like a flash of lightning, and was greeted with a thunder of applause." [25] At the end of her hunting speech the house rose and "the pit seemed to boil over." So keyed up was Boucicault

that he rushed from the theatre, wandered aimlessly to Waterloo Bridge, and returned just in time for curtain calls and em-
braces from Madame Vestris and Louisa Nisbett. During the remainder of the season *London Assurance* was played almost
nightly, and Boucicault wrote exultantly to his mother, "I have
made my fortune and my name. . . . I am now looked upon as
the great rising dramatic poet of the age."[26]

Election to the Dramatic Authors Society did not make him

William Farren as Sir Harcourt Courtly and Mrs. Nisbett as Lady
Gay Spanker in *London Assurance*. (*Harvard Theatre Collection*)

less buoyant, but in the preface to his published play he expressed himself more soberly. "It will not bear analysis as a literary production. In fact, my sole object was to throw together a
few scenes of a dramatic nature; and therefore I studied the
stage rather than the moral effect." Most reviewers agreed that
he had poured old wine in new bottles. In spite of its production, *London Assurance* could easily enough have been performed with the bagwigs and backdrops suitable to Vanbrugh
or Sheridan. Sir Harcourt Courtly, Meddle, and Dazzle have in-

numerable dramatic forebears, and Young Courtly instantly calls to mind the double-dealing heroes of Goldsmith and Sheridan. Among Boucicault's few possessions in Villiers Street was a set of *Cumberland's British Theatre*. Evidently he put it to good use, skillfully modifying the characters and plot devices to conform to contemporary taste. Grace Harkaway, a Bowdlerized version of Vanbrugh's Miss Hoyden, would have been welcomed in any Victorian drawing room, and the intrigue between Lady Gay and Sir Harcourt, though inspired by the Restoration cuckoldings, is manipulated so antiseptically that it could not have offended the staunchest member of the Society for the Suppression of Vice.

Although not yet twenty Boucicault had already developed an ear for dialogue and an eye for character. He was profoundly grateful to the actors for their contribution to his success, but they also had reason to be grateful to him, for he had given them a play with no bad roles. Mrs. Nisbett, Farren, and Mathews divided the honors, but even the actors in minor parts, Boucicault tells us, "produced effects wholly unexpected." [27] Anderson, with his loud voice and stagey manner, was ill-suited to Young Courtly, but otherwise the cast was a strong one— perhaps the strongest comedy cast since the original production of *The School For Scandal*.

Madame Vestris's attention to the settings also contributed substantially to the play's success. Reviewers singled out for particular praise the exterior of Oak Hall in Act II: "Such a house of such real old English substantiality; a security for such a cellar in that warm, genial-colored brick—they don't make such bricks now; and the confidence afforded by the verandah, with its honeysuckle and jessamines creeping up, and the apartment just half disclosed to view by the French windows." [28] The set for Squire Harkaway's drawing room, though some found it too splendid for a manor house, was even more lavishly praised. As Lester Wallack put it, "It was really the first time that the perfection of the modern boxed-in scenery was displayed to the public." [29]

With the £300 he received for his play, Boucicault launched

his career as a bon vivant and man of letters. He acquired two horses, seven new overcoats, and a vast stock of self-confidence. There is no indication that his feelings were in any way ruffled by those critics who dismissed his play as a clever pastiche. He himself recognized that he had synthesized rather than revitalized a comic tradition, but his play held the stage for the rest of the century, and its evident influence on *The Importance of Being Earnest* bolsters its claim to be ranked as the best English comedy between Sheridan and Wilde.

Mathews and Vestris enjoyed a further success with Planché's Easter entertainment, *Beauty and the Beast*. The extravaganza featured a succession of spectacular scenes beginning with the apparition of The Rose Queen, and concluding with the beast's transformation. Its success, paradoxically, imposed a crushing burden on Madame. Almost nightly, for the remainder of the season, she was appearing as Boucicault's heroine, and in the second half of the bill was reappearing as Planché's Beauty with a dozen songs to sing before the performance concluded.

At the end of the season Mathews summed up for the audience Madame's accomplishments during 1840–41. The company had performed two hundred and twenty times. Eighty-eight performances had been devoted to Shakespeare. Sheridan and various minor comedies from the standard repertory accounted for forty-two more. Noting her encouragement of modern dramatists, Mathews then alluded to the quality of her productions at Covent Garden: "Mrs. Mathews had the honor of beginning, at the Olympic, a system of minute attention to the accessories of the stage, until then unknown in British Theatre. That she was right has been proved, first by your applauding sanction, during nine seasons of success at that theatre, and subsequently by two at Covent Garden." [30]

On the subject of their plans for next season Mathews maintained "a most mysterious and melodramatic silence," but their course was clear enough. Macready, fretting at his servitude under Webster, had completed negotiations with the patentees of Drury Lane and was preparing to resume his managerial career in October. He was anxious to strengthen the comic wing of Drury Lane and was eyeing the Covent Garden company speculatively, hoping for possible defections. It was imperative for Madame to keep her company intact and to bolster her comic repertory with additional new plays.

During the summer of 1841 she and Mathews toured extensively in *London Assurance*. They played it in Dublin. They played it in Liverpool, where so great was the public's curiosity that the manager went to the unusual expense of commissioning new scenery for the occasion. But in the course of these travels they were constantly corresponding with potential performers and playwrights. They engaged the soprano, Adelaide Kemble, the daughter of Charles Kemble, for an eight-week operatic season, and they contracted for several new plays.

Their first major production of the 1841–42 season, Mark Lemon's *What Will the World Say?*, had a chilly reception. "As a picture of life today it is ridiculously unreal," one reviewer commented. "It is just such a slight, artificial, fabric of old theatrical materials as a practised playwright might produce, without any draught upon his invention or great effort of skill." [31] If it proved nothing else, it proved that it was no easy task to carpenter together "old theatrical materials" as Boucicault had done. Much was hoped for from Sheridan Knowles's new comedy, *Old Maids*, but this too proved a failure. Although it was tailored to the talents of Madame, Mathews, and Mrs. Nisbett, Knowles's trivial comedy of two court beauties in the Caroline period limped along in the blankest of blank verse and disappeared from the repertory after sixteen performances.

Most disappointing of all was Boucicault's contribution. In *The Irish Heiress* he attempted to duplicate the success of *London Assurance*. The play had virtually the same cast, playing virtually the same parts—with one exception. Madame preempted for herself the role of the Irish heiress, a Hibernian Lady Gay. The results might have been anticipated. The novelty of Madame's brogue and the satire of London life mildly amused the audience but not sufficiently to overcome their sense of déja vu. They applauded the production more than the play, and after only two performances *The Irish Heiress* disappeared.

By far the most warmly received of the new comedies was Douglas Jerrold's *Bubbles of the Day*. "Had it come down to us stamped with the name of Congreve, [it] would be cited as a model of pungent satire, of raillery and of repartee," [32] wrote one critic. "It is undoubtedly the only real comedy produced for many a long year; it abounds in caustic irony and brilliant wit," [33] wrote another. But audiences failed to share their enthusiasm. Jerrold's play, like Bulwer-Lytton's *Money*, was Jonsonian in conception, but the gulls and knaves of *The Alchemist* and *Volpone* throb with life, those in Jerrold's play remain mere puppets. It too vanished from the repertory, though it was subsequently performed with some success at a number of other theatres.

Madame Vestris's attempts to revive the comic muse proved almost as disappointing as Macready's campaign to restore tragedy to her throne. But five-act comedy and tragedy were virtually extinct forms. For nearly fifty years dramatists had channeled their energies into farce and melodrama. Raw as their products were, they were at least preferable to pseudo-Sheridan or pseudo-Shakespeare.

Although Madame had little to show for her efforts to encourage legitimate comedy, in other respects the 1841–42 season was a successful one. As one journalist noted with approval, under the direction of Bradwell and Sloman the Covent Garden stage had been brought to perfection. "There is not a joint in its boards, a flap in its scenery, a twinkle in its lights which is not replete with mechanism; and effects follow each other with a rapidity and precision that defeat calculation in the proportion they excite astonishment." [34] Making full use of these facilities, the twin genii produced *Guy, Earl of Warwick; or, Harlequin and the Dun Cow*, hailed as the best Christmas entertainment seen at that theatre in twenty years. It culminated in a panoramic scene with the hero mounted on a charger which "kept prancing and curvetting in one spot on the stage while landscapes, cottages, forests and lakes glided on behind him." [35]

Adelaide Kemble's operatic performances proved another major attraction. She had studied in Italy with Mercadante and

Pasta and had enjoyed a brilliant success at the Fenice in the title role of Bellini's *Norma*. At Covent Garden she was to make her debut in the same role, performing in Planché's English version. Every precaution was taken to ensure her London success. Cast in the important role of Adalgisa was Elizabeth Rainforth, a much-admired singer. The orchestra was supplemented and the chorus was drilled to the point of exhaustion. The results were gratifying. Such was the opera's success that it was performed no less than forty-two times. In Mercadante's *Elena Uberti* Miss Kemble had a cooler reception, but she concluded her engagement with a series of highly successful appearances as Amina in *La Sonnambula* and Susanna in *The Marriage of Figaro*, with Madame Vestris as Cherubino.

The only other major musical production of the season was a revival of *Comus* with a score drawn from Handel, Purcell, and Arne. No less eclectic was the libretto, with passages from Dryden and George Colman grafted onto Milton's text. Designed to rival Macready's *Acis and Galatea* at Drury Lane, the production was a lavish one exploiting to the full such scenes as the rout of the Bacchanals and the parade of illusions before the lady. Most applauded of all were the effects in the final scene: "The groupings and arrangements of the tableaux were admirable, and some of the mechanical effects were almost magical; especially that exquisite scene in which . . . Sabrina appeared at the head of the waterfall, immersed in the cup of a lily up to the shoulders, and in this fairy skiff floated over the fall and descended to the stage." [36] Such improvements might have offended the noble audience at Ludlow Castle, but the tastes of Covent Garden spectators were less chaste, and during the latter part of the season the company repeatedly performed *Comus* and *Norma* as a double bill. No doubt Madame often thought back longingly to nights at the Olympic theatre where entertainments concluded at eleven o'clock.

Such marathon performances were a measure of the desperation of Mathews and Vestris. Despite crowded houses, they were sinking deeper and deeper into debt. In January the Bail Court issued a writ of *distringas* to compel Mathews to appear in court. Until then the actor had eluded the most resourceful process servers, but his court appearances during the next three months became increasingly frequent. The success of *Norma* had compounded his problems. "As soon as the money began to flow in my sufferings became almost intolerable. At the first sniff of blood the tigers were let loose. While I paid no one, no one seemed to care; but the moment Jenkins got his money Jones became rampant." [37] Writs and executions showered upon him. He was learning the truth behind Bulwer's bitter observation: "Bills are like trees and grow standing." [38] Faced with the spectre of 60 percent interest, he nonetheless appeared so buoyant on stage that "everyone seemed to believe that I revelled in it, and every allusion I had to make to duns and bailiffs was hailed by the audience as the emanation of a light heart." [39] Audiences could hardly be blamed. His performances offstage were often equally ebullient. On one occasion, he tells us, he had two moneylenders in adjacent rooms and coolly played one off against the other, borrowing from Peter to pay Paul. One can see why his admirers looked forward to his appearances in court and why Mr. Lewis, his solicitor, often waived his legal fees, feeling himself amply compensated by the pleasure of Mathews's company.

It was in keeping with the comic scenario of Mathews's life that Adelaide Kemble's triumph ruined him. Her success caused the proprietors of Covent Garden to reexamine the potential value of their property, and before long they began to complain of the lack of return on their investment. The turn of events gravely alarmed Fanny Kemble. It was she who in 1829 had been instrumental in rescuing her father from bankruptcy at Covent Garden. Adelaide's triumph had revived his ambition to manage that theatre—an ambition which had proved ruinous to so many managers.

Madame Vestris, it seems, foresaw the same possibility but she accepted it stoically. Planché describes it thus:

> Madame Vestris said abruptly, after a short silence, "Charles! we shall not have this theatre next year." "What do you mean?" he and I exclaimed simultaneously. "Simply what I

say." "But what reason," inquired Mathews, "can you possibly have for thinking so?" "No particular reason, but you'll see." "Have you heard any rumor to that effect?" I asked. "No; but we shall not have the theatre." "But who on earth will have it then?" we said, laughing at the idea; for we could imagine no possible competitors likely to pay so high a rent. "Charles Kemble," was her answer. "He will think that his daughter's talent and popularity will be quite sufficient and we shall be turned out of the theatre." [40]

Her prophecy proved unerringly accurate. The annual rent had been fixed at something over £5,000 but, provided that that sum was paid yearly, it had been understood that Mathews "was not to be molested for the difference." [41] At the end of April, because of some £600 deficit, they were "bowed out of the building" [42] and the proprietors coolly confiscated some £14,000 worth of properties which Madame Vestris and Mathews had acquired for the theatre.

Public sympathy ran high in favor of the ousted lessees. In contrast to other managers, they had never canceled a performance or shortened the season. Among actors, the reaction was particularly strong. It was widely reported that Mathews and Madame had often waived their own salaries in order to meet their obligations to the rest of the company, and James Anderson spoke for many in the profession when he observed: "Never had actors and actresses kinder or more considerate managers than Madame or her husband." [43]

Their failure had been a gallant one. They had had two main objectives: first, to inaugurate a school of modern comedy, and second, to give such comedies productions that accurately mirrored contemporary life. Only in one instance had they really succeeded, and even then their success had been limited. *London Assurance*, while it "lent itself perfectly to the Vestris methods of staging," [44] broke no new ground as a play nor did it contribute to the development of modern comedy. There were too many deterrents. For almost half a century comic dramatists had been writing for individual comedians, tailoring their material to suit the talents and eccentricities of Liston, Keeley, or Buckstone. After such an apprenticeship they were

ill-suited to write realistic comedies of modern life. The theatrical monopoly and the vast size of the patent theatres were also
discouraging factors. Only at the Haymarket could such a
school of comedy have developed, but Ben Webster, for all his
talents, was no innovator, and John Buckstone, his successor,
was even more staunchly conservative. Nevertheless, during her
three seasons at Covent Garden Madame had made a lasting
contribution to the theatre. She had set a new standard of production for contemporary comedies, and although she had not
succeeded in developing a modern repertory, she had paved the
way for the success of T. W. Robertson and Marie Wilton at
the Prince of Wales's Theatre in 1865.

She and Mathews made their farewell to Covent Garden on
April 30, 1842. The occasion was as emotional as their most fervent admirers could have wished. They had remained on good
terms with Adelaide Kemble and she contributed her services
by appearing in *La Sonnambula*. Mathews in his usual fashion
romped through *Patter versus Clatter*, and Madame wound up
the evening as Prince Paragon in Planché's extravaganza, *The
White Cat*. Despite the exhausting length of the bill the audience's enthusiasm never flagged. They showered Madame with
bouquets and applauded to the echo Mathews's good-humored
and generous-spirited speech of farewell. Ten days later he declared himself bankrupt.

chapter 8

"*P*layers! poor players!"

Mathews's bankruptcy proceedings make singularly disheartening reading. He had two hundred and twenty-five creditors and debts totaling nearly £27,500. Since 1838 his troubles had multiplied. The failure of the American tour, losses incurred at the Olympic and Covent Garden, legal expenses, and usurious rates of interest had all contributed to the debacle. A hearing was set for early June. During the interim Mathews was committed to the Queen's Bench Prison, but his confinement, as he describes it, was a relatively agreeable one. "A wild young nobleman who had been sentenced to confinement there for some early prank, had fitted up a room over the porter's lodge into a really elegant little boudoir, and interest was made to get it for me." [1] He spent a week there, then retired to the country until the official hearing on June 9 in the Insolvent Debtors' Court. Only one of his creditors put in an appearance. He was a manufacturer of theatrical spangles to whom Mathews owed £48. Granted permission to question the actor, he brought a note of comic relief to the proceedings. Addressing himself to the matter of Madame's jewels and Mathews's sale of some books, he spoke with a thick Scots accent and gestured in an emphatic manner that brought frowns from the bench and laughter from the spectators. Mathews's replies were candid and explicit. Madame Vestris had sold her jewels four years earlier, and those currently in her possession were on hire from a jeweler at £3 per week. They were indispensable to her appearance, particularly on provincial tours. As to his books, they were of little value and he had pledged them to a dealer hoping to redeem them at a later date. Queried about a testimonial gift of silver plate from the Covent Garden company, Mathews further explained that its presentation had been deferred until the hearings were over. A sympathetic commissioner, impressed by his testimony, promptly discharged him. Elated by the outcome, Mathews then offered to make himself responsible for certain personal debts. It was an honorable proposal, but one which he later bitterly regretted.

Momentarily, however, life had brightened. He had shed a crushing burden and the future seemed hopeful. For some weeks he and Madame had been quietly negotiating with Macready for an engagement at Drury Lane. The eminent tragedian had made them a preliminary offer of £40 per week. He raised it to £50, then finally capitulated to their terms. Testily he noted in his journal on April 9, 1842: "I agreed to give Mr. and Mrs. C. Mathews the terms for which they stood out, viz. £60 per week. It is a very great salary, but it is paid in consideration of enfeebling an opposition as well as adding to my own strength." The engagement was to be for two years, but the alliance was from the start an uneasy one. Macready disdained them as "Players! poor players!" [2] He resented their success and felt some indignation that their financial difficulties had so little affected their way of life. "Parted with them," he noted sourly, "they starting off in their carriage, I in my shattered old hack cab!" [3] Mathews and Vestris, on their part , felt an equal distaste for his imperious and patronizing manner.

Preparations for the Drury Lane season began in early September. From the beginning, Vestris and Macready were at odds. Both were perfectionists, dedicated to raising theatrical standards, but both were highly autocratic. Vast as Drury Lane was, it was not big enough for two such strong-willed individuals. By the time the season began, on October 1, the tension had risen. The opening production, *As You Like It*, had been rehearsed and produced with exemplary care, as even Madame would have admitted. Macready, suitably enough, was playing the melancholy Jaques, but the role of Rosalind was assigned to Mrs. Nisbett. Her performance, it seems, was a lamentable one, but nonetheless Macready promptly announced that she would next appear as Lydia Languish in his forthcoming production of *The Rivals*. The casting was not unjustified. Madame was too old for both parts. She had never excelled in legitimate comedy, and critics had often pointed out that she was unsuited to roles which called for passion or pathos. It was clear to her, however, that Macready was trying to reduce her to insignificance.

Her suspicions were soon confirmed. She was to make her first appearance on October 5 in Planché's new afterpiece, *The Follies of a Night*. On the same evening Macready was to appear in Byron's tragedy of *Marino Faliero*. Macready's name figured prominently in the preliminary advertising. Hers did not. Planché's vaudeville was a trifle of the sort that Macready despised, with a masked ball, a disguised duchess, and a debauched duke. But, happily, members of the audience were of another mind. Mathews and Madame were so warmly welcomed that during the remainder of the month Planché's afterpiece was performed sixteen times.

Relations between Macready and the Mathewses did not improve however. Madame was offered the secondary role of Mrs. Frail in *Love for Love*, but rejected the notion of playing Congreve's scheming female. Furthermore, she discovered to her dismay that her name was appearing on the playbills in steadily diminishing type size. Still more demeaning was Macready's treatment of Mathews. The fact that his range, like Madame's, was a limited one, played into the hands of the lessee. He had always refused to engage actors for a specific line of business and made it a point of pride to cast minor roles as strongly as possible. Exercising his prerogative, he assigned to Mathews the trifling role of Fag in *The Rivals*. Following that, he asked him to play Roderigo in *Othello*.

The notion of casting Mathews in a Shakespearian tragedy was in itself novel. His performance, it seems, was no less novel. The play was strongly cast, with Macready in the title role,

Phelps as Iago, Helen Faucit as Desdemona, and Mrs. Warner as Emilia. Reviewers, as usual, divided on Macready's merits. (In his woolly wig he is said to have looked like "an elderly negress, of evil repute, going to a fancy ball.") [4] Reviewers agreed unanimously, however, on Mathew's interpretation. He did not play Roderigo—rather, "Roderigo appeared as Mr. Charles Mathews." [5] If one can credit John Coleman's account, said to have derived from Mathews himself, the performance reached its nadir in the fifth act when Phelps inadvertently drove his sword into "that portion of Roderigo's anatomy which he was least equipped to defend." [6] A few moments later Phelps compounded the injury by scalding the inert Roderigo with wax droppings from a lantern. Unable to contain himself, the outraged actor rose in protest, leaving behind him, on the floor of the stage, his flaxen wig.

Mathews was perhaps taking his revenge. Phelps, as Iago, may even have abetted him. He too was chafing under Macready's usage and periodically complained of being "held back." The critic in *The Athenaeum* confirms that Mathews's performance was a comic one, but it seems unlikely that Coleman's account is entirely accurate. Such an enormity would surely have been recorded in the journal of the eminent tragedian.

Relations between the two men were increasingly strained, though Macready extracted from Mathews the reluctant admission that he had been courteously treated. Madame, on her part, was also more and more displeased. With the exception of one performance as Don Carlos in *The Duenna*, she had appeared only in *The Follies of a Night*. Macready had made it unmistakably clear that he preferred Mrs. Nisbett as a comedienne. He made it equally clear that in musical entertainments young Priscilla Horton would have precedence, though Madame's contract specifically provided that she was to appear only as a principal performer.[7] Offered the minor role of Venus in a revival of Purcell's *King Arthur*, she indignantly rejected it and subjected the lessee to a three-hour-long torrent of abuse. Macready's subsequent announcement that he intended to close the theatre two nights a week and deduct a proportionate amount from the company's salaries precipitated the final break.

By the end of the week they had concluded an agreement with Webster, and on November 14 they opened at the Haymarket in *The School for Scandal.* As a part of Macready's campaign to depreciate Madame's value he had offered her the trifling role of Maria in Sheridan's comedy. Under Webster's regime she returned to playing Lady Teazle, with her old friend William Farren as Sir Peter, Mathews as Charles Surface, and Mrs. Glover as Mrs. Candour. The theatrical public was clearly sympathetic, for when Madame made her entrance in the second act, "the house rose *en masse* and made the 'welkin ring' with their shouts. . . . A like reception awaited Mr. Mathews." [8] Though their relationship with Webster was not always serene, they found the Haymarket lessee a far less abrasive personality than Macready. He was cheerful and without pretensions. In his production of *The Rivals* he promptly cast Madame as Lydia Languish and, perhaps in compliment to Mathews, himself assumed the role of Fag. Still more commendably, despite his engagement of Mlle. Celeste, the famous dancer-mime, he made no attempt to diminish Madame's attractions in the public eye. In December he produced Charles Mathews's vaudeville, *The Dowager,* which gave full play to her talents as a comedienne, and as a Christmas entertainment he revived Mathews's successful vehicle, *Riquet with the Tuft.* He also revived for them *The Way of the World,* in an adaptation by Planché. The comedies of Wycherley and Vanbrugh had long since been emasculated to avoid giving offense to genteel audiences. Planché tells us that by the simple expedient of transforming Mrs. Marwood into a man, he removed "a stumbling block to the revival of the play" and "phrases which would not have been tolerated . . . from the lips of a female, became perfectly inoffensive when uttered by an unprincipled man of the world." [9] Yet even with Madame Vestris as Millamant, Mathews as Witwoud, and Mrs. Glover as Lady Wishfort, the revival enjoyed only a brief run. Scrubbed up as it was, Congreve's elegant charade did not appeal to Mrs. Grundy. Even Henry Crabb Robinson, a sophisticated playgoer, while he enjoyed the production, felt a twinge of uneasiness about the play itself. "The essential profligacy and worthlessness of the characters is not perceived; because the gracefulness and gay tones quite absorb the attention. . . ." [10]

In real life Mathews was playing a role of a more sombre character. Creditors were again plaguing him, and in a moment of desperation he borrowed money from Joshua Anderson, his brother-in-law. Anderson had given up his stage career and taken to an even more speculative way of life—betting on the horses. He and Mathews were barely acquainted, for since Madame's bankruptcy, relations between her and the Andersons had been cool. At the urging of Madame Bartolozzi, Anderson offered to lend Mathews £200 interest-free, though he himself was heavily in debt. The offer was accepted at once, and for a time the Andersons and their children moved into the Mathewses' house. However prickly relations may have been between the adults in the household, the Mathewses were genuinely devoted to the children and developed a deep affection for them.

They remained at the Haymarket until the end of the season, then signed a three-year agreement with Webster at a salary of £60 per week, with £10 in addition for providing their own costumes. Life at the Haymarket had proved unexpectedly agreeable and the future seemed promising. A three-month tour, from January to April, took them to Dublin, Edinburgh, Glasgow, Newcastle, and Liverpool. Between them they were earning £30 to £40 a night, and Mathews had begun to pay off some of his debts, but as he had found earlier, "The moment Jenkins got his money Jones became rampant." Jenkins's law was an inexorable one, and once again the vultures were gathering. In Liverpool he was arrested and released only after pawning Madame's hired jewels. When they returned to London, in April, they found an execution on their house. They moved into a smaller one in Westbourne Grove and resumed playing at the Haymarket, but under increasingly difficult circumstances. Mathews was reduced to every sort of subterfuge to slip past the creditors who besieged the stage door. Even more embarrassing was the ignominy of dodging tradesmen. As the months passed and autumn came, the situation worsened.

Finally at the end of his tether, Mathews decided to flee to France. He pledged the furniture, Madame's jewels, and their linen and silver, and with the proceeds, some £350, he paid off their servants and some small debts. On November 4, alone, he embarked for Calais. The next day Madame Vestris followed him. Accompanied by D'Egville and her maid, she left secretly by railway for Folkestone. Her flight was not without its comic aspects. At Tunbridge she discovered to her surprise that the railway went no further. Fearful of recognition in a public coach, she engaged an omnibus and two extra horses. Her departure was not unnoticed, however, as the omnibus rumbled off, topped by a mountain of luggage. Once arrived in Paris, she found that their troubles were far from over. Mathews had been persuaded by M. Bouffé, the comedian, that they could obtain an engagement in the French capital without difficulty. He soon discovered, however, that he "was no safer abroad than at home, as all legal documents could be passed to foreign holders, and be enforced more rigidly on that side of the water. . . ." [11] Worse still, the rumor spread that he had fled England with Madame's jewels. In an open letter to his creditors he attempted to justify his flight, [12] but the folly of his action became increasingly apparent to him and by December 6 he and Madame Vestris were back in England.

During their absence Anne Mathews had frantically busied herself trying to bring some order to their affairs. She had called on Webster and succeeded in patching up matters to some extent. It was hoped that Mathews and Vestris might appear in Planché's Christmas piece, *The Fair One With The Golden Locks*, but it was produced without them. Mathews and Vestris had fled to the countryside where they remained in hiding. They were grateful to Webster for his kindness and eager to be back at the Haymarket, but could not bring themselves to perform under their present circumstances. "Let them set our minds and bodies free and we will work cheerfully," wrote Mathews, "but no longer will I dance with sheriff's officers for partners and usurers for fiddlers." [13]

On December 23 Mathews once again filed for bankruptcy. A few days later they resumed their engagement at the Haymarket. For the moment, at least, the pressures had been lessened. Mathews was over £8,000 in debt, £4,000 of which had been contracted since his previous bankruptcy. To the extent of £6,000, creditors were agreeable to the terms which Mathews proposed for gradual liquidation of his debts, but one steadfastly opposed him—his brother-in-law, Joshua Anderson. At the first examination, which took place on February 8, he accused the actor of reckless extravagance and bitterly protested his attempt to take advantage of the insolvency act. Under oath Anderson affirmed that he had lent Mathews money with no knowledge of the fact that he had renewed some of his earlier debts. Mathews categorically denied this, and under examination recapitulated the unhappy events of the last year and a half. From time to time a flash of humor drew a ripple of laughter from the crowded courtroom. Queried as to whether he had received £30 from Mathews, Anderson replied, "Upon my oath, I had not a farthing from Mr. or Mrs. Mathews—she is very reluctant in parting with money." "I wish she were," Mathews replied. "That is certainly making her appear in a new character!" [14] But outside of an occasional exchange of this sort, there was little levity during the proceedings.

A second hearing on February 27 probed Mathews's finances in still greater detail. Mr. Anderson remained adamant, but the Commissioner was clearly impressed by Mathews's candor and the generosity of his proposal to assign one-half of his yearly earnings, some £1,350, to his creditors. Under these conditions, Mathews was discharged. He and Madame Vestris were permitted to retain a few trifling pieces of jewelry, but their wardrobes, which had been seized, were put up for auction. The sale of their effects was a pitiful affair. Held at short notice and without publicity, it attracted few buyers. A dozen muslin and cotton dresses were knocked down for £2. "A superfine court dress coat and a pair of breeches" fetched only 18 shillings.

The Commissioner's decision temporarily staved off Mathews's creditors, but in reassuming responsibility for his debts, Mathews was in actuality no better off than he had been in June 1842. Only in one minor respect had their financial situation improved. The death of Madame Bartolozzi in June 1843 had relieved them of a £200-a-year obligation. Though they tried to minimize their expenses, both were constitutionally unable to effect real economies, and once again they began living on credit. It was only too easy to justify their expenses as professional necessities—their carriage, Madame's dresses and jewels, and Mathews's own impressive wardrobe.

So celebrated was he as a man of fashion, both offstage and on, that the public avidly followed his career in both worlds. On February 6, two days before his first examination by the bankruptcy commission, he created perhaps his most famous role—Sir Charles Coldstream in Boucicault's two-act farce, *Used Up*. The part of the jaded exquisite fitted him as impeccably as his frock coat, and as usual spectators were quick to detect affinities between the actor and his role. What could have been more apropos than his opening line: "James, bring in the *pâtés de fois gras* which arrived from Paris last week!" It set an appropriate tone for Boucicault's comedy in which the dialogue, at its best, has the dry sparkle of good champagne.

> *Saville.* You should go to Switzerland.
> *Sir Charles.* I have been—nothing there—people say so much about everything—there were certainly a few glaciers, some monks, and large dogs, and thick ankles, and bad wine, and Mont Blanc! yes, and there was ice on the top too; but I prefer the ice at Gunter's—less trouble and more in it.
> *Leech.* Then if Switzerland wouldn't do, I'd try Italy.
> *Sir Charles.* My dear Leech, I've tried it over and over again, and what then?
> *Saville.* Did not Rome inspire you?
> *Sir Charles.* Oh, believe me, Tom, a most horrible hole! People

talk so much about these things—there's the Colosseum, now—round, very round, a goodish ruin enough, but I was disappointed with it; Capitol—tolerable high; and St. Peter's—marble, and mosaics, and fountains; dome certainly not badly scooped, but there was nothing in it.

Leech. Come, Coldstream, you must admit we have nothing like St. Peter's in London.

Sir Charles. No, because we don't want it; but if we wanted such a thing, of course we should have it. A dozen gentlemen meet, pass resolutions, institute, and in twelve months it would be run up; nay, if that were all, we'd buy St. Peter's itself, and have it sent over.

Leech. Ha, ha! well said, you're quite right.

Saville. What do you say to beautiful Naples?

Leech. Ay, *La Belle Napoli!*

Sir Charles. Not bad,—excellent water-melons, and goodish opera; they took me up Vesuvius—a horrid bore! it smoked a good deal, certainly, but altogether a wretched mountain;—saw the crater—looked down, but there was nothing in it.

Disguised as a ploughboy in the second act, Mathews was less convincing. Whether by accident or design, he failed to remove the rings from his fingers, although as Lewes observed, "a jewelled hand is not usually seen directing a plough." [15] But however unconvincing he may have seemed as a ploughboy, as the weary dandy he was matchless. D'Orsay, the ultimate arbiter in such matters, attended a performance with Lady Blessington and reported to Anne Mathews: "We went to see Charles in *Used Up*. He played admirably. . . . The fact is, that the part must be acted by a real gentleman who has been a great deal in society." [16]

Mathews also found an effective vehicle in Planché's *The Drama at Home*, a diverting view of the state of the theatre in 1844. The Theatre Regulation Act of 1843 had finally freed the theatres by abolishing the almost two-hundred-year-old monopoly of the legitimate drama by the patent theatres. But no theatrical renaissance had taken place. A prize of £500 offered by Ben Webster for the best original play had failed to turn up any striking new dramatists, and Drury Lane and Covent Garden, the traditional temples of the drama, were either dark or given over to such spectacles as M. Jullien's musical fantasia, *The Destruction of Pompeii*.

Satirizing the drama's plight, Planché sets his scene in a desert. Lost in contemplation of the dreary prospect, the Drama is suddenly confronted by the irrepressible Mr. Puff who rushes in to comfort her. Mathews had often played Sheridan's stagestruck playwright, and as Puff he presided over a satrical survey of the current theatrical scene. More topical than *The Critic*, *The Drama at Home*, like *Success* (1825) and *The Drama's Levee* (1838), wittily anticipates the modern topical revue.

While Mathews was romping through these roles, Madame was growing increasingly restive. She had reached the age of forty-seven. She still sang charmingly, but she could hardly expect to do so much longer. After attending one of her performances Henry Crabb Robinson sadly noted: "Only downright comic talent can ally itself to old age." [17] Madame had never succeeded in establishing herself as a first-rank comedienne, still less did she show any indications of developing as a character actress.

Since the debacle at Covent Garden she had been at a loss, and only in touring did she find an outlet for her energy. While she and Mathews continued to appear intermittently at the Haymarket, they spent an increasing amount of time out of London, gravitating restlessly from one town to another, performing in the stock pieces of their repertory. Their relations with Webster had cooled perceptibly, and from Plymouth Mathews wrote: "I don't care what the consequences may be, I will either have things restored to their original comfort and quiet or I will leave the Haymarket at once. . . . The first month or two of our engagement was Heaven, the next five or six Purgatory, the last eight Hell. It is your business, if you wish it, to make the next season Paradise Regained." [18]

Sheer fatigue, perhaps more than anything else, triggered his irritation. Still in the shadow of debt, neither he nor Madame Vestris could afford to decline an engagement, much as they sometimes longed to do so. "If I were a rich man I would say 'damn the whole salary for the rest of the season,'" Mathews wrote Webster, "but that cannot be." [19]

Despite their reluctance, they returned to the Haymarket for the 1844–45 season. It began in early October with a revival of Vanbrugh's *The Confederacy*, featuring Madame Vestris as Flippanta and Mathews as Brass. But Vanbrugh's robust comedy offended critics who smugly dismissed it as "a satire upon the morals and habits of a dissolute age." [20] *A Match for a King*, an adaptation by Mathews of the Porte-St.-Martin melodrama, *Don César de Bazan*, followed soon after. One of three English versions of the play, it failed to match the popularity of the more swashbuckling version played by James Wallack. Dispirited and fatigued, Mathews and Vestris were reluctant to undertake new parts. They rejected the roles offered them in Mrs. Gore's prize-winning comedy, *Quid Pro Quo*—with good reason, as it turned out, for the play proved a total failure. They were unhappy as well when called upon to rehearse Boucicault's new five-act comedy, *Old Heads and Young Hearts*. Webster had high hopes that it might prove another *London Assurance* and, contrary to his usual practice, was planning an elaborate production. Gratifying as this was to Madame Vestris, she found her role as Lady Alice thin and inconsistent and so expressed herself to the author. But Boucicault was no longer a callow young playwright, eager to make use of any suggestion. Evidently he responded hotly, as Mathews makes plain in a letter which he promptly fired off to Webster:

> After the gross impertinence of Mr. Bourcicault [*sic*] this morning in your presence you cannot be surprised at my returning the parts. . . .
> His last words were these: "I want no one's opinion but my own as to the *consistency* of the characters I draw—*your* business is to utter what I create."
> As I differ *in toto* from this inflated view of the relative positions of the actor and dramatist I at once decline subscribing to it.[21]

In some fashion they patched up their differences, and when the play had its premiere on November 18 they had resumed their roles. Hailed by the critics, the comedy, like Jerrold's *Bubbles of the Day*, proved a nine-day wonder. Hampered by a plot of staggering complexity, its success, such as it was, was attributable largely to Webster's and Farren's skill as character actors.

Without question Webster was finding it increasingly hard to cope with Mathews and Vestris. The former could perform brilliantly, but only within a limited range of comedy. Time had narrowed Madame Vestris's repertory, her voice was fading, and her career as a manager made her a difficult subordinate. No doubt he was relieved when in February, 1845, they set off once again into the countryside. But even so, he was constantly obliged to communicate with them—particularly in regard to Planché's forthcoming extravaganza, *The Golden Fleece*.

A recent production of *Antigone*, after the Greek manner, on a raised stage, with a chorus, Mendelssohn's music, and Miss Vandenhoff's declamation, had made a sensation at Covent Garden. Taking his cue from this, Planché concocted a burlesque version of the Medea legend. Madame Vestris was to play the Greek enchantress and Mathews the Chorus. In earlier years Madame would have accepted the part eagerly, but Webster also planned to cast her in a major role in Douglas Jerrold's forthcoming five-act comedy. The prospect appalled her. In quite uncharacteristic fashion, she was agitated by the notion of the raised stage, disturbed by the length of her roles, and dreaded the possibility that Jerrold's and Planché's entertainments might be offered as a double bill. "It is somewhat too much," Mathews complained, "to expect her to rehearse a 5 act comedy, play in a 5 act comedy, and play in a 2 act afterpiece at the same time." [22] There were limits even to Madame's endurance.

Nonetheless, they returned to the Haymarket. Madame was in a bad mood, but one eminently suitable to Medea, and three weeks later the curtain rose on the palace of the King of Colchis. On the pediment, in Greek and English, appeared the legend: "All in my eye and Betty Martin." Madame, for the moment at least, felt thoroughly at home. The doggerel verses, the torrent of puns, and the musical parodies all recalled bygone Olympic entertainments. Equally at ease was Mathews, as an urbane one-man chorus, bending over the footlights to explain the action or rattle off a patter song. Both Mathews and Madame enjoyed a considerable success, and Planché's extravaganza was at once incorporated into their standard repertory.

In Jerrold's *Time Works Wonders* they were distinctly less happy. The playwright did not want to interfere with the casting, but in a letter to Webster he made plain his opinion: "I'd rather that the comedy should be without them." [23] He had good reason. Mathews was forty-two—a somewhat mature age for the juvenile lead, Felix Goldthumb. Still worse, Madame was to play Bessy Tulip, a schoolgirl. The embarrassment, one suspects, was mutual. Madame performed the role, but her position at the Haymarket made her increasingly uncomfortable. Mathews was no less uneasy. Periodically he was indisposed and unable to perform. He refused, however, to waive his salary or return an advance—a refusal which provoked yet another quarrel with Webster. Angrily, Mathews wrote him:

> No one more than myself regrets the pecuniary obligation I am under to you, especially now I find you capable of so coarsely reminding me of it, but you must excuse my observing, at the same time, that when the money was advanced I considered it was somewhat to serve me and somewhat to serve yourself, it being a moment when the services of myself and [my] wife were more appreciated by you than they now are, and when it would have been most detrimental to have done without either of us in your theatre.[24]

In July they broke off relations altogether and left the Haymarket for good.

After a month's holiday in Brighton they resumed their travels, and from October 1845 to May 1846 they toured wherever there was a theatre with a manager willing to engage them. Though they were accustomed to the hardships of "provincializing," even they were sometimes shaken. Booked to appear at a small town near Bath, they refused to perform when they discovered that the theatre was a wooden booth with no backstage facilities, "men and women stripping and dressing in sight of each other without the least regard to decency." [25] They had problems as well with fly-by-night promoters, on one occasion refusing to play for a manager faced with imminent bankruptcy. They could hardly afford to do so.

In June, 1846, they returned to London to appear at the Surrey. The transpontine theatre, long associated with circus and melodrama, was looked down on by legitimate performers, but Madame Vestris and Mathews were willing to swallow their pride—for a price. They were induced as well to accept a four-months' engagement at the Princess's at £90 a week. Situated on the north side of Oxford Street, the building had originally been used as a concert hall, but after the passage of the 1843 Theatre Act it had been converted to a legitimate theatre. Its appointments were the most modern and comfortable in London, but the excessive summer heat discouraged theatregoers, and in October Mathews and Vestris returned to the Midlands.

The competition they faced there was formidable— General Tom Thumb, Macready, Charlotte Cushman, Ira Aldridge, and The Ethiopian Serenaders. In addition, Madame's health appeared to be failing. By mid-October Mathews, in a letter to a friend, informed him that "various circumstances have made me come to the determination that Mrs. Mathews shall retire altogether from the profession." [26] Mrs. Mathews may or may not have concurred with his opinion, but she at least recognized the box-office value of such an announcement, and from January to June, 1847, she toured the provinces in a series of well-advertised farewell engagements. *The School for Scandal, Know Your Own Mind, The Belle's Stratagem,* and *The Golden Fleece* made up the bulk of her repertory, along with a number of the afterpieces she had made famous. She also devised a graceful speech of farewell, adaptable to any theatre.

> Ladies and Gentlemen: The moment has at length arrived when I must take my leave and close a long acquaintanceship with a long farewell. Let not the phrase alarm you—though my farewell will be a long one, the address, I assure you, shall be very short. I made my first appearance in . . . —I will not say how many years ago, though I believe I might do so with-

out surprising anyone—since it appears notorious that with respect to the date of my birth I am in the exact position of the late snowstorm—it is an event that cannot be remembered by the oldest inhabitant. [Cheers and laughter.] Believe me, however, ladies and gentlemen, whatever my age may be, my memory is as fresh as ever, I am still young enough to entertain a grateful recollection of the many favours you have conferred upon me, and I beg to offer you my humble and heartfelt thanks.[27]

But even as Madame was pressing to her lips the bouquets from her ardent admirers, Mathews was discreetly investigating the theatrical situation in London. On April 1 his mother informed him that the Lyceum would shortly be vacant. Within the month he had arranged for its lease and he and Madame Vestris were once again London managers.

chapter 9

Lyceum Lessee

Few London theatres have had as curious a history as the Lyceum. Built in 1765 for exhibitions by "The Society of Artists," it subsequently housed a bewildering variety of attractions ranging from puppet shows, equestrian displays, and a School of Defence, to Madame Tussaud's waxworks. In 1810 it became a home for English opera, melodrama, and wild-beast shows. Converted to a legitimate theatre in 1843, it came under the management of the Keeleys who for three years delighted playgoers with their famous Caudle Curtain lectures and their vivid dramatizations from Dickens. In June 1847 they left the Lyceum to accept an engagement at the Haymarket. Mathews and Madame, with the aid of a loan from Frederick W. Allcroft, a Bond Street ticket agent, signed an agreement with Samuel Arnold, the owner, renewing the lease at £2,500 a year. His confidence in them was surprising, but not altogether misplaced. In recent years a parade of lessees great and small had passed through the bankruptcy courts, but in two important respects his new tenants differed from the majority of their hard-pressed brethren. They were experienced managers and they had retained the affection and respect of their theatrical colleagues.

As a result they had little trouble in assembling a company. Before long they had engaged thirty-nine principal actors— eighteen women and twenty-one men. Some were veteran co-

163

medians, such as John Harley and Frank Matthews, who had often appeared with them before. Others were comparative newcomers—Fanny Stirling, a soubrette, and Miss Fairbrother, who had been performing with the Keeleys. The greatest catch of all was John Buckstone, the great farceur, who deserted the Haymarket to join them, bringing with him his *chère*

Interior of the Lyceum Theatre, with Madame Vestris in
Pride of the Market.

amie, Mrs. Fitzwilliam, and her attractive young daughter, Kathleen.

They were joined as well by many of the backstage staff who had previously worked for them. Planché had been dickering with M. Jullien about superintending the *mise en scène* at Drury Lane, but agreed to assume the same duty at the Lyceum.[1] Mr. Sloman, their chief machinist at Covent Garden, returned to them in the same capacity, and Oscar Byrne, who had been associated with Madame since 1831, resumed his post as choreographer. As stage manager they appointed Robert Roxby, a useful all-around actor. Finally, they engaged William Beverly as their scene painter. He was a gifted young artist who had the advantage of a theatrical background. For six years his father, Henry Beverly, had struggled to make a success of the Tottenham Street Theatre. Young William had grown up backstage. Not only could he paint a scene—he had a thorough knowledge of stage machinery as well.

Although the Theatre Regulation Act of 1843 had freed the minor theatres and Mathews and Madame were consequently permitted to present legitimate five-act dramas, they felt little inclination to do so. At Sadler's Wells, Samuel Phelps in his solid, thoughtful productions had successfully introduced Shakespeare and the classic English playwrights to the working-class citizens of Islington, but the talents of Mathews and Madame were not suited to such a repertory. They longed to play modern comedy, but their experiences at Covent Garden had convinced them that good five-act comedies—*London Assurance* excepted—were not being written. Webster's futile search for good new scripts for the Haymarket confirmed their pessimistic opinion. Although the theatres had been freed, the drama still languished.

They had decided to present much the same type of repertory that they had offered in Wych Street although the Lyceum, which could accommodate eighteen hundred spectators, was about one-third larger than the Olympic. They hoped once again to attract a fashionable audience, but they knew that it would not be easy. The Lyceum had an unsavory reputation. Rumor had it that a secret underground passage linked the theatre to a brothel.[2] But seventeen years earlier Madame had transformed the Olympic from a dingy hole-in-the-wall to a well-appointed theatre. At the Lyceum she felt confident that she could once again create a milieu in which the world of fashion felt at ease. She had long since decided that the drama's patrons were to be found in the boxes, not in the pit or gallery, and consequently the alterations which she commissioned at the

Lyceum closely paralleled those she had previously brought about at the Olympic and Covent Garden.

Under the direction of Mr. Bradwell the balcony was replaced by a dress circle. The number of boxes was increased, and patrons were provided with separate entrances on both sides of the house. Bradwell also provided a private entrance for the Royal Box and removed the stall seats from the pit. Stall seats were increasingly favored by the world of fashion, but Madame despised them as a modern innovation. In addition to these structural changes, Bradwell also redecorated the house, transforming it into a triumphant example of Victorian baroque. In place of the vast central chandelier he substituted eight smaller chandeliers and sixteen gilt gas brackets. Painted cupids sported on the frescoed ceiling and sculptured cherubs swarmed around the boxes festooned with gold-fringed crimson draperies. Adding a rococo touch were porcelainlike medallions of flowers, fruit, and birds, modeled in delicate relief against pale rose and blue backgrounds. Simple white muslin curtains, dividing the boxes, completed the decor.

While these alterations were in progress, Mathews and Madame also settled into a new house. For months Anne Mathews had been looking for something suitable for them. In August she found it at last—Holcroft Hall, a charming house set among the trees and fields at the west end of the Fulham Road. They took it at once, and Gore Lodge, as they rechristened it, became their permanent home.

Somehow they found the time for a fortnight's holiday in Brighton before the opening of the Lyceum on October 18. On the first-night bill were two adaptations from the French, Planché's *Pride of the Market*, with Madame improbably cast as a market woman, and *The Light Dragoons*, with Mathews as an equally unlikely military man. Both were trifling vaudevilles, but both actors were warmly welcomed. Members of the audience also welcomed certain changes of policy which Madame had effected in the newly decorated theatre. The boxkeepers had been forbidden to accept fees for any reason. The noisy basket-women, peddling ginger beer and lemonade, had vanished from the scene. Madame had also taken the important step of abolishing half-price admission and no longer was the theatre overrun by the raffish crew who swarmed in after nine o'clock. As a result, the Lyceum, like the Olympic before it, soon began to draw the most fashionable audiences in London.

On November 1 it had its first resounding success— Morton's *Box and Cox,* perhaps the most famous of all Victorian farces. Put together as meticulously as a Swiss watch, it gave Buckstone and Harley the chance to show off their comic virtuosity. As two distraught lodgers, sharing the same bed and the same fiancee, they played at breakneck speed, exchanging a cross fire of dialogue as they bolted in one door and out the other. As one critic put it, Morton's play was "a 'touch and go' piece, requiring great rapidity of action and dialogue, and very dangerous if the audience are permitted for half a minute to let their laughter or attention die away." [3] But never for a moment did Buckstone and Harley allow the comic pace to slacken, and for a joyous half-hour they projected the audience into the manic world of farce, midway between the wild imaginings of Box and Cox and the solid realities of Mrs. Bouncer's boarding-house.

During their regime at the Lyceum, Madame Vestris and Mathews also produced a number of other highly successful farces. W. B. Jerrold's *Cool as a Cucumber* (March 24, 1851) provided Mathews with one of his best roles, and for over twenty years he delighted audiences as the outrageous Mr. Plumper who coolly invades a well-ordered Victorian household. Admired by Shaw as a prime example of the genre, it typifies the aggression of farce in which, as Eric Bentley observes, "one is permitted the outrage but spared the consequence." [4] Mathews had strong views, however, on the limits of permissiveness. In most instances the farces offered at the Lyceum were of French origin and necessarily had to be adapted for English audiences. In his *Letter . . . to the Dramatic Authors of France* (1852) he deplored "the indecency, anachronism, immorality and dirt" [5] of French drama. The emphasis on adultery particularly distressed him. It could be included in melodrama, perhaps, but in comedy

Charles James Mathews, Miss Oliver, and Miss Martindale.

and farce "we surely have a right to expect a little wit and inge-
nuity, a little novelty in the plot, drollery in the characters,
[and] fun in the incidents . . . [without] running the risk of
stumbling upon adultery, seduction, and all the worst passions
of our nature."[6] His views reflected the prevailing climate of

opinion. One looks in vain for a Victorian equivalent to the boudoir epics of Georges Feydeau. But if English farce-writers were reluctant to violate sexual decorum, they had free license in other respects and gave joyous expression to the obvious discrepancies between "Nature red in tooth and claw" and the Victorian Vision of Progress.

While farce was featured at the Lyceum, the theatre's chief glory, however, lay in its Christmas and Easter extravaganzas, no less than eleven of which were by Planché. At the Olympic he had perfected this type of entertainment. At the Lyceum his formula remained essentially the same. In the manner of the French *féeries* and Carlo Gozzi's *fiabe*, he freely mixed fantasy and farce, song and spectacle. Typical of the species is his *Island of Jewels*, first performed on December 26, 1849, and divertingly summarized for us by a contemporary critic.

Gingerbread the Great, King of Pharitale and his Queen Tinsellina, with that melancholy forgetfulness so common in all such cases, in summoning the fairies to attend the birth or christening of their twin daughters, Princess Bellotta and Princess Laidronetta forget that notoriously malevolent old fairy Magotine, who avenges the slight in the ordinary course of nature by rushing in at the festival and casting such glamour around Laidronetta as to make her appear odiously ugly to her parents, who very properly banish her from court, for such a grievous offence, to a lonely tower by the seaside. Here, however, she is consoled by the fun and kindness of her maid Fidelia and by the delicate attentions of a large specimen of the boa constrictor species, which hisses vows of eternal fidelity from all manner of impossible places. Princess Bellotta is about to be married to Prince Prettiphello and Laidronetta, having in vain attempted to get an introduction to the ball, returns to the sea-shore to deplore her fate. The transition from the ball-room of the royal pavilion, filled with a glorious company of cavaliers and ladies in sky-blue turned up with gold (in which too a tolerable attempt was made to render the perspective complete by introducing some very tiny children at the back of the stage), to the lonely tower was very well managed. A boat without any one in it appears by the seaside; the Princess and Fidelia embark; Magotine raises a storm at sea, which does great credit to her creative powers, and but for the serpent, who, in this case turns out to be the real sea animal, the Princess would be lost on a reef of rocks off the Gold Coast. She and her faithful attendant, however, are safely landed in the Island of Jewels and express their satisfaction in a very pretty duet. Here the courtiers and suite of the master of the territory—Viscount Carbuncle, Earl Topaz, Lord Onyx, Lady Pearl, &c—visit them, and announce that King Emerald (an invisible-green Prince, or rather an invisible green-prince) claims the hand of the Princess on the understanding that she will wed him without seeing his face; to which, as there is abundant proof of his being well-to-do in the world, she consents. The King . . . is carried on in a golden litter and sings a song, in which he certainly does not make the most of his voice. It is needless to say that the King is the serpent lover held in durance vile by Magotine; and that the devotion of the Princess, a little impeded by her curiosity, however, and the assistance of the fairy Benevolentia, restore him to his proper form, that of an interesting young monarch, and bring about a happy matrimonial conclusion.[7]

In dramatizing this fairy tale Planché, as in his earlier entertainments, relied heavily on puns and parodies, operatic and literary. He expected his public to recognize such musical selections as a *duettino* from Verdi's *Macbeth*, premiered only one year earlier. He also counted on their familiarity with Shakespeare and the standard theatrical repertory. Shipwrecked on the Island of Jewels, the distraught Fidelia exclaims:

Hung be the heavens with black of deepest dye,
And one great mourning warehouse make the sky.

Planché expected a good deal of his audience if he hoped that they would recognize his reference to the opening lines of the *Henry VI* trilogy, but for playgoers less on the *qui vive* he provided grosser examples. The King of Pharitale, caught in the open during a violent storm, angrily cries out:

Blow winds and crack your cheeks, the clouds go spout!

Seconds later he cheerfully adds:

A thought has struck me, rather entertaining,
I am a king more rained upon than reigning.

But his extravaganzas were, above all, occasions for spectacle. Almost inevitably they included occasional dances and a ballet.

The Island of Jewels calls for a grand "Row Polka" and a cho-
reographic interpolation at the end of Act I. Forbidden to look
upon the King of Emeralds before her marriage to him, Laidronetta is warned once again by means of a ballet on the legend of
Cupid and Psyche. Devising such a ballet, an incidental danse,
or a tableau were routine assignments for Oscar Byrne. Only in
one instance does he seem to have been baffled. A pair of goats,
hired to supplement a procession in *Theseus and Ariadne*, behaved so disgracefully at rehearsals that he was forced to cancel
their engagement and return them to their owner.

Of far more consequence, however, were the contributions of
William Beverly, Madame's new scene painter. His sets for
Planché's first Lyceum extravaganza, *The Golden Branch*, won
him golden opinions. One read: "The grand scene in Arcadia,
with vistas of flowers, and tall crystal columns ranged in avenues, and the golden wood produced by the fertility of the
branch, and afterwards opening into a novel fairy tableau, be-
long to the very first order of fanciful scenery, and do the
greatest credit to that rising painter, Mr. Beverly." [8] His subsequent designs for *Theseus and Ariadne* were no less admired
and critics showered him with praise for *The King of Peacocks*
(1848) with its chinoiserie decor which culminated in the final
vision of an immense fan of brilliantly colored peacock feathers.

Even more breathtaking, however, was the concluding scene
in *The Island of Jewels*. Since the story required no final tableau, Planché had left the ending up to the designer. Rising to
the occasion, Beverly devised a finale in which the branches of a
vast, gilded palm tree slowly opened to reveal a group of fairies
supporting a coronet of jewels.[9]

So notable was this scene that it set the standard for all subsequent extravaganzas. Each year Beverly was called upon to perform still greater miracles, and to Planché's dismay, "the last
scene became the first in the estimation of the management." [10]
The playwright was gradually being painted into a corner, but
the trend was irreversible. The public clamored for ever more
dazzling effects and for still more tinsel, gauze, and red fire. In
Planché's *King Charming*, produced one year after *The Island
of Jewels*, the final stage direction reads: "CHARMING and

Final scene in *The Island of Jewels*.

Final scene in *King Charming*.

FLORINDA rush behind pedestal—Thunder, lightning, crash—pillars fall, pedestal sinks—Scene changes to the throne of Fan-sea." The engraved music cover for this scene clearly shows its relation to *The Island of Jewels* and the increasing scenic elaboration. These extravaganzas with their transformation scenes, elaborate groupings, and opulent decor unmistakably point the way toward the later fantasies of Florenz Ziegfeld and Busby Berkeley.

Successful as these entertainments were, Planché was increasingly uneasy. He was beginning to feel the same sense of exasperation that Ben Jonson had voiced in his *Expostulation with Inigo Jones*.

> O Showes! Showes! Mighty Showes!
> The Eloquence of Masques! What need of Prose
> Or Verse, or Sense t'express Immortal you?

The ascendancy of Jones had signaled the dissolution of the masque. The rise of Beverly similarly threatened the extravaganza and in later years Planché, as he had feared, presided over its obsequies. It was left to his successor, W. S. Gilbert, to revitalize the genre by boldly abandoning the pun, rejecting doggerel, and insisting upon original music.[11] Planché lacked his courage. He also lacked his originality and satiric bite, but nonetheless he brought to the Lyceum extravaganzas a touch of elegance, of good humor, and of wit, and for six years they proved the main staple of Madame's repertory.

Although some of the critics complained of her fading charms, she continued to perform in these entertainments, donning tights to appear as Theseus or the King of the Peacocks. She was resigned, however, to also playing less youthful roles. In *The Golden Branch* she good-naturedly played a waiting-woman and Planché saluted her gallantry by interpolating into the score the song of "Cherry Ripe" which she had made famous so many years before. Quite unabashedly she further appealed to sentimentally minded playgoers by reviving many of the entertainments which she had made popular at the Olympic. She recreated Planché's *Court Beauties* with the same attention to detail that she had lavished on the original. The costumes were as sumptuously authentic, the accessories as perfect, down to the pack of well-bred spaniels that bobbed at the heels of the Merry Monarch. Further revivals followed, of *Blue Beard, The Beggar's Opera*, and *The Merry Wives of Windsor*. Even the new pieces often seemed like revivals. To introduce John Reeve, Jr., son of the great singer, she commissioned *My Father Did So Before Me*, shamelessly patterned after *The Old and Young Stager*.

Although she was performing less frequently, as always she could be relied on to take part in her colleagues' benefits. She had frowned upon benefit nights at the Olympic, but she had mellowed in this respect, and at the Lyceum she condoned the practice. She participated also in more general theatrical benefits, among them the famous Shakespeare Night on December 7, 1847, organized to help purchase the poet's birthplace. The entertainment, made up of short extracts, began with Macready playing the death scene of Henry IV. It concluded, some three hours later, with the resurrection of Hermione, performed by Mrs. Warner. In between, virtually every distinguished mid-nineteenth-century actor put in a brief appearance, Madame Vestris and Mathews contributing their services as Mrs. Page and Slender.

Busy as they were in the theatre, they had much to preoccupy them in private life. For some years Josephine Anderson had been living quietly in St. John's Wood, devoting most of her time to her growing family. On May 1, 1848, she died of tuberculosis.[12] Madame and Mathews promptly removed the children to Gore Lodge. It was a gesture of characteristic generosity that no doubt Mr. Anderson welcomed, but it placed heavy additional responsibilities upon them.

Their debts were pyramiding and the London theatre was in an even more critical condition than usual. The year 1848 was a year of revolution and its reverberations were felt even in the theatre. London society had increasingly patronized visiting French companies at the St. James's and the Queen, in particular, had been harshly criticized for neglecting the English theatre.

Shortly after the abdication of Louis Philippe, no less than four French troupes simultaneously invaded London. One of them was ill-advised enough to perform at Drury Lane. Outraged, a group of English actors hissed through the entire performance of *Monte Cristo*. The following evening they hooted the visitors off the stage.

Madame could not condone such excesses, perpetrated by the "scum of the profession," as *The Times* called them, but she understood their motives. Victoria also understood their resentment, and after the riots her patronage of the English theatre markedly increased. She attended a benefit for the Charles Keans, another for Macready, and initiated ambitious plans for a series of private theatricals at Windsor. Her quickened interest in the drama was gratifying, but Madame realized that she herself had little to gain from it. Virtually all of the pieces at the Lyceum were of French origin. Victoria pointedly aimed at the encouragement of English drama. Madame also had little expectation that she would be invited to perform at Windsor, since the theatricals were to be under the direction of Charles Kean, an actor she found pompous and mannered.

Equally dispiriting, from her point of view, was the increasing admiration for Macready. During the Drury Lane riots he had taken it upon himself, as a spokesman for the profession, to apologize to the visitors. A group of actors headed by Charles Kean, Mathews, and Webster hotly disclaimed his right to speak for them. Mathews was particularly incensed, and in the draft of a letter preserved among his papers he savagely attacks Macready charging

> that the whole course of your theatrical career (though in private an avowed democrat) has been tyrannical and oppressive especially to those you supposed were beneath you. That the style you imperatively insisted upon when in power, being opposed to the true principle of acting & the admirable law laid down by Shakespeare in his advice to the player, has engendered a school in tragedy of guttural & spasmodic enunciation joined with exaggerated and melodramatic action. . . .[13]

The humiliations they had endured at Drury Lane had not been forgotten.

The death of Josephine, the fatigues of management, and the theatrical tensions of 1848 made them anxious for a holiday. The summer was a warm one, almost Italianate. They could not afford Brighton, but they found a cottage that suited them in the less fashionable seaside resort of Littlehampton. Pleading with him to keep their address a secret, Mathews wrote to Planché apologizing for the arrears in his salary and urging him to visit them. "We have a small house, and have but to add that there is a spare bed in it, with a knife and fork and a cup and saucer at your service." [14] Once again Mathews was playing hide-and-seek with the bailiffs.

> Every piece had to be got up on credit, and the outlay had always to be repaid before a profit could be realised; and all the large receipts accruing from the brilliant houses from Christmas to Easter were more than swallowed up by the utter blank that followed from Easter to Michaelmas. The stone was no sooner rolled up to the top of the hill than down it went to the bottom again.[15]

The world he had known as a young man was falling apart. On April 1, 1849, Count D'Orsay, the prince of dandies, threatened with arrest for debt, fled from London with his valet and one valise. Two weeks later Lady Blessington followed him to Paris. Her fortune had dwindled to nothing, and the drawing room at Gore House, the scene of so many brilliant soirees, was shuttered for good. Within two months she was dead. It was the end of an era—the long golden days at the Palazzo Belvedere had vanished forever.

The letters of Mathews during this period vividly reveal his mounting sense of frustration. He was angry at Kean's unwillingness to let Madame Vestris perform Lady Teazle at Windsor, attributing it to her refusal to engage him at the Lyceum. He was also piqued by Kean's reluctance to let him double the roles of Puff and Sir Fretful Plagiary in a forthcoming command production of *The Critic*. In a letter to one of Victoria's equerries he testily observes: "Mr. Kean has been repudiated as an actor for so many years by the members of the profession he follows and is completely indebted to the talents of his wife and the friendship of his Eton associates for his position in London, that his want of feeling for his poorer brethren is no matter of surprise to them." [16] Far from rejoicing in the honor of playing before the Queen, he bitterly complained that it would cost him "at least £80." [17]

His correspondence with Planché shows him no less harrassed, fretting at the perenially debilitated state of the Lyceum. "It would be madness," he writes, "to begin a season without [a] complete fresh bill. Everything we have is worn to rags." [18] But flashes of humor enliven even his gloomiest letters. Discussing a possible future production, he suggests to Planché "a tapestry curtain for instance to draw aside and discover a lake with an illuminated palace and people dancing within it—the lake by moonlight." In a flurry of postscripts he jocosely adds: "Oh—couldn't you? no—that won't do. Stop—what if you were to—no. Or—why not make—no, you couldn't." [19]

But like Sheridan, that perennially harassed manager, Mathews had a talent for survival. He could wheedle a loan from an enraged creditor and send him off in a high good humor. Madame Vestris, in her own way, was no less resourceful, and the production of Planché's *King Charming* in December, 1850, is a testimony to their powers of persuasion. Despite the fact that they were also in debt to Beverly, he conjured up for them vistas of palaces, groves, and gardens as breathtaking as ever. If Mr. Sloman, the machinist, resented the fact that he often paid the crew out of his own pocket, it was not evident in the marvels he produced—most notably a giant pie with four-and-twenty jeweled blackbirds perched on boughs of silver and precious stones. Madame herself, in the title role, made as dazzling a figure as ever, attired in a costume copied from the dress of the Nepalese ambassador—"a pale pink satin tunic embroidered with pearls, Turkish trousers, a turban hat, one mass of pearls, and hung with pendent diamonds, surmounted by a spray of bird of paradise feathers." [20] She was performing less and less frequently, and in less demanding roles, but her appearance in the Christmas entertainment was indispensable.

Successful as it was, their creditors were increasingly clamorous, and on April 2, 1851, Mathews petitioned the Bankruptcy

Madame Vestris as King Charming.

Court for protection against arrest under the Debtor and Creditor Private Arrangements Act.[21] He was over £17,000 in debt, with assets of slightly over £6. The Act was about as serviceable to him as an umbrella to a drowning man. As one of the bankruptcy commissioners put it, "These arrangement clauses, as they are called, are little better than a mass of gibberish." Even more dishearteningly, he added, "It is almost impossible to understand them. I have never attempted it." [22] Nevertheless, Mathews was granted immunity under the act and a temporary reprieve.

The respite came at a critical time, for theatre managers were preparing to entertain the hordes of visitors streaming into London for the Great Exhibition. Planché had concocted for the Lyceum a new extravaganza, *The Queen of the Frogs,* designed to appeal to the eye rather than to the ear. The piece disappointed their expectations. To the dismay of theatre managers, visitors saved their money and their energy for the Crystal Palace. Tireless a sightseer as she was, the Queen came home from her visits "quite dead beat," and even the energetic Dickens, after examining everything from absinthium leaves to zithers, found himself "used up." In place of the *Queen of the Frogs* Madame Vestris restored *King Charming* to the repertory. Business revived somewhat and the Lyceum remained open throughout the summer with Mathews and Vestris alternating in the title role of Planché's extravaganza.

The season had been a generally undistinguished one, but during its course Madame had produced one play which was a distinct departure from her usual repertory. Her previous experiments with serious drama had been discouraging, but on December 4, 1850, she ventured into the field once again with Planché's *Day of Reckoning,* adapted from Emile Souvestre's *Enfant de Paris.* In France the drama of the clash between a young French workingman and a corrupt aristocrat had provoked an outcry. In adapting it for English audiences, Planché modified its strident republican tone and stressed the drama rather than the dialectic. But even in its emasculated state, it stirred British theatregoers. It came as something of a shock to see Madame playing a pathetic French countess, not in Louis XIV costume but in contemporary dress, and playing her, furthermore, without a trace of artifice. No less surprising was Mathews's performance as a dissolute count. They "were natural," George Henry Lewes wrote, "nothing more, nothing less." [23]

> They were a lady and gentleman such as we meet with in drawing-rooms, graceful, quiet, well-bred, perfectly dressed, perfectly oblivious of the footlights. He is a polished villain —a D'Orsay without conscience, and without any of the scowlings, stampings, or intonations of the approved stage villain. There are scoundrels in high life—but they are perfectly well-bred. Whatever faults there may be in their conduct, their deportment is irreproachable. [24]

For the first time Mathews received notices acclaiming him as a "first-rate dramatic artist." [25] His talents had previously been confined almost entirely to light or eccentric comedy. His performance opened up for him a whole new range of characters.

Madame's notices were less striking but she too could take satisfaction in her reception. She could not resist inserting a song into her somewhat colorless role, but she made no attempt to win the sympathy of the audience through any of the claptrap tricks of Surrey melodrama. Analyzing her performance in some detail, Lewes above all praised her reliance on Nature.

> Her character is one which in most hands would become insipid or melodramatic: a sad, neglected wife, loving another man, of whom her husband is jealous, and solacing her unhappiness by constant beneficence to the poor—a noble, loving, suffering woman, she stands there represented with a truth, a grace, a gentle pathos I have no epithets to characterize. The sad dignity with which she bears her husband's insults, the terror which agitates her when that husband intimates his knowledge that her lover is in an adjoining room, and that he, her husband, is permitted by the law to kill him—these things are represented in a manner very unlike that current on the stage —and recall the finished art of French comedy. [26]

Critics acknowledge that the new natural style had its origins in the French theatre. Up-and-coming young actors such as Leigh Murray, Alfred Wigan, and Fanny Stirling, all of whom had appeared with Madame Vestris, were developing a style which stressed elegance, delicacy, and effective byplay.[27] Most English actors, however, had not yet attained an easy, contemporary manner, and in *A Day of Reckoning* Lewes noted an obvious discrepancy between the natural manner of Mathews and Madame and the stagey manner of the rest of the cast.

Lewes had long admired them. While still a very young man he had written enthusiastically to Mathews, then the lessee of Covent Garden, suggesting that they collaborate on a play. The

Madame Vestris, George Vining, and Frank Matthews in
A Day of Reckoning.

proposal came to nothing, but Lewes, in spite of his increasing absorption in journalism, did not lose his interest in the theatre.[28] In 1849 his play *The Noble Heart* was produced in Manchester and London. Two years later he provided Mathews and Madame with *The Game of Speculation*, an adaptation of Balzac's *Mercadet*. Even in that great age of literary piracy, few French dramas were as swiftly Anglicized. A copy of Balzac's play, just produced, was rushed across the channel and thrust into Lewes' hands. Immuring himself with several shorthand writers in a room at the top of the Lyceum, he delivered a completed manuscript to the waiting cast within thirteen hours. Within three days it reached the stage.

In making his adaptation Lewes evidently had in mind Mathews's performance in *A Day of Reckoning*. Balzac's play of modern life took as its cynical motto: "All our morals lie in dividends!" Lewes chose to omit many of the French author's satirical thrusts, but nonetheless *The Game of Speculation* has an almost Jonsonian ferocity, and as Affable Hawk, a Victorian Mosca, Mathews again had an opportunity to display his talent for glossy villainy. Though Lewes had tacked onto Balzac's play a pseudomoralistic conclusion, it is hardly persuasive. His comedy indicts the same society which Trollope so brilliantly dissected in *The Way We Live Now*. In Mathews he found an actor who understood that society only too well.

Its success induced Mathews and Vestris to put Lewes on the payroll at £10 a week. He was paid only irregularly, but during the next three years he produced eight plays for the Lyceum, all of them from the French. On two of these he collaborated with Mathews. Their first effort, *A Chain of Events*, was a four-hour-long adaptation of a seven-act drama, *La Dame de la Halle*. Needless to say, it took up the entire evening. Produced on April 12, 1852, in lieu of an Easter extravaganza, it offered something to everybody—"drama, farce, ballet, spectacle" [29] —and required the services of the entire company and backstage crew. On the same evening Ben Webster's *Queen of the Market*, a rival four-act version, had its premiere at the Adelphi. Many reviewers preferred the condensed Adelphi version to the vast, sprawling adaptation at the Lyceum, but Mathews's performance as an unscrupulous lawyer was highly praised as was the Lyceum production. Beverly's realistic Paris settings were much applauded, but even more applauded was the staging of a spectacular shipwreck scene which Lewes and Mathews tacked on to the French original. Their stage directions read as follows:

> The Scene represents the open sea in the midst of a hurricane. A large dismasted vessel tossed on the tempest in seen rolling heavily among the billows. Four or five only of the crew are left on the wreck and are clinging to the spars and broken mast.

At intervals between the roar of the ocean and the peals of
thunder broken sentences are caught from those on board. . . .
A terrific peal of thunder is heard and the lightning runs along
the sky, and the vessel goes down bodily, amidst a shriek from
those on board. The waves wash over her, and nothing is seen
but the open sea.[30]

Such scenes were a feature of nineteenth-century opera and
melodrama. Solidly built vessels rocked like cradles in seas of

The shipwreck scene from *The Chain of Events*.

waving gauze. Lightning flashed through transparent openings
in the backcloths, and sheets of silver-green paper, illuminated
by a bull lantern, cast a lurid glow upon the scene.[31] Even Macready made use of these effects, staging the opening of *The
Tempest* so realistically that the rest of the play seemed like an
anticlimax. So sensational was the staging of the shipwreck
scene in *A Chain of Events* that the cries of the spectators, we
are told, supplemented those of the crew, and so prolonged was
the applause that it seemed, for one awful moment, that the au-

dience might demand an encore. The trumpery melodrama had little to recommend it, but it gave Madame the occasion to apply her theories of production on an almost epic scale. This huge, cumbrous drama, Coleman tells us, in its stage management and mounting "as nearly approached perfection as anything I have seen." [32]

The following Easter, Mathews and Lewes collaborated on another play of still more gargantuan proportions. Written in nine "chapters," *A Strange History* (March 28, 1853) was far less successful than its predecessor and spectators were yawning long before the four-and-a-half-hour play crawled to its conclusion. Even Lewes recognized its inadequacies, and under the pseudonym of Vivian criticized himself for its rambling, leisurely pace: "When once you have taken your place in the railway carriage the train should stop as seldom as may be. You are impatient to arrive. Let the scenery through which you pass be varied, and your fellow-travellers pleasant, but let the train rush on." [33] As a long-suffering *vivandiere*, Madame Vestris had little to do, and Mathews was ineffectively cast as a young Swiss peasant. The hero of the occasion, once again, was William Beverly, but even he was faulted. Mathews and Lewes had set him an an almost impossible task. The script called for an avalanche. Such a scene was not unprecedented. A dramatization of *Frankenstein* had demanded a similar effect, and in Birmingham, so the story goes, a harassed manager attempted to meet the requirement by whitewashing a pasteboard elephant and dropping it from the flies.[34] If Mr. Beverly's avalanche was somewhat less ludicrous, it was not much more convincing. He redeemed himself, however, with a scene depicting a real waterfall in a Swiss glen and the performance was not allowed to continue until he stepped forward to acknowledge the applause. But audiences applauded only the scenery.

The failure of *A Strange History* was all the more disturbing in that the other major production of the 1852–53 season, Planché's Christmas extravaganza, *The Good Woman in the Wood*, also proved a disappointment. Although Lewes lavished superlatives upon it, other journalists were less enthusiastic. The

critic on *The Morning Chronicle,* in particular, found the entertainment cold and heavy and the sets faded and dingy.[35] Stung
by this heresy, Mathews promptly posted bills informing the
critic and his friends, "if any," that the Lyceum doorkeepers
had strict instructions to refuse his money and bar him from the
theatre. He also withdrew from *The Morning Chronicle* the
privilege of writing orders of admission. Over twenty years earlier Madame Vestris had imposed a similar ban at the Olympic,
but the practice was still widely prevalent.[36]

During the winter of 1852 and the spring of 1853 Vestris and
Mathews often played to almost empty boxes and benches, and
during the last three months of the season the theatre was oper-
ating at an average weekly loss of about £250. F. W. Allcroft,
who had initially helped them to engage the Lyceum, refused
them any further credit, and Arnold, the theatre's owner, flatly
demanded £2,000 in cash to renew their lease. They faced other
problems as well. Planché's contract with them had expired and
he had retired to Kent. In June, William Beverly regretfully announced that he too was leaving. The news was catastrophic. So
uncertain was their future that Mathews, at the conclusion of
the season, decided to resume "provincializing." Madame Vestris longed to go with him, but her health precluded such exer-
tion, and Mathews set off on his travels accompanied by Hin-
ton, his dresser, who had been with him since his American
tour. Provincial playgoers who had seen little of him since 1847
found him a trifle bulkier, but still superbly turned out and, on
stage at least, as high spirited as ever.

Although stories of his extravagance continued to circulate,
his tastes had become increasingly simpler and his habits increasingly regular. He smoked only the cheapest cigars, and friends
deplored his taste in wine. His whole life was disciplined to the
demands of the theatre. Rehearsals occupied most of his morn-
ings and early afternoons. At their conclusion he had a light
dinner, flung a handkerchief over his head, and napped for an
hour. Then, with clockwork regularity, he dashed off a note to
Gore Lodge or Littlehampton before the evening performance.
On August 1, from Liverpool, he wrote:

My own dearest love
> Pouring! pouring! pouring! Such a rehearsal! Such a com-
> pany! I really cannot but rejoice that you are not here, to
> sit in this melancholy place with nothing to do but wait
> for me from 11 till ½ past 4 and then again by the light of
> two wretched candles till my return at night. . . . The the-
> atre is in a state of delapidation and as to properties &c
> something beyond belief.[37]

His letters reveal an intensity of emotion that would have astonished those critics who contended he was incapable of feeling or
conveying real passion: "My own beloved wife. . . . I want
your comforting communication—tell me that you love me
dearly as ever and that nothing shall ever part us. I doat on you
more and more the more our misfortunes thicken." [38]

Madame Vestris, often similarly accused, responded no less
emotionally. However calculating and selfish she may have been
in her twenties, in her fifties she was as deeply in love with her
husband as he with her. Although she realized the necessity for
Mathews's summer engagements, with the querulous irrational-
ity of an invalid she could not resign herself to his absence. The
trip to Littlehampton with the Anderson children had exhausted
her and only occasionally did she venture out for a carriage
ride. "I feel that another separation will half kill me," she writes,
"I have not a kindred creature who loves me as I thought you
always did till now. Ah money, money, what a curse it is on all
hearts, good or bad." [39]

They exchanged letters daily, sometimes twice a day, Mathews was also in correspondence with ruffled members of the
Lyceum. Whether the threatre would open in October was seri-
ously in question, but Mathews's pen was no less persuasive than
his tongue, and on September 8 he wrote exultantly to Planché:

> Beverly, Planché, and the Theatre lost to me there was only
> one thing left to be done—viz to begin again, better than
> ever. I first tackled with Arnold and made *him* find the
> money to pay himself with—got the lease signed without
> putting down a penny, and then got my company together
> and looked forward to go in and win. No sooner was this
> done than I had a visit from Beverly at Littlehampton to

say how much he regrets being obliged to secede from the
Lyceum. Knocked *him* on the head and nailed him to the
old flag staff. Away he went shouting "Lyceum for ever!"
My next point was to secure [Edward] Wright [a popular
low comedian from the Adelphi]. Nailed *him;* and now,
having a clean bill of health, write to *you* to say that all is
in order for your winter campaign: you are of course unable to write for me in consequence of past circumstances.
This *won't do.* The human mind naturally looks forward
and after so many years you must not let the oldest friend
be the first to desert the ship. I know you can't work for
nothing and therefore I ask you what *you* mean to do. I
will tell you what I am going to do. From the opening of
the theatre I have put you down at a weekly salary of £10.
For this you will have to do—nothing. If you do not write at
all, your weekly £10 will at all events be paid and I think you
are not the man to let Wright lack for novelty (depend upon it,
he can act your material, in the farce way, as well as Buckstone) nor let Christmas pass without an Extravaganza from
your pen as usual. That's all.

With Mrs. M's best regards

My dear Planché

Faithfully yours,

C.J. Mathews

redivivus [40]

Like the others, Planché capitulated, and in October the Lyceum reopened. Madame's health was such that she did not appear during the earlier part of the season, but at Christmastime
she returned in *Once Upon a Time There Were Two Kings.*
Her performance was as assured as ever, but the irony of her
role as a dethroned queen can hardly have escaped her, and the
presence in the cast of James Bland was another sad reminder of
the passage of time. Planché's last extravaganza for the Lyceum
lacked the sparkle of his earlier efforts, and the production was
plagued with problems. Mr. Wright, the low comedian whom
Mathews had wooed away from the Adelphi, proved so inadequate that he was replaced by Robert Roxby, the stage manager, and Madame herself was frequently indisposed. In addition, the winter was an exceptionally severe one, with heavy
falls of snow. As a result, box-office receipts plummeted, and by

February creditors were again hounding Mathews. Convinced that his primary obligations were to his company, he privately informed the principal actors that he would set aside enough from the receipts to cover their salaries. The news leaked out to his creditors, and on February 7 he was arrested. He was to have performed at the Lyceum that evening, but the audience refused to allow another actor to read his part, and consequently the performance was canceled. Released the next day, Mathews rushed to the theatre and found it deserted. The following evening performances were resumed and the season went limping on.

Lackluster as it was, it included at least one attractive production—*A Charming Widow*, an adaptation by John Oxenford of Alfred De Musset's *Un Caprice*. For over twenty years the French playwright had delighted sophisticated Parisians with his dramatic *proverbes*. Mathews and Madame could have played them to perfection. Of all the English actors of the period they were best suited to do justice to the delicately inflected dialogue, to suggest the emotions behind the exquisite veneer. Their reluctance to play De Musset perhaps stemmed from their suspicion that his *proverbes*, like some French wines, traveled badly. When they finally decided to risk a production it was too late—at least from Madame's point of view. Both of the women's roles were too young for her, but nonetheless her influence made itself felt in every aspect of the production. The drawing-room set might have been transported intact from the faubourg St. Germain. Miss Oliver played the neglected wife with a touching simplicity. Mathews, as her careless spouse, struck exactly the right note of easy nonchalance, and Miss Paton, as the dashing young widow, had obviously been well rehearsed. Although she was making her theatrical debut, she radiated assurance and gave the impression "of one accustomed to shine in the fashionable salons." [41] The quiet tenor of the play, the perfection of the setting, the effortless style of the actors—it was all too understated, perhaps, for English taste, but it typified Madame's productions at their best.

Nonetheless, the production may well have had a subtle influence on the later course of English comedy. Stationed in the wings was T. W. Robertson, an unsuccessful young dramatist, who for £3 a week was functioning as the prompter. His stay at the Lyceum was a short one but, in the words of one of his biographers, it gave him "the opportunity to study at close quarters the realistic techniques of the Mathews." [42] *A Charming Widow*, in particular, anticipates the restrained naturalism of Robertson's later comedies.

While Mathews found his part in De Musset's play thoroughly congenial, in real life he was forced to play a far less agreeable role. Irresistible pressures again impelled him to appear in Bankruptcy Court. He had appeared there so often that he and the Commissioner had perfected a routine. The script began with an exchange of courtesies. The Commissioner would sigh and then remark, "With deep regret, Mr. Mathews, I see you in this court again." [43] With a graceful bow Mathews would reply, "Our regrets are mutual, your Honour, and would to me be unbearable, only I always have the pleasure of seeing you." As usual, he brought with him a pile of ledgers, as voluminous as they were confused. But one fact emerged with chilling clarity—he owed over £22,000.[44] He had virtually no personal debts, but the list of his creditors ranged from his friend the Marquis of Abercorn to the London Gas Company and included almost all his associates at the Lyceum. After years of harassment Mathews was tempted to take full advantage of the Bankruptcy Act and renounce his debts altogether, but to do so would be to betray his friends and colleagues. The dillemma was an agonizing one.

Not only his friends but even casual acquaintances commiserated with him. "To think of such a man being in difficulty!" exclaimed one admirer after seeing him in *Speculation*. "There ought to be a public subscription got up to pay his debts!" [45] Many shared his opinion. Sympathetic fellow members of the Garrick Club called for an investigation of Mathews's finances and on May 15, 1854, Mr. E. W. Edwards submitted his findings:

> That the Lyceum Theatre, notwithstanding the difficulties by
> which it has been surrounded, has yielded a satisfactory
> profit, during the last seven years, to warrant Mr. Math-
> ews's friends in assisting him to continue the speculation.
> That Mr. and Mrs. Mathews's private expenditure, apart from
> all outlays entailed upon them by the theatre, during the
> same period, has not exceeded £1000 a year.
> That the causes which have led to their present embarrassed sit-
> uation date back as far as 1838, at which period Mr. and
> Mrs. Mathews were lessees of the Olympic Theatre, and
> that, from that time to this, they have never been able to
> recover their position.[46]

In proposing a committee to solicit funds, Edwards announced
that Mr. Arnold, the owner of the Lyceum, had already offered
to subscribe £500. During the investigations Mathews had been
cheerfully performing in two ominously entitled farces—
Serve Him Right, and *Give a Dog a Bad Name*. Elated by the
findings, he decided once again to avail himself of the Arrangements Act, which permitted the liquidation of debts over a period of time. The court assented but, as the Commissioner put it,
he was still in the position of a man trying to swim with a stone
around his neck.

His problems had left him with little time to devote to the
Lyceum, and from May 6 to June 5 the theatre remained closed.
Only four weeks were left before the end of the season, but on
June 16 the premiere took place of George Henry Lewes's *Sun-
shine Through the Clouds*, adapted from Mme. Girardin's *La
Joie Fait Peur*. A month earlier it had been performed by a
French company at the St. James's. So praised was the produc-
tion that it served as a pattern for Madame's. In the leading role,
as a grieving mother who mistakenly believes her son is dead,
she differed markedly, however, from her French counterpart.
Mme. Allan had played the part in the grand style of tragedy.
Madame Vestris played it in a more subdued and realistic manner, and the deep pathos of her performance was much applauded.

The generous response to the fund for Mathews had virtually

assured the renewal of his lease at the Lyceum, but his concern over the state of his wife's health was steadily increasing. At the close of the season he was again compelled to go on tour, but he did so reluctantly.

> My own dearest love
>   It was indeed with a heavy heart that I drove away from you this morning and I could not recover my spirits the whole way. It was really most afflicting to see you in such a wretched state of low spirits and illness and yet to be obliged to leave you. Pray let me try and arrange for you to go with me next time for I really feel like a *brute* to leave you behind. . . .[47]

Madame Vestris in reply tried her best to be cheerful, chattering on about Jenny and Eliza Anderson and their sister Josephine's determined efforts to make a dress for her doll. But she was evidently deeply disturbed by his absence and she describes herself as walking around the living room and dining room "as pale as a ghost." [48]

They were together again, briefly, three weeks later, for on July 26 the leading London managers organized a benefit for Mathews at the Lyceum. Webster of the Adelphi, Buckstone of the Haymarket, Allcroft of the New Strand, E. T. Smith of Drury Lane, Alfred Wigan of the Olympic, and even Charles Kean of the Princess's all contributed to the occasion in one way or another. If the admission prices were steep, the audience that packed the house to the rafters had little reason to complain. The cast was all-star, and the bill almost twice as long as usual. In addition to *Sunshine Through the Clouds* and *Patter versus Clatter* it included three more farces and a divertissement from *La Favorita*. The occasion would have been a still more emotional one could the audience have known that they were witnessing Madame Vestris's final performance.

Seemingly, things had taken a turn for the better and Mathews went back to the provinces, but when he returned to London after his long summer tour, he found that his situation had worsened. The subscribers to his fund had quarreled among themselves and many had failed to make good their pledges of support. Mathews was again tenant of the Lyceum, but on the strength of unfulfilled promises he had incurred additional debts of about £2,000. He deferred opening the theatre until late in November, but Londoners hardly noticed. Madame Vestris was no longer appearing and what novelties he offered failed to draw. Planché had again retired, and in the hope of replacing him Mathews engaged William Brough, a young playwright. His first contribution, *A Comical Countess*, proved a disappointment. His Christmas extravaganza had a more kindly reception, but even so it was evident that he could never take Planché's place.

The winter was a bitterly cold one and Londoners, gloomily preoccupied by the Crimean War, felt little inclination to venture out after dark. For four months Mathews kept the Lyceum open, but on March 24, 1855, he finally gave up. On the following day notices plastered on the billboards outside the theatre advised the public that Mr. Mathews had abandoned management forever.

chapter 10

Epilogue

The year 1855 was proving almost as disastrous for theatrical managers as had the year 1833. Charles Kean, at the Princess's, was running deeply into debt, and John Mitchell was finding the St. James's equally expensive. Mathews attributed the closing of the Lyceum to want of capital and to Mrs. Mathews's declining health, but the critic of *The Athenaeum* suggested that the real reason for its failure was its almost exclusive dependence upon French adaptations. "The English stage for English genius!" he trumpeted.[1]

Mathews had disbanded the company, but a number of his actors, headed by Mr. and Mrs. Frank Matthews, reassembled for a fortnight's engagement at Sadler's Wells where they appeared in a number of short pieces from the Lyceum repertory. The audience was for the most part a working-class one, and though the first few performances drew good houses, subsequent attendance dropped off sharply. Once again the critic of *The Athenaeum* was ready with an explanation. "With an audience composed of persons engaged in the real struggle of life, and sternly occupied in daily efforts to keep the wolf from the door, the serious drama is preferable to the comic, and the poetic element the very thing that has the needful influence and the fitting interest."[2] No doubt there was some truth to his observation. After Phelps's robust productions of Shakespeare, Islington playgoers may well have found the light French confections too insubstantial for their taste. But the simplest explanation was perhaps the most logical one—without Mathews and Madame Vestris, the company had lost its chief attractions.

Mathews and various other members of the Lyceum—notably William Beverly, Robert Roxby, and Rosina Wright, the ballerina—had accepted engagements with E. T. Smith at Drury Lane, but Mathews was not to appear there until autumn. In the interim he embarked on a punishing tour. It took him to Manchester, Liverpool, Edinburgh, and Glasgow, then back to Manchester and on to Dublin.[3] A handsome offer of £150 a week from the City of London Theatre permitted him to return home briefly during the month of June, but from July to September he was again constantly on the move provincializing in the Midlands.

He returned to London in early October, having agreed to serve at Drury Lane both as a performer and as stage manager. Smith, a showman in the Barnum tradition, had been presenting a dizzying variety of entertainments—*Uncle Tom's Cabin*, Chinese conjurors, a human fly, and fire-breathing performances of Shakespeare by Gustavus Brooke. When Mathews joined the company the season was already under way and rehearsals were in progress for an ambitious production of Edward Fitzball's *Nitocris*. Prompted perhaps by his sense of duty, but more probably by his sense of the ridiculous, Mathews, as stage manager, insisted on reading Fitzball's tragedy of ancient Egypt to the assembled company. The result was predictable. "The more serious he became, the more laughable it became." [4] Even the good-natured author succumbed, though Smith, the lessee, found the occasion somewhat less hilarious. A back wall of the theatre had been removed to accommodate a vast set of the Temple of Memphis, and his expenses had already soared to over £3,000. Though the dress rehearsal of the five-act tragedy passed off tolerably well, its first public performance was a debacle of epic proportions. According to Edward Stirling, Mathews took so contemptuous a view of the play that he nonchalantly omitted one act and played the last act first.[5] Fitzball records that the play inexplicably concluded after three acts with a procession of hundreds of supernumeraries "bearing sumptuous properties, vast idols of silver and gold, whose heads absolutely touched the top of the theatre." [6] An indignant audience, totally bewildered, left the theatre hissing and booing. Subsequent performances of the play, in both the cut and full-length versions, failed to alter their verdict. Remarkably, neither Smith nor Fitzball seems to have blamed Mathews for the disaster, nor did the public hold him accountable, and when he made his first appearance of the season, in Poole's *Married for Money*, he was warmly welcomed.

He remained at Drury Lane through February, appearing in various stock pieces. Madame Vestris had for almost a year been confined to Gore Lodge. Much of the time she kept to her bed. Occasionally she sat up in a chair. She was suffering from cancer of the uterus, and only morphine could alleviate her agony. She saw almost nobody except for her physician, Dr. Jones, and a few friends such as George Henry Lewes and Robert Morrisson, of Somerset House. Compelled to accept provincial engagements, Mathews could hardly bring himself to leave her, and in his letters to her he fluctuates between despair and hope.

> I am weary of my life and the task grows more irksome every day. . . . The [Manchester] company is execrable and by daylight the most miserable set of barndoor fowls you ever saw. . . . The weather is gloomy, cold, and cheerless and the town itself, as you know, at any time horrible. . . . You don't mean to say that you *dined* up on Wednesday!!! Come, this is cheering, indeed. Morphine forever! [7]

He was deeply concerned as well about his finances. Skyrocketing interest rates had frustrated every effort to pay off his debtors, and in June he intimated to Madame that the vultures were again beginning to gather. On July 4, while he was in his dressing room at Preston, preparing for his performance, the event which he had for so long dreaded finally occurred. A sheriff's officer announced himself, produced a writ, and arrested him. Turning a deaf ear to his plea that he be allowed to perform, since the audience was already assembled, the officer clapped him into a chaise. They rumbled through the dark in a cold, drizzling rain and at eleven o'clock arrived at Lancaster Castle. The turnkey, as Mathews describes him, might have stepped out of an Adelphi melodrama. A huge bunch of keys in one hand and a flickering lantern in the other, he worldlessly beckoned to the actor to follow him, and together they mounted the flights of stone steps as grating after grating clanged to behind them. Wild peals of laughter and raucous cries echoed through the corridors. It was a scene that Hogarth might have painted.

The distraught Mathews was thrust into a common cell with twenty-one other debtors. The fact that he had just received a part of his salary from a previous engagement spared him the in-dignity of the paupers' cell, but the debtors' cell was bad enough. Instantly recognizing him, the inmates greeted him with jeering references to *Used Up* and *Speculation.* Exhausted, he fell asleep upon a makeshift bed.

The next morning he and the other debtors washed in the common sink and ate breakfast in John of Gaunt's former ban-queting hall. The rest of the day they whiled away with the fencing foils, boxing gloves, and fiddles which the authorities provided for their recreation. At night they returned to their cell and were again locked up. The routine was unchanging. Al-though they were not handcuffed or fettered, there was little else to distinguish them from convicts.

Each day Mathews poured out his despair in letters to his wife. She longed to visit him, but he instantly rejected the suggestion. Ill and distraught, she accused him of wanting to re-main away from her. In anguish, he replied: "From anyone else I would think it was only done to taunt me and drive me to des-peration. . . . I hear from moment to moment of the dreadful and increasing suffering and despondency of a beloved wife and not only to be unable to fly to her but to be accused of the bru-tality of remaining here from *choice!*" [8] To some extent she succeeded in making his imprisonment more bearable. She man-aged to send him some butter, some seltzer, and a few bottles of wine. A chess set helped to pass the time. Gradually he adjusted to the routine of prison life, and when his painting box arrived he set to work on a watercolor of the banqueting hall. But his wife's condition preoccupied him far more than his own troubles. On July 18 he and Madame would have celebrated their eighteenth wedding anniversary. An allusion to this in one of her letters drew from him perhaps the most poignant expression of his feelings for her.

> Your reminder of our wedding-day brought the tears into my eyes; for though I may be inattentive to such anniversaries generally, my heart must be made of stone not to call to mind and contrast the happiness experienced on that blessed day and the misery endured yesterday. Believe me, my darling Lizzie, when I swear that my love for you is as true at this moment as it was eighteen years ago, and that your sufferings and your fortitude under all the ills of the world endear you more to me every hour.[9]

On August 1 he appeared in court. After an examination by the judge, he was formally discharged as a bankrupt. The ordeal was finally at an end. He at once dispatched a telegram to his wife: "Discharged today; shall be home on Monday. God bless you." He also wrote to her an account of the hearing. Characteristically, he added to it a sketch of himself thumbing his nose at the gloomy castle.

On Monday he was back in London. On Friday, August 8, Madame Vestris died. A few days later she was buried. To quote *The Era's* summary account: "The funeral took place quite privately at Kensal Green in accordance with her last request. Only one mourning coach followed, containing her husband, her medical adviser, and a friend." [10]

It was a grim conclusion to an extraordinary career. Her death had come slowly and painfully, but in another sense she had been dying since her retirement, so totally had she devoted herself to the life of the theatre.

Obituary writers, as might be expected, recalled her youthful extravagances and her performances *en travestie*, but they also pointed out the paradoxes in her career. She had never succeeded in establishing herself as an operatic singer of the first rank, yet she had distinguished herself as a singer of simple unassuming ballads. She had had serious limitations as an actress, yet she had brought to comedy a touch of elegance and ease that foreshadowed the Robertsonian revolution. She had helped to bring about a number of important reforms by discouraging overlong bills, nine o'clock half price, "puffing," benefits, and orders of admission, yet her policy in these matters had not always been consistent.

As a producer she had contributed much to the English stage.[11] With the assistance of Planché she had set new standards of accuracy for costume and setting. Like Macready, Phelps, and Charles Kean she saw each production as an individual unit, and in her extravaganzas, in particular, she had harmoniously integrated the script, the performance, and the physical production. To a lesser extent she had achieved the same fusion in the modern comedies she had produced. Though many of the minor lessees persisted in their old ways,[12] few self-respecting managers still put on contemporary plays in the shabby, makeshift style that had prevailed before her production of *London Assurance*. Time had paid her the ultimate compliment—the reforms for which she had struggled were becoming commonplace.

Mathews's subsequent career can be briefly related. A generous offer to tour in America induced him to return there in 1857. In the course of his stay he met and married Mrs. Elizabeth Weston Davenport. She shared Madame's Christian name, she was an actress, and she too was devoted to Mathews, but there the resemblance ended. Mathews describes her as a "prudent, economical, industrious little helpmate." [13] They returned to London late in the summer of 1858 and soon after, at the Haymarket, she made her debut as Lady Gay Spanker in *London Assurance*, with Mathews playing opposite her as Dazzle. An engagement at Drury Lane followed, and in 1861 they initiated a series of *At Homes* modeled on the famous entertainments of Mathews, Sr. Mrs. Mathews appeared infrequently from then on, but her husband remained as active as ever. Not only did he perform in London and the provinces, but he appeared in Paris as well, astounding playgoers by his volubility and ease in the French versions of *Cool as a Cucumber* (*L'anglais Timide*) and *Used Up* (*L'Homme Blasé*).

In 1869 his mother, Anne Mathews, died at the age of eighty-seven, and shortly afterward Mathews and his wife embarked on a world tour. More properly, it might be described as a progress. Fêted at every port of call, they made their leisurely way to Egypt, to Ceylon, and finally to Australia, where they had been engaged for a prolonged tour. In its initial phase their engagement proved a disappointment, but it concluded triumphantly, and at his wife's farewell benefit Mathews happily summed up his impressions: "Perfect pleasure combined with plenty of profit!" [14] On the voyage home they stopped briefly in New Zealand and the Hawaiian Islands. Their stay in Honolulu particularly delighted Mathews and there, in a little palm-shaded theatre, he performed *Patter versus Clatter* before King Kamehameha and an audience as enthusiastic as any he had ever encountered.

Not until late in the summer of 1872 did they return to London. At the Gaiety Mathews resumed playing the stock pieces which he had made famous. His round-the-world trip had invigorated him, and during the intervals between his London engagements he toured intensively. Full days of rehearsals and long evenings on stage had no apparent effect on his energies. in 1875, at the age of seventy-two, he leaped at the chance to visit India and eagerly accepted an engagement in Calcutta. In the course of the same year he produced his last farce, *My Awful Dad*. Like his father, he had become a national institution. As a young man, his easy naturalistic manner had helped to bring about a profound change in acting style, but so thoroughly had these reforms been assimilated that toward the end of his life audiences regarded him as a slightly old-fashioned actor of extraordinary verve. But even Mathews was not indestructible. In the course of a performance in Glasgow he was found insensible in his dressing room. Fifteen minutes later, after copious libations of brandy, he was back on stage. The applause of the audience proved even more stimulating, and the next morning he appeared to have totally recovered.

His last performance took place at Staleybridge on June 8, 1878. Ironically enough, he was playing Adonis Evergreen in *My Awful Dad*. He contracted a chill, developed bronchial complications, and on June 24 he died. It seemed almost unbelievable that he was dead. Westland Marston, the dramatist, recalling his last glimpse of Mathews, remembered him as smiling and agreeable but silent and thoughtful.[15] John Coleman's last recollection of the actor is more in character. Musing on the subject of the afterlife, Mathews breezily observed, "If there are no theatres in the hereafter, the hereafter must be a very dull affair." [16] No epitaph could have suited him better.

He was buried in Kensal Green. Twenty-one years later, his second wife was buried at his side. A few feet away lies Madame Vestris. Her grave is neglected and the rains have long since effaced her name from the stone half-hidden beneath the nettles and the ivy.

Notes

CHAPTER I. PROLOGUE

1. [Pückler-Muskau], *A Regency Visitor*, p. 81. Letter III, November 21, 1826.

2. For an account of Therese Jansen's friendship with Joseph Haydn see Strunk, "Notes on a Haydn Autograph," *Musical Quarterly*.

3. I have found no official record of Madame Vestris's birth, but a manuscript letter in the Folger Library addressed to her by her father, Gaetano Bartolozzi, and dated Sunday, March 4, 1821, refers to her birthday as "last Friday." This date is corroborated in Charles James Mathews's manuscript diary in the Princeton Library. On March 2, 1846, he makes the entry: "My wife's birthday." There is some confusion, however, as to her Christian names. On the occasion of her marriage to Vestris she is listed on the parish register as Lucy Bartolozzi. When she married Mathews she signed herself Eliza Lucy Vestris. The name recorded on her death certificate is Lucia Elizabeth Mathews. Her father apparently favored the name of Lucy while she herself preferred Eliza.

4. Tuer, *Bartolozzi and his Works*, I, 14–15.

5. *Memoirs of the life . . . of Madame Vestris* (London, [misdated 1839]), p. 7.

6. *The Daughters of Thespis*, p. 102.

7. José Sasportes, "The Dance in Portugal," *Dance Perspectives*, no. 42 (Summer, 1970), p. 45.

8. See Guest, *The Romantic Ballet in England*, pp. 29–32.

9. See *The Times*, July 21, 1815, and *British Ladies' Magazine*, II (August 1815), 120.

10. June 20, 1816.

11. Pearce, *Madame Vestris*, p. 43.

12. Manuscript letter from Vestris to Benelli, Eddison Collection.

13. Quoted in Leathers, *British Entertainers in France*, p. 48.

14. *Gazette de France*, December 8, 1816.

15. *British Stage and Literary Cabinet*, I (March 1817), 67.

16. Affidavit by Madame Vestris printed in *The Times*, November 27, 1826.

17. *Memoirs of the life . . . . of Madame Vestris* (London, 1826), p. 67.

18. Manuscript letter, undated, Harvard Theatre Collection.

19. Manuscript letter, from Madame Vestris to Elliston, docketed "September 8, 1819 answered," Shevelove Collection.

CHAPTER 2. ADONIS IN BREECHES

1. See manuscript letter in the Princeton Library from Madame Vestris to Elliston, dated September 28, 1819, and manuscript draft of an agreement between them in Harvard Theatre Collection, dated December 13, 1819.

2. *The Examiner*, February 27, 1820.

3. Robinson, *The London Theatre 1811–1866*, p. 91. February 19, 1820.

4. *The Examiner*, February 27, 1820.

5. *The Theatrical Inquisitor*, April 1820, p. 237.

6. William Hazlitt quoted in M. Willson Disher, *Clowns and Pantomimes* (London, 1925), p. 265.

7. Quoted in Marshall, *Lives of the Most Celebrated Actors and Actresses*, p. 42.

8. See Oscar Mandel, *The Theatre of Don Juan* (Lincoln, Nebraska, 1963), *passim*.

9. John Bannister, *Memoirs* (London, 1839), I, 69.

10. *The Mirror of the Stage*, I (1823), p. 8.

11. *The Examiner*, July 30, 1820.

12. During the month of August she appeared in Birmingham.

13. See entry for November 2, 1820, James Winston's manuscript diary, Huntington Library.

14. *The British Stage and Literary Cabinet*, V (January 1821), 3.

15. *Ibid.*, April 1821, p. 106.

16. *The Examiner*, March 18, 1821.

17. Christopher Murray, "The Great Lessee: The Management Career of Robert William Elliston (1774–1831)," (Ph.D. diss., Yale, 1969), p. 215.

18. Christopher Murray, "Elliston's Coronation Spectacle, 1821," *Theatre Notebook*, Vol. XXV, no. 2 (winter 1970/71), p. 62.

19. Manuscript letter, Folger Library.

20. *The Daughters of Thespis*, p. 120.

21. She appeared as Pippo on April 20, 1822, but Ebers does not include her on his salary list for that year.

22. See the account in *The Times*, June 26, 1822.

23. The affidavit appeared in *The Times* on November 27, 1826.

24. *The Theatrical Observer*, October 18, 1822.

25. *The Times*, October 28, 1822.

26. She played the role once more with Young and on three occasions with Kean: December 14, 1822; February 23, 1824; and March 11, 1824.

CHAPTER 3. THE SIREN OF MAYFAIR

1. Manuscript letters, undated, author's collection.

2. Pearce, *Madame Vestris*, p. 196.

3. Much of this correspondence was acquired by me in 1971. A few supplementary letters are in the Columbia University Library. Some others are quoted and reproduced in Pearce. I have been unable to trace their present whereabouts.

4. Draft manuscript, undated, author's collection.

5. Manuscript, dated December 3, 1822, author's collection.

6. Quoted in Pearce, *Madame Vestris*, p. 191.

7. Manuscript letter, undated, author's collection.

8. Manuscript letter, undated, author's collection.

9. Manuscript letter, author's collection. In an undated manuscript letter Madame Vestris returns to Montague Gore his settlement and his check for £700; Columbia University Library.

10. [Pückler-Muskau], *A Regency Visitor*, pp. 334–338. Letter XX. July 8, 1827.

11. See *The Great Metropolis*, I, 231.

12. Ebers, *Seven Years of the King's Theatre*, pp. 371–372.

13. See manuscript letters in the collection of Mrs. John F. Wharton.

14. See manuscript draft of an agreement between Elliston and Madame Vestris, dated September 22, 1823, Harvard Theatre Collection.

15. Ebers, *Seven Years of the King's Theatre*, p. 214.

16. See *Don Juan*, Canto XVI, stanza 45. These verses were published in 1824.

17. *The Mirror of the Stage*, IV (1824), 144.

18. Lawrence, "Dublin Stage History," *Dublin Evening Telegraph*.

19. She did not appear in 1826 but made a few token appearances in 1827.

20. See Marian Hannah Winter, *Le Théâtre du Merveilleux* (Paris, 1962), p. 112, and Edwin Binney III, "A Century of Austro-German dance prints," *Dance Perspectives*, no. 47 (autumn 1971), p. 14.

21. See entry for April 4, 1825, in Letter-Book of Henry Robertson for Covent Garden, British Museum Add. MS 29, 643. See also manuscript draft of an agreement between Madame Vestris and Robertson, dated March 18, 1825, Shevelove Collection.

22. [Pückler-Muskau], *A Regency Visitor*, p. 95. Letter IV, December 5, 1826.

23. Vol. I, no. 1, September 30, 1826.

24. I have based these figures on Madame's performances at Covent Garden between February 16 and June 17, 1826.

25. The identity of the author of this volume has never been established. In *The Daughters of Thespis*, pp. 120–121, it is stated that Madame Vestris was erroneously convinced that her uncle, Louis Jansen, contributed in some way to its publication.

26. See *The Times*, November 27, 1826, and *The Morning Chronicle* of the same date.

27. *The Theatrical Observer*, July 24, 1828.

28. *The Dramatic Magazine*, September 1829, p. 224.

29. *Ibid.*

30. *The Theatrical Observer*, December 7, 1829.

31. *Ibid.*, January 29, 1830.

32. See Winston Diary, April 12 and June 12, 1830, Huntington Library.

33. Winston Diary, April 12, 1830.

34. *Theatrical Street Ballads*, ed. J. W. Robinson (London, 1971), p. 66.

35. Nicholson, *The Struggle for A Free Stage in London*, pp. 309–313.

CHAPTER 4. THE OLYMPIC MUSE

1. See *The Theatrical Observer*, March 12, 1839, and *The Times*, June 22, 1839.

2. The Olympic Theatre was located approximately where Bush House now stands.

3. Brayley, *The Theatres of London*, p. 88.

4. *British Parliamentary Papers: Stage and Theatre 1: Session 1831–1832* (Shannon, 1968), p. 246.

5. *Ibid.*, p. 13.

6. Quoted in H. Barton Baker, *History of the London Stage*, p. 140.

7. See St. Vincent Troubridge, *The Benefit System in the British Theatre* (London, 1967).

8. W. T. Moncrieff, quoted in Fitzball, *Thirty-Five Years of a Dramatic Author's Life*, II, 28.

9. On theatre audiences see [Pückler-Muskau], *A Regency Visitor*, pp. 83–84, and Grant, *The Great Metropolis*, I, 43ff.

10. *The Tatler*, January 4, 1831.

11. [Mackintosh], *Stage Reminiscences*, p. 72.

12. Planché, *Extravaganzas*, I, 41. The playbill reads: "A street on earth (as unlike Regent Street as possible)."

13. *Ibid.*, p. 40.

14. J. M. Langford, "Some Olympic Reminiscences," *The Era Almanack*, p. 72.

15. *The Examiner*, January 30, 1831.

16. *The Dramatic Magazine*, April 1831, pp. 90–91.

17. *Ibid.*, January 5, 1831.

18. Clipping, undated, from *The Court Journal*, Enthoven Collection.

19. *British Parliamentary Papers: Stage and Theatre 2: Session 1866* (Shannon, 1970), p. 255.

20. This and the following quotations are from *The News*, January 23, 1831.

21. Anonymous ballad entitled "Legography." Stead Collection, Lincoln Center Theatre Library.

22. See Olympic playbill for January 10, 1831.

23. *The Athenaeum*, September 24, 1831.

24. [Mackintosh], *Stage Reminiscences*, pp. 74–75. Cf. Southern, *The Victorian Theatre*, pp. 34–35.

25. *The Theatrical Observer*, October 1, 1831. See also *The Tatler*, January 25, 1832, which notes that the Strand has a curtain like that at the Olympic.

26. September 24, 1831.

27. *The London Magazine*, October 1823, p. 433.

28. *The Examiner*, October 4, 1831.

29. *The Athenaeum*, October 29, 1831.

30. On one occasion, January 23, 1823, she appeared at Drury Lane as Columbine in *The Golden Axe, or, The Fairy Lake*.

31. Planché, *Extravaganzas*, I, 63–64.

32. Unidentified clipping, undated, Enthoven Collection.

33. *The Theatrical Observer*, March 9, 1832.

34. *The Age*, November 25, 1832.

35. See Odell, *Annals of the New York Stage*, III, 548–549.

36. Waitzkin, *The Witch of Wych Street*, p. 22.

37. Rowell, *The Victorian Theatre*, p. 19.

38. The Harvard Catalogue of Engraved Dramatic Portraits mistakenly identifies the actor in the Gaucis engraving as John Harley. It is clearly William Farren, who appeared with Madame Vestris in the revival of Bernard's play in 1837. In an engraving by Busby for *The Dramatic Magazine*, March 1829, Farren, as Charles XII, in Planché's play of that name, wears the identical costume.

39. See Edith Melcher, *Stage Realism in France between Diderot and Antoine* (Bryn Mawr, 1928), pp. 117–119, and Marie-Antoinette Allevy, *La Mise en Scène en France dans la Première Moitié du Dix-Neuvième Siècle* (Paris, 1938), pp. 80 ff.

40. December 1, 1832.

41. Butler, "Early Nineteenth-Century Stage Settings in the British Theatre," *Theatre Survey*, p. 55.

42. Allevy, *La Mise en Scène*, pp. 31ff.

43. *The Examiner*, February 24, 1833.

44. *Figaro in London*, March 9, 1833.

45. Watson, *Sheridan to Robertson*, pp. 135–138.

46. *The Satirist*, May 12, 1833.

47. Duncombe, *Life and Correspondence of Thomas Slingsby Duncombe*, I, 187.

48. Planché, *Extravaganzas*, I, 287.

49. *The London Theatre*, p. 138. October 19, 1833.

50. A French company appeared at the Olympic from April to August in 1834. Another French company appeared there in July 1835.

51. [Mackintosh], *Stage Reminiscences*, pp. 81–82.

52. *Ibid.*, p. 83.

53. Manuscript letter, undated, Princeton University Library.

54. Manuscript, dated August 7, 1835, Philbrick Collection.

CHAPTER 5. ENTER CHARLES JAMES MATHEWS

1. *The Life of Charles James Mathews: chiefly autobiographical*, I, 5.

2. De Wilde's watercolor is reproduced in Mathews, *Life*, I, facing p. 12.

3. These drawings, mounted in an album, are now in the New York Public Library.

4. Mathews, *Life*, I, 94.

5. *Ibid.*, I, 97.

6. *Ibid.*, I, 193.

7. Manuscript diary, Princeton University Library. The diary is unpaginated and has been misdated 1823.

8. Sybil Rosenfeld, "English Private Theatres Abroad," *Theatre Research*.

9. Manuscript diary, Princeton University Library.

10. *Ibid.*

11. See Mathews, *Life*, I, 255.

12. Manuscript play, British Museum P.S. 91479 Add. 42913.

13. Possibly because Mathews's play too closely resembled *My Landlady's Side Door*, produced at the Olympic in 1829.

14. Mathews's manuscript diary, entry for January 16, 1835, Princeton University Library.

CHAPTER 6. A VOYAGE TO AMERICA

1. [Mackintosh], *Stage Reminiscences*, p. 133.

2. Mathews, *The Life of Charles James Mathews: chiefly autobiographical*, II, 78.

3. *Ibid.*, II, 81.

4. *The Athenaeum*, January 9, 1836.

5. *The Examiner*, January 17, 1836.

6. *The Theatrical Observer*, March 25, 1836.

7. Duncan, *St. James' Theatre*, p. 61.

8. *The Age*, September 25, 1836.

9. Planché, *Extravaganzas*, I, 224.

10. *Ibid.*, I, 226.

11. See *The Times*, February 4, 1835, and *Theatrical Recorder*, February 10, 1835.

12. "Lament of Lord Thynne," *Figaro in London*, January 10, 1835.

13. *The Parthenon*, March 4, 1837.

14. See *The Times*, May 3, 1837.

15. *Ibid.*, June 10, 1837.

16. See *The Town*, June 11, 1837.

17. Catalogue of the auction in Harvard Theatre Collection.

18. November 19, 1837.

19. Manuscript letter, dated June 24, 1837, Princeton University Library.

20. *The Call Boy*, April 21, 1838.

21. *Actors by Gaslight*, April 21, 1838.

22. *The Times*, June 1, 1838.

23. Planché, *Recollections*, II, 5ff.

24. Unidentified clipping, undated, author's collection.

25. Vandenhoff, *Leaves from an Actor's Notebook*, pp. 72–73.

26. *Figaro in London*, December 31, 1838.

27. *Life*, II, 83–84.

28. Unidentified clipping, undated, Harvard Theatre Collection.

29. Unidentified clipping, undated, author's collection.

30. *Actors by Gaslight*, July 21, 1838, p. 106.

31. Odell, *Annals of the New York Stage*, IV, 607.

32. *The Knickerbocker Magazine*, October 1838, quoted in Odell, *Annals of the New York Stage*, IV, 274–275.

33. Butler, "The Ill-Fated American Theatrical Tour of Charles James Mathews and his wife, Madame Vestris," *Theatre Research*, p. 28.

34. *The Ladies' Companion*, December 1838, p. 98.

35. *The Albion*, November 17, 1838.

36. *Actors by Daylight*, December 22, 1838, p. 343.

37. Unidentified clipping, undated, Princeton University Library.

38. *The Penny Satirist*, March 16, 1839.

39. *The Satirist*, March 24, 1839.

40. *Ibid.*, May 19, 1839.

41. *Survey of London: XXXV The Theatre Royal, Drury Lane and the Royal Opera House, Covent Garden* (London, 1970), p. 80.

42. *The Times*, June 1, 1839.

43. Mathews, *Life*, II, 88–89.

44. Mathews's album is in the New York Public Library.

CHAPTER 7. COVENT GARDEN

1. Knowles, *The Life of James Sheridan Knowles*, p. 131.

2. Manuscript letter from Charles James Mathews to John Harley, dated August 1, 1839, Enthoven Collection.

3. Fitzball, *Thirty-Five Years of a Dramatic Author's Life*, I, 260–261.

4. Manuscript autobiography of "O" Smith, undated, Shevelove Collection. Unpaginated.

5. *The Times*, June 22, 1839.

6. Vandenhoff, *Leaves from an Actor's Notebook*, p. 51.

7. *Diaries*, II, 80. September 13, 1840.

8. Manuscript, undated, Princeton University Library.

9. *Characters of Shakespeare's Plays* (London, 1817), p. 293.

10. *The Athenaeum*, October 5, 1839.

11. *The Life of Charles James Mathews: chiefly autobiographical*, II, 90–91.

12. *The Theatrical Observer*, February 15, 1840.

13. Quoted in Jane Williamson, *Charles Kemble* (Lincoln, Nebraska, 1970), p. 105.

14. *The Athenaeum,* April 25, 1840.

15. *Ibid.* See also Planché, *Extravaganzas,* II, 67–68.

16. *The Examiner,* October 18, 1840.

17. Planché, *Recollections,* II, 51.

18. *The Satirist,* November 22, 1840.

19. *John Bull,* November 21, 1840.

20. October 13, 1841.

21. Dion Boucicault, "The Debut of a Dramatist," *North American Review,* p. 461.

22. *Ibid.,* p. 462.

23. Manuscript note by Anna Maria Boucicault (Dion's mother), dated January 14, 1842, Shakespeare Memorial Library, Shakespeare Birthplace Trust.

24. Wallack, *Memories of Fifty Years,* p. 177.

25. Dion Boucicault, *London Assurance* (London, 1841), p. vii.

26. Quoted in Irene Vanbrugh, *To Tell My Story* (London, 1948), pp. 39–40.

27. *London Assurance,* p. vii.

28. *John Bull,* March 6, 1841.

29. *Memories of Fifty Years,* p. 175.

30. Manuscript in Princeton University Library.

31. *The Athenaeum,* October 2, 1841.

32. *John Bull,* March 5, 1842.

33. *The Theatrical Observer,* February 26, 1842.

34. *The Age,* January 2, 1842.

35. *The Examiner,* January 1, 1842. Cf. Southern, *The Victorian Theatre,* pp. 24–25.

36. Vandenhoff, *Leaves from an Actor's Notebook,* p. 62. Vandenhoff mistakenly states that Sabrina was played by Madame Vestris. The role was played by Miss Rainforth.

37. Mathews, *Life,* II, 94–95.

38. *Money,* Act IV, scene 1.

39. *Life*, II, 96.

40. *Recollections*, II, 58–59.

41. *The Theatrical Observer*, April 29, 1842.

42. Planché, *Recollections*, II, 58.

43. *An Actor's Life*, p. 103.

44. Watson, *Sheridan to Robertson*, p. 201.

CHAPTER 8. "PLAYERS! POOR PLAYERS!"

1. *The Life of Charles James Mathews: chiefly autobiographical*, II, 107.

2. *Diaries*, II, 167. May 1, 1842.

3. *Ibid.*, II, 164. April 9, 1842.

4. Wallack, *Memories of Fifty Years*, p. 132.

5. *The Morning Chronicle*, October 21, 1842.

6. *Players and Playwrights I Have Known*, I, 227.

7. Manuscript letter from Mathews to Macready, dated November 8, 1842, Wharton Collection.

8. *The Dramatic and Musical Review*, 1842, p. 407.

9. *Recollections*, II, 63.

10. *The London Theatre 1811–1866*, p. 169. December 20, 1842.

11. *Life*, II, 109.

12. *Ibid.*, II, 287–289.

13. Manuscript letter to Webster, dated December 9, 1843, Enthoven Collection.

14. *The Times*, February 28, 1844.

15. Lewes, *On Actors and the Art of Acting*, p. 68.

16. Manuscript letter, dated September 9, 1846, Princeton University Library.

17. *The London Theatre, 1811–1866*, pp. 172–173. July 22, 1844.

18. Manuscript letter to Webster, dated August 23, 1844, Players' Club.

19. Manuscript letter, undated, Players' Club.

20. *The Athenaeum*, October 5, 1844.

21. Manuscript letter, dated November 5, 1844, Players' Club.

22. Manuscript letter to Webster, dated April 16, 1845, Players' Club.

23. Manuscript letter to Webster, undated, author's collection.

24. Manuscript letter, dated May 17, 1845, author's collection.

25. Manuscript note, undated, Princeton University Library.

26. Manuscript letter to Hugh Oxenham, dated October 12, 1846, Players' Club.

27. *The Theatrical Times*, April 24, 1847.

CHAPTER 9. LYCEUM LESSEE

1. Manuscript agreement, dated August 12, 1847, Philbrick Collection.

2. Kellow Chesney, *The Victorian Underworld* (London, 1970), p. 311.

3. *The Illustrated London News*, November 6, 1847.

4. *The Life of the Drama* (New York, 1964), p. 222.

5. *Letter from Mr. Charles Mathews to the Dramatic Authors of France*, p. 18.

6. *Ibid.*, p. 20.

7. *The Times*, December 27, 1849.

8. *Ibid.*, December 28, 1847.

9. Planché, *Extravaganzas*, IV, 8.

10. *Ibid.*

11. Granville-Barker, "Exit Planché—Enter Gilbert," *London Mercury*. See also St. Vincent Troubridge, "Gilbert and Planché," *Notes and Queries*, CLXXIX (December, 1940), 442–443; CC (March 1941), 200–205; CC (March 1941), 224; CCI (July 1941), 17–18.

12. For obituaries of Josephine Anderson see *The Gentleman's Magazine*, XXX (New Series) (August 1848), p. 215, and *The Theatrical Times*, May 13, 1848.

13. Manuscript draft of a letter, undated, Princeton University Library.

14. Manuscript letter, dated September 10, 1848, Princeton University Library.

15. Mathews, *The Life of Charles James Mathews: chiefly autobiographical*, II, 110.

16. Manuscript letter to C. B. Phipps, dated September 2, 1849, Harvard Theatre Collection.

17. *Ibid.*

18. Manuscript letter, dated September 17, 1850, Princeton University Library.

19. Manuscript letter, dated September 14, 1850, Princeton University Library.

20. Henry Turner, "Random Recollections," *The Theatre* (November 1, 1885), p. 263.

21. See *The Times*, April 25 and May 21, 1854.

22. Quoted in *The Era*, April 25, 1854.

23. Foster and Lewes, *Dramatic Essays*, p. 124.

24. *Ibid*.

25. *The Morning Chronicle*, December 5, 1852.

26. Foster and Lewes, *Dramatic Essays*, p. 125.

27. See Downer, "Players and the Painted Stage: Nineteenth Century Acting," *PMLA*.

28. See Hirshberg, *George Henry Lewes*, chapter 4.

29. *The Leader*, April 10, 1852.

30. Act II.

31. For accounts of this production see *The Leader*, April 7, 1852, *The Illustrated London News*, April 17, 1852, and *The Theatrical Journal*, April 21, 1852.

32. *Players and Playwrights I Have Known*, I, 217.

33. *The Leader*, April 2, 1853.

34. Manuscript autobiography of "O" Smith, undated, Shevelove Collection. Unpaginated.

35. December 28, 1852.

36. A running correspondence on ticket orders appears in *The Times* during December–January 1852–1853.

37. Manuscript letter, dated August 1, 1853, Harvard Theatre Collection.

38. Manuscript letter, undated, Harvard Theatre Collection.

39. Manuscript letter, dated August 3, 1853, Princeton University Library.

40. Manuscript letter, dated September 8, 1853, Philbrick Collection.

41. *The Times*, March 10, 1854.

42. Maynard Savin, *Thomas William Robertson* (Providence, 1950), p. 29.

43. Stirling, *Old Drury Lane*, II, 125.

44. See *The Times*, April 25 and May 29, 1854.

45. Lewes, *On Actors and the Art of Acting*, p. 66.

46. Mathews papers, Princeton University Library.

47. Manuscript letter, dated July 9, 1854, Princeton University Library.

48. Manuscript letter, dated July 12, [1854], Princeton University Library.

CHAPTER 10. EPILOGUE

1. March 31, 1855.

2. *Ibid.*, April 28, 1855.

3. See Charles James Mathews diaries, Princeton University Library.

4. Fitzball, *Thirty-Five Years of a Dramatic Author's Life*, II, 292.

5. Stirling, *Old Drury Lane*, I, 248.

6. *Thirty-Five Years of a Dramatic Author's Life*, II, 304.

7. Manuscript letter, dated May 11, 1856, Players' Club.

8. Manuscript letter, dated July 9, 1856, Princeton University Library.

9. *The Life of Charles James Mathews: chiefly autobiographical*, II, 142.

10. *The Era*, August 17, 1856. The friend was probably either George Henry Lewes or Robert Morrisson.

11. For good brief assessments of Madame Vestris's contributions see Watson, *Sheridan to Robertson*; Waitzkin, *The Witch of Wych Street*; and Armstrong, "Madame Vestris; *A Centenary Appreciation*," *Theatre Notebook*.

12. William A. Armstrong, "The Art of the Minor Theatres in 1860," *Theatre Notebook*, X (April 1956), 94.

13. *Life*, II, 127.

14. *Ibid.*, II, 219.

15. *Our Recent Actors*, II, 168.

16. *Players and Playwrights I Have Known*, I, 244.

$\mathcal{A}$ $\mathcal{S}$*elected* $\mathcal{B}$*ibliography*

A Note on the Biographies of Madame Vestris

The early biographies of Madame Vestris are largely fictitious accounts of her amatory adventures and are of little value. The first of these anonymous memoirs was printed by John Duncombe in 1826. In November of that year Madame Vestris brought action against him for libel. She was awarded £100 damages but failed to suppress publication. The privately printed memoirs of 1830 are based on Duncombe's account, supplemented by a few additional scandals. The five-page biography published by William Chubb (ca. 1830) and reprinted by J. Thompson (ca. 1838) is inconsequential. A subsequent volume of memoirs, dated 1839 but published post-1841, and the anonymous *Daughters of Thespis* (ca. 1842), although they are both based on Duncombe, contain some additional material of interest. Matthew Mackintosh in his *Stage Reminiscences* (1866) gives us some valuable observations on her productions at the Olympic, but his account of her life is, as W. J. Lawrence put it, "a tissue of specious absurdities." Charles E. Pearce's *Madame Vestris and Her Times* (1923), while it provides an attractive picture of her times, is also biographically unreliable.

1. BOOKS AND ARTICLES

Allen, Shirley S. *Samuel Phelps and Sadler's Wells Theatre*. Middletown, 1971.

Anderson, James R. *An Actor's Life*. London, 1902.

Armstrong, William A. "Madame Vestris; A Centenary Appreciation," *Theatre Notebook*, XI (1956), 11–18.

Baker, H. Barton. *The London Stage*. London, 1904.

Boucicault, Dion. "The Debut of a Dramatist," *North American Review*, CXLVIII (1889), 454–463.

Brayley, Edward W. *The Theatres of London*. London, 1826.

Brereton, Austin. *The Lyceum and Henry Irving*. London, 1903.

Bunn, Alfred. *The Stage Before and Behind the Curtain*. London, 1840.

Butler, James H. "Early Nineteenth-Century Stage Settings in the British Theatre," *Theatre Survey*, VI (1965), 54–64.

———. "An Examination of the Plays Produced by Madame Vestris during her Management of the Olympic Theatre," *Theatre Survey*, X (1969), 136–147.

———. "The Ill-Fated American Theatrical Tour of Charles James Mathews and his wife, Madame Vestris," *Theatre Research*, VIII (1966), 23–36.

Capon, Gaston. *Les Vestris*. Paris, 1908.

Coleman, John. *Fifty Years of an Actor's Life*. London, 1904.

———. *Players and Playwrights I Have Known*. London, 1888.

The Daughters of Thespis. London [1841].

Downer, Alan S. *The Eminent Tragedian William Charles Macready*. Cambridge, Mass., 1966.

———. "Players and the Painted Stage: Nineteenth Century Acting," *PMLA*, LXI, no. 2 (1946), 522–576.

Duncan, Barry. *St. James' Theatre*. London, 1964.

Duncombe, Thomas H. *The Life and Correspondence of Thomas Slingsby Duncombe*. London, 1868.

Ebers, John. *Seven Years of the King's Theatre*. London, 1828.

Fitzball, Edward. *Thirty-Five Years of a Dramatic Author's Life*. London, 1859.

Fitzgerald, Percy. *The World Behind the Scenes*. London, 1881.

Foster, John, and George Henry Lewes. *Dramatic Essays*. Edited by William Archer and Robert W. Lowe. London, 1896.

Grant, James. *The Great Metropolis*. London, 1837.

Granville-Barker, Harley. "Exit Planché—Enter Gilbert," *London Mercury*, XXV (1932), 457–466, 558–573.

Gronow, Rees H. *Reminiscences and Recollections*. London, 1892.

Guest, Ivor. "Dandies and Dancers," *Dance Perspectives*, no. 37 (1969).

———. *The Romantic Ballet in England*. London, 1954.

Hirshberg, Edgar H. *George Henry Lewes*. New York, 1970.

Knowles, Richard B. *The Life of James Sheridan Knowles.* London, 1872.

Langford, J. M. "Some Olympic Reminiscences," *Era Almanack*, 1870.

Lawrence, W. J. "Dublin Stage History," *Dublin Evening Telegraph*, June 4, 1910.

Leathers, Victor. *British Entertainers in France.* Toronto, 1959.

Lewes, George Henry. *On Actors and the Art of Acting.* London, 1875.

[Mackintosh, Matthew.] *Stage Reminiscences . . . by an old stager.* Glasgow, 1866.

Macready, William C. *Diaries.* Edited by William Toynbee. London, 1912.

Marshall, Thomas. *Lives of the Most Celebrated Actors and Actresses.* London, 1847.

Marston, Westland. *Our Recent Actors.* Boston, 1888.

Mathews, Charles James. *Letter from Mr. Charles Mathews to the Dramatic Authors of France.* London, 1852.

———. *The Life of Charles James Mathews: chiefly autobiographical.* Edited by Charles Dickens [Jr.]. London, 1879.

Memoirs of the Life, Public and Private Adventures of Madame Vestris. . . . London [1826].

Memoirs of the Life of Madame Vestris, of the Theatres Royal Drury Lane and Covent Garden. London, 1830.

Memoirs of the public and private life, adventures and wonderful exploits of Madame Vestris. . . . London [ca. 1830].

Memoirs, public and private life, adventures and secret amours of Mrs. C. M. late Mad. V. . . . London [ca. 1838].

Memoirs of the Life, Public and Private Adventures of Madame Vestris: of the Theatres Royal Drury Lane, Covent Garden. . . . London [misdated 1839].

Nicholson, Watson. *The Struggle for a Free Stage in London.* Boston and New York, 1906.

Odell, George C. *Annals of the New York Stage.* New York, 1927–1949.

———. *Shakespeare from Betterton to Irving.* New York, 1920.

Pearce, Charles E. *Madame Vestris and Her Times.* London, [1923].

Planché, James Robinson. *Extravaganzas.* London, 1879.

Planché, James Robinson. *Recollections and Reflections.* London, 1872.

[Pückler-Muskau, Prince Hermann.] *A Regency Visitor: letters (1826–1828).* Edited by E. M. Butler. New York, 1958.

Raymond, George. *Memoirs of R. W. Elliston.* London, 1846.

Robinson, Henry Crabb. *The London Theatre, 1811–1866.* Edited by Eluned Brown. London, 1966.

Rosenfeld, Sybil. "English Private Theatres Abroad," *Theatre Research,* I (1958), 24–29.

Rowell, George. *The Victorian Theatre.* London, 1956.

Scott, Clement. *The Drama of Yesterday and Today.* London, 1899.

Sherson, Erroll. *London's Lost Theatre of the Nineteenth Century.* London, 1925.

Southern, Richard. *The Victorian Theatre.* London, 1970.

Stirling, Edward. *Old Drury Lane.* London, 1881.

Strunk, Oliver W. "Notes on a Haydn Autograph," *Musical Quarterly,* XX (1934), 192–205.

Tuer, Andrew. *Bartolozzi and His Works.* London, 1915.

Vandenhoff, George. *Leaves from an Actor's Notebook.* London, 1860.

Waitzkin, Leo. *The Witch of Wych Street.* Cambridge, Mass., 1933.

Wallack, Lester. *Memories of Fifty Years.* New York, 1889.

Watson, Ernest Bradlee. *Sheridan to Robertson.* Cambridge, Mass., 1926.

Webster, Margaret. *The Same Only Different.* New York, 1969.

Wilson, A. E. *King Panto.* New York, 1935.

Wilson, Mrs. C. Baron. *Our Actresses.* London, 1844.

Wyndham, Henry Saxe. *The Annals of Covent Garden Theatre.* London, 1906.

2. PERIODICALS AND NEWSPAPERS

Actors by Daylight

Actors by Gaslight

The Age

The Albion

The Athenaeum

The British Stage and Literary Cabinet

PERIODICALS AND NEWSPAPERS

The Call Boy
Courrier des Théâtres
The Court Journal
The Daily News
Dance Perspectives
The Dramatic Magazine
The Dramatic and Musical Review
The Era
The Examiner
Figaro in London
Gazette de France
The Gentleman's Magazine
The Illustrated London News
John Bull
The Knickerbocker Magazine
The Leader
The Mirror of the Stage
The Morning Chronicle
The Morning Herald
The Parthenon
The Satirist
The Tatler
Theatre Notebook
Theatre Research
Theatre Survey
The Theatrical Inquisitor
The Theatrical Journal
The Theatrical Observer
The Theatrical Times
The Times
The Town

Index